PHARMAPOLITICS IN
RUSSIA

SUNY series in National Identities
———————
Thomas M. Wilson, editor

PHARMAPOLITICS IN
RUSSIA

Making Drugs and Rebuilding the Nation

OLGA ZVONAREVA

Cover art: iStock by Getty Images.

Published by State University of New York Press, Albany

© 2020 State University of New York

All rights reserved

No part of this book may be used or reproduced in any manner whatsoever without written permission. No part of this book may be stored in a retrieval system or transmitted in any form or by any means including electronic, electrostatic, magnetic tape, mechanical, photocopying, recording, or otherwise without the prior permission in writing of the publisher.

For information, contact State University of New York Press, Albany, NY www.sunypress.edu

Library of Congress Cataloging-in-Publication Data

Name: Zvonareva, Olga, author.
Title: Pharmapolitics in Russia : making drugs and rebuilding the nation / Olga Zvonareva, author.
Description: Albany : State University of New York Press, [2020] | Series: SUNY series in National Identities | Includes bibliographical references and index.
Identifiers: ISBN 9781438479910 (hardcover : alk. paper) | ISBN 9781438479927 (pbk. : alk. paper) | ISBN 9781438479934 (ebook)
Further information is available at the Library of Congress.

10 9 8 7 6 5 4 3 2 1

To my father

Contents

Illustrations ix

Acknowledgments xi

Introduction: Drug Development and Politics 1

Chapter 1 The Soviet Pharmapolitical Regime: Promising
Social Justice 25

Chapter 2 Neoliberal Experiments in the Post-Soviet State:
Producing an Alternative Vision of Society 55

Chapter 3 The Arrival of Commercial Clinical Trials in Russia:
Generating Multiple Value 81

Chapter 4 Pharma-2020 Policy: Defining the Problems of
the Russian Pharmaceutical Industry 107

Chapter 5 Innovation Environment: Collaborating in
Drug Development and Production 133

Chapter 6 Pharmapolitics in Russia and Beyond 169

Notes 183

Bibliography 187

Index 199

Illustrations

Tables

2.1	Dynamics of pharmaceutical production in Russia (in comparable prices)	68
2.2	Dynamics of pharmaceutical production in Russia according to therapeutic categories	68
2.3	Top-ten Russian pharmaceutical producing companies in 1996	79
4.1	Top-twenty producers in sales revenue on the Russian pharmaceutical market in 2016	130

Figures

4.1	Russian market composition in billion rubles in 2016	131
5.1	Divergent definitions of innovation	151
5.2	Types of incubators	166
5.3	Types of accelerators	166

Acknowledgments

An earlier version of chapter 4 was originally published in O. Zvonareva, N. Engel, N. Kutishenko, and K. Horstman (2017), "(Re)configuring Research Value: International Commercial Clinical Trials in the Russian Federation," *BioSocieties* 12 (3): 392–414. Part of the data used in chapter 5 on Pharma-2020 policy were included in another volume: O. Zvonareva (2018), "(Re)imagining the Nation? Boosting Local Drug Development in Contemporary Russia," in *Health, Technologies, and Politics in Post-Soviet Settings: Navigating Uncertainties*, ed. O. Zvonareva, E. Popova, and K. Horstman (London: Palgrave Macmillan).

Introduction

Drug Development and Politics

On November 30, 2009, a press conference titled "Pharma-2020: Future of the Russian pharmaceutical industry" begins with this introduction by the moderator:

> Today we are discussing an important topic related to the situation with the Russian pharmaceutical market. This is a crucial topic that is relevant for many, relevant in a personal way. Everybody knows that there is a problem of supplying Russian people with inexpensive, quality drugs produced locally. This problem has not been solved yet, and the government is continuously working on it. Also the industry experiences problems such as lack of modern equipment and nontransparency of state procurement. A strategy that does not only solve these immediate problems, but also defines the future of this market, has been developed by the Ministry of Industry and Trade.

Before the floor is given to Sergey Tsib, a representative of the Ministry of Industry and Trade, the attention of the audience is directed toward a large screen where a video recording of then-president Dmitry Medvedev's speech is played. The recording was produced earlier the same month during the traditional presidential address to the Federal Assembly. On the screen, the press conference attendees see Georgievsky Hall in the Grand Kremlin Palace with hundreds of people listening to the president, who is standing on a large podium with Russian flags in the background. Medvedev says:

In the nearest future we will substantially increase the production of our own drugs. . . . Already in five years the share of local production on the pharmaceutical market has to become not less than a quarter, while by 2020, more than half of all medicines. This is the aim.

Federal Assembly members applaud. The video is then turned off, and Sergey Tsib turns on his microphone. He explains that after about a year and a half of work, the Ministry of Industry and Trade is ready to present the first programmatic document in the entire course of the country's pharmaceutical industry, titled the Strategy for the Development of the Pharmaceutical Industry of the Russian Federation (Pharma-2020). "We have every chance to meet the targets . . . specified by the president," Tsib adds. He finishes by delineating two main tasks: to improve the competitiveness of the Russian pharmaceutical industry and to ensure pharmaceutical security of the country as a whole.

This episode goes directly to the heart of the issues this book explores. At the very beginning of the press conference, the moderator announces that the topic at hand is local research, development, and production of drugs. Yet the ensuing statements and exchange are not limited to the matters of (bio)pharmaceutical science and technology. In fact, the discussion swiftly moves to anything but science and technology as such: societal problems of access to quality drugs, economic questions of dominance in the country's internal market, and issues of national security. What stands out is how drug research and innovation have made their way to the highest political levels and become involved with questions of public good provision, national interests, and the country's international standing.

I encountered these engagements between science, technology, and politics when I watched the recordings of this press conference and other events, browsed through media publications, talked to those involved in the pharmaceuticals field in Russia, and went everywhere my research project took me. Of course, by now it is commonly acknowledged that drug development and production are not a matter of technoscientific developments alone. Media have covered how pharmaceutical industry promotion practices work to establish conditions that make specific diagnoses and prescriptions as frequent as possible. Scholars have produced critiques of burgeoning consumption of medicines and continual growth of disease categories, health risks, and costs. Widespread debates about evidence have highlighted how the pharmaceutical industry carefully curates available knowledge through publication planning when companies and their agents shape multiple steps in the research, data analysis, writing, and publication of articles in ways that remain hidden from the public eye. These instances make it abundantly clear that drug innovations are shaped and driven not only by scientific breakthroughs but also by agendas, ambitions, and profits.

While previous research has demonstrated how diseases and patients emerge together with revenues and capital, in this book I analyze relationships between pharmaceuticals and society from a different angle. My concern here is not so much with the politics of the markets already extensively discussed by other scholars; rather, it is with politics of the state—closely related, but until now much less explored by critical social sciences. I am interested in how visions of the nation emerge together with state-led pharmaceutical industry development efforts. Following this interest, in this book I trace how pharmaceutical innovation in Soviet and post-Soviet Russia has become entangled with processes of rebuilding the nation and reimagining its identity and future, merging into what I call "pharmapolitics."

The case of (post-)Soviet pharmapolitics provides a fruitful contrast to common critiques of capitalist pharmaceutical industry and allows an opportunity to reexamine our ideas about governance of pharmaceutical development and production. Many accounts of Soviet science and industry remain centered on the question of political interference that introduces bias into knowledge produced and curbs innovation. This question reemerges in relation to the Russian state-dominated pharmaceutical arena as well. Yet, in essence, both critiques of profit-pursuing capitalist pharmaceutical industry and critiques of the power-accumulating nondemocratic state share the same ideal of technoscience untainted by market influences or political interference. Critical social science scholarship, in particular science and technology studies (STS), has long sought to disabuse us of this ideal, which implies a possibility of straightforwardly distinguishing technoscience and politics and keeping them separate. In this book, a view of pharmaceutical development as always shot through with political concerns and engaged in societal transformations is taken as a starting point to examine specific forms of pharmaceutical technoscience-society interactions and their consequences in a situation where it is not politics of the market but politics of the state that comes to the fore. A question that needs answering then is not how to safeguard pharmaceutical research and development (R&D) from politics, but rather how to respond to their interconnections in a transparent and equitable way. In the final chapter I return to this question with regard to both capitalist multinational pharmaceutical industry and nondemocratic state efforts to stimulate drug innovation, which themselves will turn out to be more alike than they may seem.

This book focuses on pharmaceuticals among the entire spectrum of science and technology. Pharmaceuticals may appear to be less spectacular and impactful compared to a rocket being launched into space or nuclear reactors powering up cities and simultaneously carrying a risk of the most enormous manmade disasters. Nonetheless, today pharmaceuticals—their development, production, and use—occupy a special place in the world. First, pharmaceuticals have an immediate connection to public health and well-being as a way to respond to major, long-standing health problems, for example, various forms of cancer faced by increasing numbers of people; to tackle new health threats, such as drug-resistant tuberculosis and AIDS, that endanger large populations; and to ward off aging, infirmity, mental decline, and other conditions from which humanity has dreamed of breaking free for centuries. Second, new pharmaceuticals are also associated with vast economic profits. More generally, they appear to hold great promise of better futures, tapping into imaginaries of prosperous and cohesive societies, where wealth is generated through finding applications for new biomedical knowledge and people whose health needs are met have better and more productive lives (Abraham 2010; Williams, Martin, and Gabe 2011). The recent formulation and implementation of the Russian government's Pharma-2020 Strategy announced in the opening vignette of this introduction is one of the attempts to harvest the potential of pharmaceutical innovation in Russia, while simultaneously enacting a particular mode of relations between pharmaceutical technoscience, state, and society.

Considering the far-reaching roles of pharmaceuticals in societies, it is important to reflect on who has the power to articulate and materialize these imaginaries pertaining to pharmaceuticals, how inclusion in and exclusion from these processes are arranged, and how particular decisions are represented, framed, and justified. It is equally important to understand how exactly pharmaceutical science and technology become entangled with politics, why these entanglements take specific shapes, and how they work to direct sociotechnical change along particular paths. Therefore, from the beginning of this project, my goal was both to open up new opportunities for critical appraisal and social action in regard to connections between pharmaceutical innovation and people's well-being in Russia, and to contribute to understanding the dynamics of relations between technoscience and politics, equally relevant for many contemporary societies.

I begin approaching this task by outlining the accounts of the drug development field in the next section to provide the necessary background for the exploration to follow.

Accounts of Drug Development

The account of the drug development field can be conveyed in different ways. Two broad accounts are offered by the scholarship in the history of science, technology, and medicine and in the sociology of medicine. These accounts are complementary in that one traces the evolution of our understanding of human body and the emergence of new technologies that enable creating new therapeutic agents, while the other turns to the social life of pharmaceuticals and its role in drug development trends.

Advances in Pharmaceutical Science and Technology

The account offered by the historical scholarship emphasizes that the pharmaceutical industry is driven by advances in science and technology as are few others. The contemporary pharmaceutical industry can be traced to the beginning of the nineteenth century, and its 200-year history shows a strong record of innovation and continuous close relations with academic research in chemistry, pharmacology, life sciences, and medicine. Before describing the phases historians offer to structure the shifts in drug development and innovation over the past two centuries, I pause to note that accounts of drug development history tend to center on developments in Western Europe and the United States. This is because about 80 percent of pharmaceutical products commercialized from 1800 to 1990 came from the United States, Germany, Switzerland, the United Kingdom, and France (Achilladelis and Antonakis 2001), signaling a strong concentration of drug development activities in these countries, with more recent input from other European countries and Japan. Drug development activities, however, took place in other locations as well. In particular, as chapter 1 of this book will show, in the Union of Soviet Socialist Republics, or USSR, a considerable pharmaceutical sector emerged that, importantly, was structured and governed differently from this same sector in Western Europe and the United States. One can argue that the scant attention given to locations outside Western Europe and the US in the literature on the history of pharmaceutical science and technology is attributable to the small contribution these outsiders made to the list of widely commercialized and used drugs. I would add that such focus in the historical literature also reflects a particular view of innovation as centered around profit, entrepreneurial firms, and market, where commercialization is the primary measure of innovativeness and success. This discourse is traceable in part to the enduring legacy of the economist Joseph Schumpeter (1883–1950), whose work inspired circumscription of the meaning of innovation to a particular mode of capitalist production and circulation of goods and values. In the decades to follow, most discussions and theorizing about innovation have continued to be dominated by market-centered thinking and the imperative of making profit. Consequently, other possible modes of innovating in areas, including pharmaceuticals, tend to be excluded from consideration (Marcelle 2015).

Attention to the imperatives of commercialization and of profit making was prominent in my conversations with those currently involved in pharmaceutical innovating in Russia and in the local science and technology policies now in effect. Yet the book resists taking for granted the assumptions underpinning this view of innovation, instead highlighting the ambivalence and tensions associated with the prominence of a commercial metric in Russian pharmaceutical science and technology. Therefore, I avoid defining what innovation is from the onset to critically engage with the plurality of understandings of drug innovation in various chapters of this book, most prominently in chapters 4 and 5, where current efforts to boost pharmaceutical innovation in Russia are explored, and in chapter 1, where the Soviet socialized pharmaceutical industry is analyzed. From the point of view adopted in this book—that is, recognizing innovation beyond the realm of economics and outside the emphasis on profit making—the story of drug development generally told by historians of science, technology, and medicine can be enriched by narratives from locations outside the United States and Western Europe that illuminate innovations in, for example, systems of pharmaceutical knowledge production.

Structuring the past and present of drug development around technoscientific advances produces accounts of consecutive changes in drug development paradigms or drug generations (Achilladelis 1999; Achilladelis and Antonakis 2001; Landau, Achilladelis, and Scriabine 1999). These accounts locate the beginning of modern drug R&D in 1820–1880, when the first generation of drugs evolved. In this period, academic researchers and physicians who turned to chemistry worked mainly on natural plant products and their "active principles," including isolation of morphine from opium and quinine from cinchona bark, which in turn gave rise to a new discipline, pharmacology. Discovery of the medical properties of simple organic chemicals that were synthesized or isolated from coal tar or plants (e.g., anesthetic properties of ether) was also a landmark of this period. Finally, historians note a rise of industrial organic chemistry leading to the development of the dyestuffs industry in the second half of the nineteenth century, most prominently in Germany. It was mainly the dyestuffs industry that gradually gave rise to the influential pharmaceutical companies that we know today as "Big Pharma."

To return to the past and present of drug development as offered by historical accounts focusing on advances in science and technology, the second generation of drugs came to life in roughly 1880–1930. This period witnessed intensified collaboration between academic scientists, chemical companies, and public health institutes to construct the foundation of a research-intensive pharmaceutical industry. The first synthetic drugs and vaccines were marketed. While most medical discoveries originated in academic hospitals and universities, their development and commercialization moved to public health and medical research institutions established by the European and American governments, for example, the Pasteur Institute and the Rockefeller Institute and (predominantly German) dyestuffs companies, the most prominent being Bayer and Hoechst. These companies were also building their own drug R&D capabilities. By 1910, equipped with industrial manufacturing and pill-making machines, apothecaries, including Abbott, Lilly, Burroughs–Wellcome, and Parke–Davis in Great Britain and the United States, also began investing in in-house R&D. Most current Big Pharma companies came into existence during this second generation of drugs. Concurrently, as I describe in chapter 1, in the Soviet Union a different, public pharmaceutical industry was developing. On the basis of small entrepreneurial companies that existed in the Russian Empire, the new Soviet state was creating an integrated industrial complex focused on science and technology to produce drugs of the first, second, and, soon, third generation.

In the course of the third generation of drugs, which can be located in 1930–1960, most pharmaceutical companies became strongly committed to in-house R&D; drug marketing methods changed to intensively target health professionals, hospitals, and drugstores; and corporate structures began to be organized in a way that would solidify during the rest of the twentieth century. During World War II, governments supported development and production of pharmaceuticals to meet the needs of their armed forces. Many new hormones, vitamins, antibiotics, and anti-inflammatory drugs were developed. The number of pharmaceutical companies to introduce their versions of new types of drugs increased significantly, sharpening the competition among them and speeding the diffusion of new drug development technologies, while enlarging markets stimulated further growth of pharmaceutical companies and attracted companies from other sectors into the profitable business of pharmaceuticals. In the USSR, drug development continued along its socialized path with no private businesses and therefore no drug commercialization, but with a state-organized and state-controlled industry.

During the fourth generation of drugs in 1960–1980, the pharmaceutical industry's scientific basis shifted from chemistry and pharmacology to life sciences. Growing understanding of cellular-level processes enabled developing hundreds of new drugs, mainly for noncommunicable diseases such as cardiovascular disease, cancer, and central nervous system diseases; antidepressants, tranquilizers, and anxiolytics arrived. While the US industry retained its dominance in the field that it had gained during the postwar years, the Western European and Japanese economies recovered, and companies from these regions entered the pharmaceutical markets. With an abundance of new drugs, many of which did not offer a clear advantage over already existing ones, and the international thalidomide scandal in 1961, governments became increasingly concerned with ensuring the safety and efficacy of drugs and proper regulation of the pharmaceutical industry. Of central importance were the 1962 Kefauver-Harris Amendments to the United States' Federal Food, Drug, and Cosmetic Act, which specified critical components of contemporary pharmaceutical regulation: premarket review and well-controlled studies to prove safety and efficacy (Hogarth 2015). Following the Amendments, the US Food and Drug Administration (FDA), the federal agency tasked with regulating pharmaceuticals, was influential in spelling out and enforcing the three-phase system of clinical trials and stipulating randomized controlled trials (RCTs) as the "gold standard" of evidence (Carpenter 2010). Similar legislation and regulatory practices were adopted in most European states during the next decade. In part because of these developments, the costs of discovery, development, approval, and marketing of drugs continued to rise, promoting the dominance of larger companies. By contrast, as chapter 1 of this book demonstrates, the USSR adopted a different system to regulate drug development. This system, while being plagued by its own drawbacks, was meant to prevent the duplication of efforts and waste of resources that were perceived in capitalist drug development.

The fifth generation of drugs began in 1990, according to Achilladelis (1999); Achilladelis and Antonakis (2001); and Landau, Achilladelis, and Scriabine (1999); and it has not yet run its full course. Further developments in the life sciences allowed designing precisely targeted and highly specific drugs, particularly for cancer and viral and age-debilitating diseases, with major advances brought by the rise of biotechnology. The pharmaceutical industry underwent a massive process of mergers and acquisitions in the 1990s and at the beginning of the 2000s, which accomplished the formation of unprecedentedly concentrated global companies. Simultaneously, the promise held by new, revolutionary biotechnologies attracted investments enabling the creation of many smaller biotechnology companies. Currently biotechnology firms tend to engage in upstream research, that is, identification of drug candidates—drug discovery. Because it is mostly pharmaceutical companies that possess resources sufficient to bring drugs through the extremely costly development and registration process in the current environment, pharmaceutical companies focus on the downstream stages, further developing methodologies and substances discovered by biotechnology companies (or public laboratories) for a commercial drug (Sternitzke 2010). Pharmaceutical companies increasingly tend to in-license molecules from biotechnology firms or buy biotechnology companies with promising molecules in the pipeline to strategically assimilate new technology as a source of potential value (Henderson, Orsenigo, and Pisano 1999; Kneller 2003; Sunder Rajan 2006).

In this same period, at the beginning of the 1990s, Russia became an independent state. Then the socialist drug development system was quickly dismantled, making way for a deregulated field where large multinational pharmaceutical companies powerfully stepped in. Local pharmaceutical industry came to a halt, followed by efforts to find a workable way of organizing and governing drug development that came to incorporate elements of the Western market-oriented system together with Soviet-rooted approaches and an ambition to master and employ technologies of the fifth drug generation.

Pharmaceuticalization and the Social Life of Drugs

The sociology of medicine takes another approach to providing an account of the drug development field, focusing on the social life of drugs. This strand of scholarship highlights how pharmaceuticals increasingly have come to be seen as preeminent solutions to health problems and analyzes associated changes in patterns of their development, production, and use. It offers the concept of pharmaceuticalization to account for the growing importance of pharmaceuticals and their multiplying and diversifying roles in society.

The ongoing reflection on the contours and meaning of pharmaceuticalization was instigated by works of Abraham (Abraham 2010, 2011) and Williams, Martin, and Gabe (2011). While Abraham suggests that pharmaceuticalization is a "process by which social, behavioural, or bodily conditions are treated or deemed to be in need of treatment, with medical drugs by doctors or patients" (2010, 604), Williams, Martin, and Gabe (2011) argue that analysis of pharmaceuticalization should not be restricted to the use of pharmaceuticals by doctors or patients for treatment purposes, but rather that pharmaceuticalization "denotes the translation or transformation of human conditions, capabilities and capacities into opportunities for pharmaceutical intervention" (Williams, Martin, and Gabe 2011, 711). Furthermore, Williams, Martin, and Gabe (2011) suggest that it is useful to frame pharmaceuticalization as a sociotechnical process that is part of a so-called pharmaceutical regime—heterogeneous networks of institutions, actors, and artifacts associated with the creation, circulation, and use of pharmaceuticals. Further chapters of this book make visible the evolution and contours of the present pharmaceutical regime in Russia, contributing to the sociological scholarship concerned with pharmaceuticals, which to date has mostly been concerned with discussing changes within Western societies, as noted recently by Sariola and colleagues (2015).

Analysts have discerned several important trends in the recent transformations of the pharmaceutical regime globally, including massive growth of drug markets, changing forms of governance, and the increasing prominence of pharmaceuticals in imaginaries of societal futures. The astonishing growth rate of the pharmaceutical industry, as reflected, for example, in worldwide sales having risen 11.1 percent annually from 1970 to 2002 (PhRMA 2003 as cited by (Gassmann, Reepmeyer, and Von Zedtwitz 2008), signals profound expansion of the global pharmaceutical regime. Correspondingly, a large increase in the use of drugs has been documented. Busfield (2015), for instance, shows that in England the average number of prescriptions dispensed per person increased from 8.0 in 1989 to 18.7 in 2012, and he argues that because this rise occurred well after the introduction of the major new drugs of the previous century, such as antibiotics and antihistamines, its drivers cannot be reduced to the developments in pharmaceutical technology.

The distribution of pharmaceutical sales and consumption, however, has been uneven across the globe. WHO states that while between 2000 and 2008 consumption of pharmaceuticals has grown in countries of all income categories, and the percentage growth is higher in low-income countries than in high-income countries, the growth in absolute terms is far greater in the latter, with high-income countries as a whole consuming "very much more [pharmaceuticals] than lower-income ones" (Hoebert, Laing, and Stephens 2011). Against this background, vocal concerns about overuse of pharmaceuticals are accompanied by no less justified concerns about underuse due to inaccessibility, as exemplified by the worrisome data showing that about one-third of the world's population lacks access to essential medicines (World Health Organization 2004, 61–74). Therefore, while pharmaceutical markets are clearly expanding both commercially and geographically, this expansion is neither homogenous nor even.

Concurrently with the growth and expansion of pharmaceutical markets, related governance forms have been shifting as well, affecting drug development practices. A push toward deregulation since the end of the 1980s has been noted by researchers interested in the work of such regulatory bodies as the FDA in the United States, the Medicines and Healthcare products Regulatory Agency (MHRA) in the United Kingdom, and the European Medicines Agency (EMA) in the European Union. These regulatory agencies have been increasingly reliant on industry funding ("100% funding for the MHRA since 1989, with similar trends in the EU [70% funding] and the USA [50% funding] since the mid-1990s," according to Williams, Martin, and Gabe [2011]). This arrangement has committed regulators to significantly decrease review times for new drugs and encouraged them to introduce fast-tracking approval procedures for drugs targeting life-threatening conditions or addressing unmet health needs requiring less data to demonstrate safety or efficacy (Abraham and Davis 2007; Abraham and Lewis 2000).[1] Subjected to criticisms by industry for stifling innovation and impeding prompt arrival of new drugs to the market, and hence to patients who need them, regulatory agencies have come to embrace more flexible and open relationships with industry (Abraham 2010; Hogarth 2015). Moreover, major drug regulatory agencies increasingly position themselves as enablers of innovation. Against the background of the "productivity crisis" in the pharmaceutical industry, that is, ever-increasing spending on R&D coupled with decreasing numbers of approved new drugs (Gassman, Reepmeyer, and Von Zedtwitz 2008) and, as some authors point out, shrinking numbers of new drugs actually offering significant therapeutic advances (Martin et al. 2006), regulatory agencies have begun to play a greater role in supporting pharmaceutical innovation in addition to a more traditional role as guardians of public health. For example, in 2004 the FDA introduced the Critical Path Initiative, which is defined as a "strategy to drive innovation in the scientific processes through which medical products are developed, evaluated, and manufactured to improve and accelerate translation of recent scientific advances into innovative medical treatments."[2] Finally, along with making efforts to rethink ways of governing pharmaceuticals, the established system of regulation has been globalizing, as exemplified by the International Conference on Harmonisation of Technical Requirements for Registration of Pharmaceuticals for Human Use (ICH) and its influential Tripartite Harmonised Guidelines. ICH originally brought together regulators from Europe, Japan, and the United States, but the geographical focus of the initiative is changing. The history section of the ICH website states: "Entering into its third decade of activity, ICH's attention is directed towards extending the benefits of harmonisation beyond the ICH regions."[3] Currently, representatives of non-ICH regions are increasingly involved in ICH work, and the guidelines are being incorporated in the regulatory practices outside Europe, Japan, and the United States.[4] Efforts to expand regulations for drug development and approval facilitate access by international pharmaceutical companies to new markets and enable outsourcing some parts of drug development and production to lower-income locations. The reverse is also possible: harmonization of the regulatory system could allow drugs developed outside the high-income Western locations that historically have been the center of most commercial innovation in pharmaceuticals to enter Western markets, but this reverse movement has been much less noticeable.

The third trend in transformations of the pharmaceutical regime noted in the pharmaceuticalization scholarship is related to a heightened attention to the futures associated with pharmaceutical innovations. It is well known that expectations and visions play a crucial role in scientific and technological change through driving activities, attracting interest and resources, and providing legitimation (Borup et al. 2006). Pharmaceuticals in particular appeal to deep-seated imaginings of many people—we generally want to live healthier lives devoid of suffering and premature death. Imaginaries of (better) futures are at play on many levels of the pharmaceutical regime, from individual patients to transnational structures and discourses. Many patients participating in development of particular drugs as research subjects, especially those with currently untreatable conditions or with conditions nonresponsive to standard treatments, hope that novel medicines accessed through trials will improve their condition and prospects (Brown et al. 2015). Patient organizations engage in political activism, fundraising, and awareness raising and work to shape the field of biomedical research in attempts "to bring to fruition the many future possibilities inherent in the science of the present" (Novas 2006, 289; see also Epstein 1996; Rabeharisoa and Callon 2004). The development of new technoscientific fields such as pharmacogenetics is shaped by visions emerging of its impact on medical practice, on industrial landscapes, on research agendas, and on ethical discourses, with different visions competing and developing in synergy with each other (Brown and Michael 2003; Hedgecoe and Martin 2003).

Taken together, the two broad accounts of the drug development domain offered by the fields of history of science, technology, and medicine and the sociology of medicine suggest that changes in the area of drug development are attributable to both advances in pharmaceutical science and technology and related societal dynamics, such as growing numbers of conditions identified as suitable for pharmaceutical treatment. Consequently, in this book, changes in drug development are not viewed as a matter of technoscience or social processes alone. Rather, I consider drug development as being shaped both by advances in technoscience and changing roles of drugs in society.

The notion of coproduction of technoscience and society proposes viewing scientific knowledge and technologies as both embedding and being embedded in the social, including identities, norms, discourses, institutions, and practices (Jasanoff 2004) and conveys the gist of my approach in this book. Taking coproduction as a starting point enables me to take account of both technoscientific advances and social processes in this study of pharmaceuticals and their engagements with politics, which here I take to mean material and discursive practices of the production, exercise, and contestation of power.

Strategic Technopolitical Practices

Beyond the broad idea of coproduction, several specific concepts proved to be particularly inspiring for analyzing relations between politics and pharmaceutical science and technology in Russia. One is a notion of technopolitics that is attentive to practices of using technologies in political processes and to the workings of power in these peculiar hybrids.

The concept of technopolitics has been elaborated by Hecht (2009, 2001), who defined it as "the strategic practice of designing or using technology to constitute, embody, or enact political goals" (2001, 256). Using the example of French nuclear reactors, Hecht showed that many of the criteria that shaped technical design choices in that case were deliberately political. She moves beyond calling the resulting reactors "socially constructed technologies" in stressing that these hybrids were intended and used as tools in political negotiation. At the same time, it is also not enough to call these technologies "politics" because of their materiality and the importance of the effectiveness of these technologies for achieving material purposes for their political effectiveness. Rather, the practice of using technologies "in political processes and/or towards political aims constitutes technopolitics" (Hecht 2001, 257).

The analytical approach of technopolitics means not only taking into account how technologies, broadly defined as "artefacts as well as nonphysical, systematic means of making or doing things" (Hecht 2001, 256), become sites and objects of politics, but also tracing how political ambitions and agendas interact with technological developments and are shaped in the process of such interactions. In this sense, a technopolitical approach is in accord with the notion of coproduction of technoscience and society.

At the same time, a technopolitics approach has a particular focus on the workings of power and shades of local politics and ideologies. This focus is important to explain how authority is being established and performed, how specific meanings become prevalent, and how certain assemblages persist over alternative ones—that is, to explain the shaping of sociotechnical trajectories. Furthermore, as Gagliardone (2014) suggests in his study of technopolitics, nation building, and information and communications technology (ICT) in Ethiopia, the concept of technopolitics, being attentive to differences in power, places a greater emphasis on the role of governments in shaping technology. He explains that in many settings, the state is not just one actor among many. Rather, while it may not always be able to perform its stated functions in terms of the delivery of public services and goods, it still does tend to occupy a position of prominence among other actors involved in policy making and implementation.

Although Gagliardone's reflection refers to the ICT sector in Ethiopia, attention to power and governmental practices is important to understand coproduction of pharmaceutical innovation and politics in Russia as well. While the authoritarian Soviet state was left behind, the new Russian state inherited its elements and practices. Experimenting with new relationships between the government and the public, and still possessing significant resources to enforce its visions, the government has tried exercising varying degrees of control over various spheres of life; therefore, its activities are worth looking at in greater detail.

Here I would like to note that in analyzing entwinements of science, technology, and politics, this book looks beyond formal political organization and power centers, not taking such entities as "state" for granted or considering that their structures fully explain particularities of sociotechnical outcomes. Previous research shows that many differences in how science and technology are dealt with, how related problems are framed, and which solutions are presented as acceptable are organized along the national borders. For example, the field of biotechnology regulation in Europe and the United States demonstrates that different national discourses have arisen around risk and safety, innovation and bioethics, naturalness and artificiality, and gave rise to different approaches to dealing with biotechnological advances (Jasanoff 2005). Here comes the next concept that became important to my investigation of pharmapolitics in Russia—that of political culture. The idea of political culture reflects the importance of interpretations and attribution of meaning and offers a reflexive and dynamic way of thinking about relations between states and sociotechnical trajectories, going beyond formal structures. Jasanoff (2005) defines political culture as a "systematic means by which a political community makes binding collective choices" with political culture encompassing written and unwritten codes and practices of political decision making and institutionalized approaches to reasoning as well as less explicit cultural commitments to forms of legitimation. The concept of political culture highlights the importance of capturing stabilities in meaning making to analyze particularities of national discourses about risks, benefits, and goals of innovation, and to understand how policy problems are constructed. Therefore, while taking the analytical approach of technopolitics and paying attention to power and state, I engage in an exploration of meaning making in the pharmapolitical nexus I am studying.

Finally, the notion of sociotechnical imaginaries provides another stepping-stone to understanding the interconnections of science, technology, and politics. This notion, developed by Jasanoff and Kim (2009, 2015), builds on previous work of social and political theorists on collective imaginations. For example, Anderson (2006) highlighted the centrality of imagination in nation building. He suggested viewing the nation as an imagined community tied together through shared cultural, political, and also technoscientific practices and highlighted the necessity of paying attention to actions required to produce and maintain common imaginaries.

The concept of sociotechnical imaginaries refers to "collectively held, institutionally stabilized, and publicly performed visions of desirable futures, animated by shared understandings of forms of social life and social order attainable through, and supportive of, advances in science and technology" (Jasanoff and Kim 2015, 4). This theoretical concept attends symmetrically to both technoscientific and social processes. For example, Hecht, in her investigation of technopolitics in France, reflects on how national identity is being imagined and negotiated in the processes of coproduction of science, technology, culture, and politics. She argues that national identities do not grow by themselves; rather they require cultivation through articulation, rehearsal, and grounding in materiality of technological systems. Alternatively, as Felt (2015) shows in her study of reception of several technologies, including agricultural biotechnologies in Austria, national identities can become tied to rejection of certain technologies. In this case, a specific kind of "Austrianness" became tied to an imaginary of keeping a group of technologies out of the country and thereby becoming distinctive as a nation. Importantly, sociotechnical imaginaries not only describe what is attainable through science and technology in the future, but they also prescribe what ought to be attained, encoding societal normative visions. Relying on this notion of sociotechnical imaginaries, in this book I analyze how political culture is working to frame the rules, goals, and trajectories of drug innovation that are simultaneously describing and prescribing national futures in Russia.

Investigating Pharmapolitics

Beginning this project, I faced the question of where exactly I should do my research. Where would I be able to see how pharmaceutical science and technology relate to politics? One thing was clear: logics through which pharmapolitics are constituted and operate would not be not visible in any one particular site. Therefore, my research was not to be restricted to a single location to enable me to study the circulation and evolution of meanings, identities, and objects in time and space. This led me to adopt a multisite approach, where site is understood broadly and can include, among others, communities, technologies, and even discourses. Anthropologist Peter Metcalf wrote that "the sites of fieldwork cannot be the result of some prior theoretical agenda. Instead, they have to be discovered" (Metcalf 2001). And, indeed, it was only in the process of doing this research that it became fully clear to me where exactly to look for pharmapolitics.

My entry point was clinical trial sites—places where new drugs are tested on humans to check their effectiveness and safety. Studying these sites through interviews with investigators, trial participants, and representatives of business (twenty-seven in total) and observations of the work performed there together with continuous informal talks with those doing this work directed my further search. There I learned about how sweeping political changes that followed the dissolution of the USSR allowed globalized clinical trial enterprise to arrive in Russia and how this enterprise found and secured its uneasy place amid decaying welfare provision and new market institutions. But apart from this, my informants kept telling me that most advanced-stage and large-scale trials are sponsored by foreign pharmaceutical companies and volunteered to offer their opinions on the dismal state of the local pharmaceutical industry and current governmental attempts to revive it.

Following this lead, I started to go through materials and documents pertaining to these attempts to boost local drug development. I read programs and strategies, regulations, minutes and records of regulatory meetings, statements of regulators made in the press and during public events, and comments on these developments made in popular and professional media. But to understand how these relate to day-to-day practices of actors involved in pharmaceutical science and technology and how those actors themselves perceive and respond to the government actions, I needed to go beyond documents. So I went on to have thirty interviews with individuals involved in local drug innovation: those from academia, with a few of these academics also having positions in relevant regulatory structures; those from business, with one of those businessmen being involved as a consultant in a relevant regulatory structure; and those from development institutes and R&D infrastructure organizations such as industrial parks. Furthermore, I participated in events that allowed me to observe firsthand discussions among professionals and between professionals and regulators pertaining to infrastructure for innovative drug development and regulation and practices of drug development. During this stage, I learned about how attempts to revitalize local pharmaceutical science and technology link to the wider political aspirations and why actors involved in pharmaceutical innovating find it difficult to deliver the expected material results. When discussing the current state of drug development in the country and its political significance, my informants often referred back to the strengths of Soviet pharmaceutical sector and to the period immediately following the end of the Soviet Union, which in their narratives marked the destruction of local pharmaceutical science and technology.

It became clear that to understand current pharmapolitics in Russia and how actors involved make sense of it, I also needed to dig deeper into the relations between politics and pharmaceutical science and technology in Soviet and early post-Soviet times. In doing so, I relied on stories of my older informants, who witnessed these transformations firsthand, and documents and publications of Soviet and foreign authors. Then I was able to reconstruct how the pharmapolitical nexus in which I was interested was changing shape with time and producing different imaginaries of the nation and its future. I finalized the main period of data collection for this project by organizing two focus groups with drug developers, where I posed questions regarding governance and trajectories of pharmaceutical innovations in Russia. These questions arose from my research, and having them discussed by relevant actors allowed me to ascertain and refine my interpretations.

It must be noted, though, that it was not possible for me to treat all sites uniformly in terms of the kinds and amount of data collected; nor was it necessary, because the aim was to bring into the same frame of analysis different sites where pharmaceutical technologies and politics in Russia meet and ascertain relationships between them. These sites are distributed in time from the period of the USSR to the beginning of the new Russia's existence at the turn of 1991 to 2015. They include drug discovery and development, clinical trial conduct, and spaces where related policies are developed, articulated, and appraised, as well as some wider interconnections between them.

What emerged from my study of politics and pharmaceutical technoscience in Russia is a picture of four interconnected processes that together shape both pharmaceutical and political trajectories. While the notion of coproduction of technoscience and society was a starting point, it remained important to specify how exactly this coproduction occurs and to what effect. My analysis suggests that pharmaceutical technoscience and politics underwrite each other's existence through vision production, problem definition, collaboration, and value generation. Vision production refers to the process whereby the organization and practice of pharmaceutical development interact with political imagination to enable the emergence of specific visions of societal futures, which in turn feed back into the governance of drug innovation and wider regulatory agendas. Problem definition here is taken to mean a mutual dynamic where drug innovations define possibilities for solving societal problems, while simultaneously the ways in which societal problems to be solved through pharmaceutical R&D are defined shape directions of drug innovations. Collaboration denotes how relations between actors in the pharmaceutical arena are influenced by political culture and, conversely, how the ways in which actors on the ground choose to engage with each other affect implementation of the national political agendas. Value generation highlights that the type of value that is generated through pharmaceutical technoscience depends on which visions of the future animate drug development efforts, how the problems to be solved with the use of pharmaceutical science and technology are defined, and how the actors in the drug innovation domain engage with each other. At the same time, the value generation process here also highlights how potential and actually generated value contribute to formulating political priorities and strategies. How these four processes unfold defines the specific shapes that pharmapolitics take.

The chapters in this book, arranged in a chronological order, systematically attend to vision production (chapter 2), value generation (chapter 3), problem definition (chapter 4), and collaboration (chapter 5), the processes that take part in the configuration of the pharmapolitical nexus. I begin by exploring the emergence and consolidation of the Soviet national pharmapolitical regime in chapter 1. Here I trace how a constellation of institutions, technoscientific practices and artifacts, political programs, and ideologies came to act together to direct development of the pharmaceutical sector and pursue politics. Immediately after the beginning of the Soviet state, its pharmaceutical industry was reorganized into a centrally managed and planned sector with no involvement of private capital. Gradually the system settled into a situation where new drugs developed at the state research institutes would move into state production factories and then into state health-care organizations and pharmacies under the guidance and control of expert scientists, government decision makers, and bureaucrats. The effectiveness, safety, and quality of medicines were established without making use of the three-phase clinical trial system introduced in the United States in the 1960s and currently dominant in drug development globally. The chapter argues that Soviet drug research, development, and production were shaped by an imaginary of an ultimately socially just society and organized in explicit opposition to the capitalist system of countries such as the United States whose drawbacks included bias introduced by profit motives, resource duplication, and exploitation of clinical research participants. Simultaneously, Soviet pharmaceuticals enabled a forceful articulation of communist ideas about society and contributed to shaping Soviet political agendas. My analysis of Soviet pharmaceutical science and technology as a case of pharmapolitics additionally suggests that it was not particularly good or bad in developing innovative drugs. Rather, it operated with its own definition of innovation that involved the ability to quickly develop and produce required drugs, irrespective of how such ability was achieved.

After the end of Communist rule at the beginning of the 1990s, Russia quickly adopted many of the previously rejected elements of pharmaceutical research, development, and production, such as strong involvement of private interests and withdrawal of the state from managing and organizing the sector. In chapter 2, I investigate what enabled such radical transformation and explicate how the process of *producing visions* operates to shape pharmapolitical practices. At the time of the USSR's collapse, conflicting visions of the Russian nation and its future were being articulated. One vision originally became particularly powerful: a set of neoliberal ideas championing the market, which has to be safeguarded from state intervention, and placing entrepreneurship at the center of economic and social development. The power of this neoliberal view, initially articulated by a small group of young politicians, came from the full support of the new government, which swiftly put to force such radical reforms as privatization and decentralization, embodying and disseminating neoliberal ideas. I show that specifically in the field of pharmaceuticals, the neoliberal agenda has exercised significant influence in other settings, such as Western Europe and North America, but nowhere was it put into action so quickly and to such an extent as in post-Soviet Russia. The chapter analyzes how the Russian pharmaceutical sector was molded by neoliberal ideas and shows that, despite their impact, these ideas failed to take root among those involved with pharmaceutical science and technology. Rapid deterioration of the already troubled Russian pharmaceutical sector in the 1990s greatly contributed to a wide resistance to the neoliberal vision of the Russian future both among those involved with pharmaceutical science and technology and in the wider society. This rejection then enabled a major turn in the regulation of the pharmaceutical industry in Russia away from neoliberal aspirations toward the currently dominant idea of a strong state and protectionist measures, animated by another, alternative vision, analyzed in chapter 4.

Chapter 3 investigates the arrival and conduct of international commercial clinical trials to Russia after the opening up of the Russian borders in the 1990s, and analyzes how *generating value* operates as another process that shapes pharmapolitics. Value generation is central to pharmaceutical science and technology, because the development and production of drugs entangles multiple kinds of value, including potential therapeutic benefits for patients, soaring profits for industry, and opportunities to advance academic research and to promote state interests. Correspondingly, questions loom large about what kind of value is being generated and for whom in the drug development and production systems. It is well established that the international clinical trials enterprise, currently an integral part of the drug development process, has come to rely on global health inequalities, with people living in situations of a health crisis often coming to sustain medical research whose results are mainly used by more affluent populations. At the same time, I show how, in the context of limited access to adequate health care and lack of support for academic research, Russian investigators and research participants through their personal work translate trials into academic capacity building, development of local medical expertise, and public health benefits. My analysis shows that while the rhetoric of improving public health is central in the pharmapolitical arena, the value in pharmapolitical processes is not a given; rather it is multiply configured in the clinical, scientific, and economic domains.

Chapter 4 turns to an important milestone in the enfolding of pharmapolitics in Russia. The Strategy for the Development of the Pharmaceutical Industry in the Russian Federation to 2020 (Pharma-2020) was adopted by the Russian government in 2009 and followed in the next years by other related initiatives. The Strategy aims to ensure "innovative development of the Russian pharmaceutical industry" with one of its primary objectives being the "fostering of research, development and production of innovative drugs." Chapter 4 analyzes this attempt to revitalize local pharmaceutical science and technology, links it to the wider political aspirations that gradually superseded radically neoliberal ideals, and elaborates how the process of *defining problems* to be solved through pharmaceutical science and technology shapes the pharmapolitical nexus. In the policy documents and statements of officials and professionals involved, the lack of locally developed and produced drugs has been defined as a paramount threat to national security. The country's dependence on foreign companies in delivering medicines and a current failure of local companies to harvest profits from the growing Russian pharmaceutical market have been assessed as long-term risk factors. This pharmapolitical problem definition draws on preexisting, historically rooted aspirations with respect to self-sufficiency, on recent national experiences of living through drastic reforms, and on novel technoscientific opportunities in the field of pharmaceuticals. The problem to be solved through the employment of pharmaceutical science and technology thus has been defined in economic terms and has focused largely on the local market. Consequently, the implementation of Pharma-2020 so far has concentrated on enhancing the research, development, and production capacities of the local industry, while leaving out the issue of translating the newly built industrial capacities into the improvement of public health, and has also inhibited the internationalization of Russian pharmaceutical business practices. The development and implementation of Pharma-2020 has then worked to articulate, rehearse, and strengthen a particular vision of the nation and its future: that of an independent and self-sufficient Russian nation.

Innovations in pharmaceuticals are nowadays generated in complex networks involving scientists, physicians, firms, and state agencies. Chapter 5 investigates the implications of the Russian government's efforts to boost local drug research, development, and production for collaboration between actors involved in pharmaceutical innovating and thus for their ability to work together in introducing new drugs. It analyzes *collaborating* as yet another process that shapes pharmapolitical practices. The political aspirations of Pharma-2020 suggest that the current situation in which foreign pharmaceutical companies dominate the internal country market is considered problematic, because it is the Russian pharmaceutical industry that should be reaping the benefits from this market. To rectify this situation, Pharma-2020 was translated into quick, state-defined measures to rapidly produce the required results. The measures have included the introduction of new pharmaceutical research funding schemes, the establishment of new infrastructural organizations, such as biomedical clusters, and the development of new rules for obtaining state support. These measures have been characterized by nontransparency, continual change, top-downness, and a lack of opportunities for dialogue between the actors working on drug development and regulators. It became clear that these characteristics contribute to the general atmosphere of disorientation and uncertainty that inhibits the opportunities for interaction and collaboration between actors involved in pharmaceutical science and technology. Correspondingly, this atmosphere also inhibits the changes policy makers are trying to achieve because the described lack of collaboration opportunities in the Russian pharmaceutical arena is inimical to drug innovation.

Chapter 6 concludes by bringing together all four processes that shape pharmapolitical trajectories—*producing visions, generating value, defining problems, and collaborating*. This analysis highlights how pharmaceutical science and technology become sites and objects of politics, and how political ambitions and agendas are being shaped through their interaction with technological opportunities and constraints, together constituting pharmapolitics. The ways in which the four processes function in particular contexts account for the specific directions pharmapolitical developments take. In this chapter, I also analyze the implications of the current pharmapolitics in Russia for governing drug innovation there. I question the reigning assumption—that the development of the capabilities of the pharmaceutical industry, supported by the state, will necessarily lead to meeting population drug needs in a better way and thus will positively affect public health. Also, I link the Russian case with the global pharmaceutical arena to suggest that both are characterized by oppressive imagination practices that prevent alternatives to the dominant visions of the pharmaceutical futures from emerging, which is detrimental to linking pharmaceutical science and technology with people's health and societal well-being.

This book is concerned with the relations between politics and pharmaceutical science and technology, and with explicating the processes whereby relations between them are configured, which introduces certain limits to research presented here. I am exploring these relations through engaging with a number of specific drug R&D sites. Transformations in Russian political life, including the evolution of political institutions and policy-making processes, form an important background of my study. However, I engage with them only insofar as it is necessary to achieve the primary goal of this book. Also, this book may disappoint those who attempt to read it as a history book. I simply rely on several specific sites in the USSR and post-Soviet Russia that provide fruitful vantage points to reflect on the questions raised in this book; therefore, a historical account of the regulatory and technological change in the field of pharmaceuticals is necessarily limited and makes no claims on comprehensiveness. To further stake out a manageable field of work that fits within the cover of one book, in this study I am concerned with the R&D of pharmaceuticals, rather than with the issues involved in their circulation and consumption. This is not because the latter topic is unimportant, but because the issue of drug circulation and consumption revolves around special considerations and circumstances that distinguish it from drug R&D.

Chapter 1

The Soviet Pharmapolitical Regime

Promising Social Justice

Immediately after the beginning of the Soviet state, its pharmaceutical industry was reorganized into a centrally managed and planned sector, production moved to state factories, and modern science was invoked to develop drugs and ways to manufacture them. Public research institutes and laboratories became linked to public medicine production and distribution facilities, with state institutions commanding the flow of resources and drugs within this system. This chapter analyzes the formation of the Soviet pharmaceutical industry through the pharmapolitical lens, that is, paying attention to "the strategic practice of designing or using technology to constitute, embody, or enact political goals" (Hecht 2001, 256). Viewing Soviet pharmaceuticals from this analytical angle, we see that they enabled a forceful articulation of the communist ideas about society, on one hand, and contributed to shaping Soviet political ambitions, on the other. In the USSR, pharmaceuticals and politics coproduced a vision of an ultimately socially just society that, as becomes clear in the following chapters, later was superseded by other dominant visions of the nation and its future.

In this chapter, I focus first on the early years of the Soviet pharmaceutical industry; second, on the organization and practice of developing drugs that gradually solidified in the Soviet Union; and third, on the culture of collecting and evaluating evidence in Soviet drug research and development (R&D). In conclusion, by focusing on these three key points, I elaborate on the contours of the Soviet pharmapolitical regime. The chapter is based on my reading of existing accounts of various periods in the history of Soviet pharmaceutical industry. Through a close reading and comparison of these accounts, I bring to the fore ideals and assumptions at play in the formation of the Soviet pharmapolitical regime.

Previous analyses of the Soviet pharmaceutical industry, some of which I draw on here, often emphasize the inefficiencies of the USSR's drug development, production, and distribution and the USSR's modest innovation record for medicines. These inefficiencies tend to be explained by a lack of relevant knowledge and understanding of business operations on the part of those who directed the industry. I offer an analysis of the Soviet pharmaceutical industry that makes visible the imaginaries of a particular kind of society at work in building the industry. Not disputing the shortcomings of the Soviet pharmaceutical industry, I argue that to understand the formation of the Soviet pharmaceutical project, it is also necessary to take account of how this sociotechnical endeavor came to be entwined with the vision of a future society saturated with a specific kind of social justice; this vision, in turn, was shaping the governance of the pharmaceutical arena.

The Foundation of the Soviet Pharmapolitical Regime

The Soviet pharmaceutical industry began when chemical and pharmaceutical enterprises were nationalized after the Great October Socialist Revolution of 1917. Nationalization began in April 1918 when a special administrative body called Pharmcenter was created within the Supreme Council of the National Economy to oversee the reform of the pharmaceutical industry. First, of all chemical and pharmaceutical production facilities and laboratories located in the Russian Soviet Republic, the twenty-two most sizeable ones were nationalized. Previously these enterprises belonged to private individuals, joint-stock companies or nongovernmental organizations (such as the International Red Cross), and all but six of them were located in Moscow (Natradze 1967). By the end of 1919, all sixty-two enterprises that produced medicines in the Russian Soviet Republic, which altogether employed about five thousand people, were managed by the state (Natradze 1957). The Soviet strategy further focused on consolidation: many of the nationalized units were closed or reorganized so that the largest plants received most equipment and resources to hereafter scale up the production of pharmaceuticals.

I build my account of the Soviet pharmaceutical industry's early years, decisive for its further developmental path, on placing two scholarly sources in a dialogue: Mary Schaeffer Conroy's *The Soviet Pharmaceutical Business During the First Two Decades (1917-1937)* (2006) and Onisim Magidson's "History of the Development of the Chemical and Pharmaceutical Industry in the USSR" (1970). The two texts I selected represent two major narratives on which existing accounts of the inception of the Soviet pharmaceutical industry rely. Divergences and silences, made visible by reading them together, provide a fruitful vantage point for discerning joint workings of technology and politics.

Let us first take a look at how these two sources assess the state of the pharmaceutical industry in late imperial Russia and, correspondingly, of the industry development strategy chosen by the Soviets. Mary Schaeffer Conroy (2006), author of three meticulous books on the Soviet pharmaceutical industry, cites the presence of "one hundred or more Russian pharmaceutical enterprises . . . within the Russian Empire," adding that "many concerns were small, owned by individuals or families" (11). She describes these enterprises as engaged mostly in botanicals rather than in medicines developed from advances in chemistry and related technologies (11–45). The latter was the broad domain where drug innovation (Achilladelis and Antonakis 2001, 536) clustered in the late nineteenth and early twentieth centuries—and during the First World War, Russian industry began turning its gaze toward medical chemistry (Conroy 2006, 33–35). Conroy suggests that these data demonstrate that the pharmaceutical industry in imperial Russia was quite viable.

Onisim Magidson, a chemist who actively participated in establishing the new Soviet drug R&D system (Ministerstvo meditsinskoi promishlennosti 1971), writes of the pre-Soviet pharmaceutical industry rather dismissively:

> Before the Revolution, the chemical and pharmaceutical industry of Russia consisted of small primitive enterprises the proprietors of which occupied themselves mainly with commercial medicaments, articles for the care of patients, and perfumery and cosmetic products. Production was only subsidiary to trade and was a secondary affair. Consequently, the enterprises of the chemical and pharmaceutical industry mainly carried out the mechanical treatment of the pharmaceutical raw material (grinding, mixing, tableting, packaging) or the preparation

of galenicals from plant and animal raw material (tinctures, extracts, ointments, etc.). In addition, some technical and perfumery and cosmetic articles were manufactured (soap, creams, face powders, etc.). (53)

While the two authors' assessments of the state of the pre-Soviet pharmaceutical industry are conflicting, the basic premises on which their assessments are based are similar: the industry consisted largely of small enterprises and barely engaged in chemical synthesis of drugs. The authors, however, interpret the situation in precisely opposite ways. Conroy sees it as supporting freedom of entrepreneurship and encouraging innovation and therefore being the best for development and growth of the pharmaceutical industry. From this point of view, multiple small private enterprises driven by the desire to obtain profits would be creatively coming up with novel technologies, while market mechanisms would ensure their responsiveness to the health needs of the population. In this picture, chemically synthesized medicines and other novel drug groups would arrive soon, through entrepreneurs' energy and creativity.

But Soviet reformers, including Magidson, viewed the pharmaceutical industry's makeup of multiple private enterprises as disorderly and primitive. In their point of view, private entrepreneurs working in market conditions would be operating inefficiently, duplicating efforts, and overlooking population health needs in pursuit of profit maximization. Also, the introduction of medical chemistry and modern science and technology more generally in drug development and production would be too uncertain and dependent on the self-interest of business. Against this background, the Soviet reformers were determined to modernize the pharmaceutical sector into one that was centrally planned and directed and in which the most scientific and efficient approaches were employed to develop and produce medicines. The entire industry was to be centrally coordinated to achieve such ultimate efficiency. The system envisioned can be described by a statement by L. Ia. Karpov, the head of the Department of Chemical Industry in the Supreme Council of the National Economy, on May 30, 1918. Karpov conveyed that the state through its governance mechanisms had:

> . . . the tasks to regularize and coordinate the activity of factories, review and approve budgets of the state factories, supply them with [financial] means, unite accounting and control,

guarantee raw materials and fuel, [coordinate] technical control over production, supervise administration, review and approve the order of sales of the products. (Russian State Economic Archive [RGAE], fond 8126, opis 1, cited in Conroy 2006)

Therefore, Magidson, who viewed the Soviet way of building the pharmaceutical industry as the most rational and efficient one, considered the late imperial Russian industry to be in a dismal state.

The differences described between Conroy and Magidson in assessing the pre-Soviet pharmaceutical industry and, correspondingly, in their views on how industry was to be organized and governed cannot be explained by their drawing on different data, because they agree on initial facts, that is, on what the pre-Soviet Russian pharmaceutical industry looked like. I suggest, rather, that these differences are reflective of divergent sociotechnical imaginaries of the pharmaceutical industry and the society that this industry is to serve. The Soviet society was held strongly by an imaginary of how the country's industry, including the pharmaceutical sector, would come to the forefront of science and technology and become the most rational and efficient in the world through its central coordination and planning and the exclusion of private profit motives and, in these ways, support progress toward a society of ultimate social justice. Entrepreneurial, private, diverse industry developing in a market society, where individuals are free to pursue private initiatives and profits, does not sit well with this imaginary. The Soviet insistence on building a pharmaceutical industry not subjected to market forces can be illustrated by the following statement:

> ... all medicines, to the last gram, have to be accounted by the state that knows how to rationally use them. ... In our circumstances products will belong to the state only when the state itself makes them. (Archives of the USSR Ministry of Health, file #979-a from March 15, 1920, cited in Natradze 1967, 98)

This statement was made by the Board of the State Chemical-Pharmaceutical Factories in response to foreign pharmaceutical companies' requests for concessions to operate pharmaceutical factories in the Soviet territory. In the same document, the authors also stressed that apart from not being willing to rely on market forces to satisfy the country's needs in medicines generally, they found involvement of foreign businesses particularly dangerous because "[a]s a result we will have not the medicines we need, but the medicines that foreign capitalists deign to give us."

Therefore, the divergent assessments of the starting conditions of the Soviet pharmaceutical industry can be understood as underpinned by the conflicting sociotechnical imaginaries implicit in Magidson's and Conroy's positions. Magidson envisions a society of ultimate social justice, not plagued by inequality and exploitation associated with private business operations, and a pharmaceutical industry organized without duplication of effort, resource waste, or biases of private interests in serving such a society. Conroy, by contrast, sees the freedom to engage in entrepreneurial activities as in fact a driver of societal development and a way to create both economic profits and societal value. Consequently, Magidson defines the state of the pharmaceutical industry in late imperial Russia as primitive and disorderly because it does not facilitate progress toward a society of ultimate social justice as conceived by him and the Soviet reformers. At the same time, Conroy perceives this state as vibrant and developing as it contributes to the emergence of a society of free enterprise and creativity, beneficial for the well-being of the individuals and groups who populate it.

After reviewing the two contrasting perspectives on the initial conditions of the Soviet pharmaceutical industry, I now turn to early Soviet drug R&D. I continue comparing the texts by Conroy and Magidson to analyze practices of drug R&D through discrepancies revealed.

Soon after the nationalization and initial consolidation, the early Soviet pharmaceutical industry gained another element decisive for its shaping—a centrally positioned R&D institute. In 1919, Pharmcenter received a programmatic document from one of its members, Aleksei Chichibabin, who was a prominent organic chemist, a professor at Moscow University (Zaitseva 2001). In this document, Chichibabin argued that creating such a pharmaceutical R&D institute was paramount for the systematic growth of the Soviet pharmaceutical industry, which required a technoscientific foundation (Magidson 1967). The response was positive, and from November 30, 1920, building 15 on Bolshaia Nikolskaia Street in Moscow, where the private Ferrein Laboratory was located before the revolution, housed Pharmaceutical Chemical Scientific Research Institute (NIKhFI) (Mashkovskii 2000). NIKhFI was tasked with:

1. Development of methods for synthesizing medicines and their verification for use in production factories;

2. Substitution of imported raw materials with domestic ones;
3. Research and utilization of medicinal plants;
4. Technoscientific support of the industry. (Natradze 1957, 5)

Confronted with a lack of import opportunities due to frictions in the international political arena, the Soviet state expected pharmaceutical science and technology, concentrated in the NIKhFI, to swiftly find ways to substitute previously imported items and catch up with development and production processes from abroad.

The achievements of early Soviet pharmaceutical science and technology are again assessed differently by the authors whose texts I compare here. Conroy (2006) writes that in 1927, among nineteen new medicines developed by the NIKhFI and introduced into production on a factory scale were

> Pantopon (a Roche and, in 1922 a Poehl product); Dionin and Stypticin; the hormone products Adrenalin, Mammin, Ovarin and Tyreoidin (in 1922 a Poehl product for skin diseases).... Exactly *how* these new preparations ... heretofore imported from abroad were developed was not disclosed. Undoubtedly it was through reverse engineering." (131, italics in the original)

She stresses that most formulations and production methods developed by the NIKhFI in the first years of its existence were not original; rather, its staff found ways to manufacture drugs already available elsewhere. Therefore, Conroy's evaluation of the NIKhFI's work is not especially positive.

Magidson (1970), on the other hand, also does not claim that the first achievements of the Institute were highly original, writing that "[i]n a comparatively short time the institute developed and introduced into practice several manufactures new to Russia" (295), that is, admitting that the newly produced drugs were new to Russia, not necessarily to the world. But, he added, "even in the first years of its existence and in spite of various kinds of difficulties (the small number of personnel—60–70 [people], poor equipment), the Institute proved to be of real use to industry and acquired scientific authority" (295). This addition shows that Magidson saw the job of the Institute, where he worked for many years, differently, and, against this background, his evaluation of the NIKhFI's achievements is much higher than Conroy's.

To Magidson, the task at hand was to move forward from an industry heavily focused on botanicals and natural remedies and catch up with the technoscience-based pharmaceutical industry abroad, first of all, in Germany, which had already produced two generations of radically innovative drugs based on advances in chemistry, physiology, and bacteriology, and was preparing for a leap to the third generation (Achilladelis and Antonakis 2001). The urgency of the task was aggravated by the continuing reliance on importing drugs from countries not too sympathetic to communism building. This reliance was not considered a suitable option for the Soviet Union, as illustrated by Magidson with an example: "The complete lack of anesthetics and the necessity of replacing imported cocaine made it necessary to create a basic assortment of synthetic preparations of this group" (1970, 55). If it took reverse engineering to reach these goals, Magidson and others involved in these efforts did not see it as problematic; rather, success was perceived as building internal capacity to synthesize and produce modern drugs.

Divergent views on what innovation is can be discerned in these conflicting assessments of achievements of the early Soviet pharmaceutical science and technology, although Magidson does not use the term innovation in his writing. For Conroy, consistent with her implicit view of a free entrepreneurial society as beneficial for people's well-being, innovation is associated with a concrete, commercializable pharmaceutical product that had not existed before. An important part of this conception is patenting, because innovation is protected by a patent, and those who violate patents, as the Soviets did, engage in anything but innovating. Thus Conroy's view on innovation is consonant with the influential view of innovation as centered around profit, entrepreneurial firm, and market. This view has dominated most scholarly discussions and theorizing about innovation. By contrast, Magidson, consistent with his aspiration for a society of ultimate social justice as conceived by the architects of Soviet reforms, views innovation in a different way. In his writing, he recalls how the establishment of the NIKhFI itself became a new form of organizing drug development, embedded in the novel socialized institutional structure of the Soviet pharmaceutical industry. Learning how to produce modern drugs and finding ways to do so in the circumstances of scarcity and societal turbulence was innovative for the Soviet reformers, who were opposed to the capitalist mode of production and circulation of goods that form the crucial background of the understanding of innovation articulated by Conroy.

Consequently, understanding innovation in divergent ways, Conroy and Magidson assess in divergent ways the achievements of the NIKhFI and early Soviet pharmaceutical science and technology more generally. For Conroy, these achievements were only imitations that therefore had little value; for Magidson, these were valuable innovations in the organization and processes of drug development and production that were uniquely suited to the harsh conditions of the early Soviet Union. Again, these authors do not disagree on basic data; Conroy writes that "the Soviet Union prototypes rolled off the assembly line at dizzying speed" (2006, 221). It is the interpretation and significance of these facts that are the basis for the disagreement, which can be understood as grounded in opposing ideas about what innovation is and in conflicting sociotechnical imaginaries of the societies these innovations are meant to serve.

To complete an overview of the early years of the Soviet pharmaceutical industry, I briefly describe below the types and quantities of drugs that it came to develop and produce. By 1920, in the conditions of civil war, lack of raw materials, and drastic reforms, the volume of medicines produced fell and constituted about 80 percent of the volume in 1916 (Natradze 1957). The centrally set production plans could not be fulfilled. For example, in the first quarter of 1920, pharmaceutical factories in Moscow managed to produce only 45 percent of the volume of drugs expected from them (Natradze 1967, 96). Gradually the production volume did begin increasing, exceeding pre-revolutionary levels, in part because of the changes in pharmaceutical industry governance. Because prior to the mid-1930s all pharmaceutical production units were governed by the People's Commissariat for Heavy Industry, which was not closely concerned with health-care needs, capacities of those units were often occupied by non-medicinal production tasks. The USSR People's Commissariat for Health Care (from 1946 named Ministry of Health) was created in 1936 and immediately began governing drug development and production. This merger of health-care provision and pharmaceutical industry within one governing body took place because the pharmaceutical industry was considered to be an essential part of the Soviet socialized medicine, as I elaborate in the next section. During its first years of work, the People's Commissariat for Health Care also formed the foundation of the pharmaceutical regulation system in the USSR, which I analyze in the third section of this chapter. In short, from 1937, production of new pharmaceuticals could begin only by permission of the People's Commissariat for Health following a review of the content of the drug, its production methods, its purpose, its testing methods and results, and its package design. Each pharmaceutical that received such permission was included in a special registry, and production without permission would result in criminal charges.[1] The increase in the production of the pharmaceuticals can be gaged from the following numbers: in 1913, medicines produced amounted to 16.2 million rubles in 1926–1927 prices; in 1940, medicine production amounted to 244.8 million rubles, and in 1947, to 341.1 million rubles at the same prices (Magidson 1967). To make these numbers more concrete, between 1916 and 1938, production of salicylic acid went from 12.8 to 441.6 tons, aspirin from 0.6 to 169 tons, and iodine from 0.5 to 200 tons (Natradze 1967, 139). Numbers of pharmacies also increased: whereas in 1914 there was one pharmacy per 37,000 people, in 1940 there was one pharmacy per 17,000 people and new factories began to operate, including the Akrikhin factory, the factory named after M. V. Lomonosov, the Krasnaya Zvezda factory, the factory for endocrine drugs, and a number of smaller units for vitamin production (Sherstneva 2018). Yet, despite these increases, shortages of drugs also persisted.

> Enter any pharmacy and ask for the most mundane medicine—boric acid, iodine. In most cases the response will be that such medicine is not available. Healthcare organizations' demand for essential medicines and disinfectants is met by our pharmaceutical industry at no more than 20 percent.

In January 1935, these words by Grigory Kaminsky, at the time People's Commissar of Health of the Russian Soviet Republic and in 1936–1937 first People's Commissar of Health Care of Soviet Union, were addressed to delegates of the All-Russian Congress of Soviets, the supreme governing body of the Russian Soviet Republic (Sixteenth All-Russian Congress of Soviets 1935).

In terms of types of medicines, by 1940, the Soviet pharmaceutical industry produced 570 different pharmaceutical drugs (Natradze 1967). The "prototypes" mentioned by Conroy did come to include several medicines novel to the world. For instance, the antimalarial plasmocid (Plasmocidum) was produced from 1933 and became part of the strategy that led to eliminating malaria in the USSR. Production process innovations were also introduced; for example, a method for obtaining synthetic vitamin C, ascorbic acid, was developed and put in industrial production at the end of the 1930s. A method for extracting iodine from brine water, which is a byproduct of oil and gas production, was developed, and the first Soviet iodine factory in Nefte-Chala began to operate in 1931 followed by five more factories in 1932. As a result, by the mid-1930s the USSR stopped importing iodine. The organization of the Soviet pharmaceutical sector with its centralized and state-directed R&D facilities, whose findings were then implemented in the state production factories, was very different from that in other countries, where pharmaceutical innovation was mostly concentrated in the twentieth century (see Achilladelis 1999, and introduction to this book). But, all in all, the types of drugs that were developed and produced by the Soviet pharmaceutical sector prior to World War II were much like the kinds of drugs that constituted the first, second, and third generation of drugs in the West: anesthetics, analgesics, antipyretics, soporifics, antiprotozoals, vaccines, sulfonamides, and vitamins. In the postwar years, natural antibiotics and their synthetic analogues (for instance, levomycetin), as well as steroids, were introduced, which also was generally in line with what constituted the third generation of drugs in the West.

Overall, the ascent of the Soviet pharmaceutical industry was animated by a broader Soviet futurist vision of progress to socialism through large-scale industrialization (Hecht 2011). Achievements in industrial technologies and science appeared to offer a modern means to transcend inequalities, including those in health, and establish a society of social justice. The pharmaceutical industry specifically was to be modernized to rely on the latest science and technology for developing and producing medicines. Its efficiency and rationality were to be achieved through excluding private interests and centralizing planning and coordination. We can therefore discern in these developments the beginning of the Soviet pharmapolitical regime, where new drug research institutes, a reformed drug production structure, a socialist political program, and pharmaceuticals themselves were converging to govern the industry and also to pursue pharmapolitics. Thereby pharmaceutical technoscience became involved in constituting, embodying, and enacting political goals.

Drugs: From Bench to International Politics

The drug R&D system in the USSR was from its beginning intended to be organized in such a way that the points most often criticized about the Western commercial pharmaceutical industry could be avoided: duplication of research and corresponding resource waste, unreasonably high prices, and aggressive advertising. Details of its organization changed from time to time, especially in the early years, but by the later period of the Soviet Union (from the 1960s onward) the drug development system generally remained unchanged. In this section I offer an analysis of this system through, again, placing a number of existing narratives in a dialogue. I do not intend to provide a comprehensive history of the governance of the Soviet pharmaceutical industry here. Rather, I analyze divergent takes on key elements of the drug R&D system during the later period of the Soviet Union in comparison with its opposite—the US system—to discern joint workings of technologies and politics. This analysis also provides a foundation for revisiting a question already raised in the previous section: the contribution of the Soviet pharmaceutical industry to the world's pool of innovation.

From 1967, the Soviet pharmaceutical industry was governed by two ministries: the Ministry of Health (MoH) and the Ministry of Medical Industry (MMI); before 1967, the MoH oversaw the entire system. Once a candidate drug was developed by MoH laboratories or by those of the Academy of Medical Sciences, the MMI had to find a plant willing and able to produce a pilot batch of the candidate drug. The pilot batch manufactured was returned to the MoH to organize clinical trials that, if successful, would lead to the MoH granting a license to the drug to be produced and included in the pharmacopoeia. Manufacturing of the approved drugs again became the responsibility of the MMI, which assigned a manufacturing plant. A separate state inspectorate external to the factory and accountable to both the MoH and the MMI checked the quality of the drug being produced for mass distribution. Yet another group of professionals from the MoH was responsible for distribution and information dissemination about the drug.

The organization of this drug R&D system thereby embodied the Soviet vision of society: it excluded financial profit motives that were deemed to be responsible for the ills of the commercial system and was designed to ensure efficient channeling of resources and efforts for developing products needed by society. Let us take a brief look at the dangers the Soviet drug development system was intended to combat. The private pharmaceutical industry had a long history of questionable marketing practices. The Kefauver hearings on the US pharmaceutical industry held in 1959–1963 brought to light that drug advertisements tended to omit details about side effects and contraindications (Tobbell 2009). Tobbel (2009), detailing testimonies and statements made during the Kefauver hearings, adds:

> A group of prominent academic physicians which included
> Louis Lasagna of Johns Hopkins University, Maxwell Finland
> of Harvard Medical School, Walter Modell of Cornell Medical
> School, and Harry Dowling of the University of Illinois, criticized the industry for each year introducing a "plethora of poor
> compounds," with little to no therapeutic advantage over existing
> drugs and yet marketing them as if they were groundbreaking
> therapeutic innovations. Most troubling for these physicians
> was the industry's recent practice of combining two or more
> old drugs and marketing—and patenting—the resulting drug
> as a new drug without any evidence that the combination drug
> had any therapeutic advantage over its constituent drugs. (454)

That is, duplication and resource waste paired with problematic practices were indeed a part of the commercialized US pharmaceutical arena, a part criticized also from within American society. It is therefore hard to argue that the Soviet authorities and professionals were completely misguided in trying to avoid it. Even after the Kefauver-Harris Amendments were put into force in the United States in 1962, obliging manufacturers to disclose information on side effects, contraindications, and effectiveness, as approved by the FDA, the industry found ways to circumvent the regulation. This can be illustrated by other hearings initiated by Senator Gaylord Nelson in 1976, when the FDA questioned the pharmaceutical companies' practice of using "throwaway journals"—journals whose content resembled peer-reviewed publications but instead was controlled by their sponsors—to encourage physicians to prescribe medicines for off-label uses, that is, uses not approved by the FDA (Greene and Podolsky 2009). The head of the FDA at the time argued that "[t]he issue here is whether such an article in a controlled industry circulation journal presents, in the guise of a scientific paper, promotional information which otherwise could not be legally published as drug advertising or drug labeling" (quoted in Greene and Podolsky 2009, 371).

Nonetheless, the Soviet drug R&D system had its own problems, and to avoid presenting an idealized view of it, I further summarize criticisms of its functioning as formulated by two medical researchers from Birmingham University, United Kingdom, at the end of the 1980s. In practice, the Soviet drug development system that was expected to efficiently supply reasonably priced drugs accompanied by balanced and unbiased informational materials did not function smoothly. Jack and Mason (1987) describe its shortcomings in the following way: the complicated institutional system could produce delays at almost every step. Factories mostly were not particularly interested in producing new drugs because they were assessed based on fulfilling quotas calculated in quantities produced rather than qualitative composition. Investing time and effort in producing a new drug could even lead to factory managers being penalized if as a result smaller quantities of pharmaceutical output were produced. Producing old, familiar drugs was less risky and did not necessitate searching for ways to obtain new equipment and personnel expertise. Expertise accessibility constituted a problem in itself, because scientists who developed the drug were located in their institutes and not in the factories, which could be far away. Finally, quality control by an external inspectorate took place mostly when the drug was already produced; that is, quality control was not always involved in the manufacturing process itself. Problems were reported on the distribution side as well, resulting from a rigid retailing system that often did not respond to the drug needs of the population and from both doctors and pharmacies being provided with insufficient information about new drugs. Jack and Mason (1987) thus argue that the time needed for a drug to travel from bench to bedside was nearly unpredictable, and researchers trying to deliver their drugs to patients faced bureaucratic nightmare.

At the same time, during my fieldwork in 2013–2014, those of my informants who had worked in the Soviet drug development system told a different story. The picture of institutional constraints in drug R&D presented by Jack and Mason can be enriched by an understanding of experiences of drug developers themselves. My informants explained that they found it easy to work in the Soviet system and get things done. They portrayed the ministries, also staffed mostly with scientists, as their allies. For instance, one researcher contrasted his present relationship with the Russian MoH with his experiences with the Soviet MoH. This researcher explained that he could discuss his drug development projects and optimal ways to design and bring them forward with the Soviet MoH, while such a dialogue would be impossible now with the Russian MoH:

> Previously I would take a document proving that I am a staff member of a cardiology research institute. Here it is. I would come, there is a policeman. I show that I am a staff member. Make a call and I can enter any office of the Minzdrav [MoH]. There were several of them, Minzdrav organizations. You come in and talk to people, who understand [what you are doing], and they even give you advice. (11SD, 2014)

Overall, my informants who had worked in the Soviet drug R&D system argued that they knew how to navigate the constraints of its bureaucratic organization and established working relations with various decision makers, many of whom were their scientific peers. Another illustration of this thesis can be derived from a description another scientist provided, explaining to me how his team brought their first diagnostic radiopharmaceutical to clinical practice in about a year:

> In principle, we made our first drug, bringing it from the first experiments to clinical use, in approximately one year. It is because back then to obtain permission for clinical trials of radiopharmaceuticals there was a commission where we would bring data about functional suitability (specific activity) of pharmaceuticals and, in a very condensed way, about toxicology. They would look and say: "Ok, guys, you can perform clinical trials. Finished clinical trials? Ok, guys, please, produce." Now all this, of course is two or may be even three times more bureaucratized. Back then it was clear, who you are communicating with. You were given useful advice, because people were interested in development of this area. . . . Back then it was easy and we needed our patients to have such an opportunity [to use the radiopharmaceuticals developed to improve diagnostic processes]. (10SD, 2014)

While the descriptions provided of the Soviet system of drug R&D and of actual experiences of drug developers within it appear to be contrasting, I suggest viewing them not as contradictory, but rather as complementary. The institutional system indeed was complicated and could produce delays and constrain the drug development processes. At the same time, those involved in drug R&D were not cogs in a machine but active contributors to shaping the Soviet pharmaceutical industry. They developed knowledge and skills to effectively direct and perform their work using this system. They established personal connections with each other and various decision-making institutions to facilitate bringing new drugs from bench to bedside. Finally, they also shaped the institutional system in question themselves because people responsible for the planning and administration of drug R&D were the scientists and medical professionals themselves.

This latter point has been artfully articulated by historian Anna Geltzer. When discussing Soviet biomedical science and technology, she stresses that it "was an integral part of the larger health care system that blended curative and preventive concerns. This system, in turn, was an integral part of the Soviet state, a point that is frequently lost sight of by Western analysts and observers, who often conclude that because the health care system was centrally planned it was strictly subordinate to the state and its employees were nothing more than civil servants required to do the state's bidding" (Geltzer 2012, 53). This is an important point to consider in analyzing the Soviet pharmaceutical R&D system.

Indeed, Geltzer describes how American biomedical scientists who participated in a US–USSR scientific exchange program in 1956–1977 viewed Soviet biomedical scientists as being controlled by a planning system that coordinated their activities and set their research agenda. In the words of an American virologist who spent six months in the USSR in 1962, the operation of this system resulted in "all planning and thinking [being] centered in one man at the head of each institute," "serious difficulties in establishing or changing programs," and excessive deference to authority that "tends to inhibit the evolution of concepts" (Brody, cited in Geltzer 2012, 45). Many scholarly analyses of Soviet (pharmaceutical) science and technology suggest that exactly these governance characteristics, which stifled initiative and creativity, explain why the Soviet record of major innovations, including drugs, is rather modest (see, for instance, Conroy 2006, for the pharmaceutical industry, and Etzkowitz and Leydesdorff 2000, 111–12, for technoscientific innovation more generally).

At the same time, other scholars and accounts of my informants suggest, as did Geltzer herself, that scientists and administrators who staffed the Soviet science and technology institutions were "surprisingly effective at exploiting the contradictions in the Soviet system of planning and administration in pursuit of their own scientific and political goals" (2012, 42). The practices of planning and control in the Soviet healthcare system, of which biomedical science and technology were a part, in fact were flexible and porous, and, while bureaucratic constraints had to be negotiated on a daily basis and some were impossible to circumvent, individual scientists found ways to exercise control over their own work. As an illustration of this thesis, Geltzer demonstrates how a program of intensification of the US–USSR exchange in biomedicine was tacitly approved by the Communist Party apparatus only retroactively, when the exchange had been effectively underway for several months after being debated and planned by the scientists from the Academy of Medical Sciences and other scientific institutes together with Ministry of Health officials. More generally, historians argue that even amid the Stalinist repressions, Soviet scientists did not completely surrender their agency and attempted to leverage the bureaucratic machinery in pursuit of their agenda (Krementsov 1997) and that this trend intensified after Iosif Stalin's death (Ivanov 2002).

Before moving to the last section of this chapter, I return to the issue of the contribution of the Soviet pharmaceutical industry into the world's pool of innovation. I reflect on this question, again, from the analytical angle of pharmapolitics, looking at how pharmaceuticals and systems of their development, production, and circulation became embroiled in the international politics of the Cold War period.

As I mentioned above, Soviet pharmaceutical R&D was an integral part of the wider Soviet health-care system that, according to Dmitrii Venediktov, a surgeon and Soviet deputy minister of health care for international affairs from 1965 to 1980 (Serebrianyi 2016), had three main goals:

1. Development of medical science as the only possible foundation for comprehensive measures aimed at protecting and improving human health.
2. Individual and public disease prevention, first and foremost child health protection, and environmental sanitation control as a primary factor influencing human health.
3. Universal accessibility of early diagnosis and qualified treatment of diseases, including rehabilitation and work reintegration. (Venediktov 1977, 55)

These goals were far from being fully realized in practice but nonetheless guided the development of structure and function of the system. Therefore, the significance of the Soviet pharmaceutical science and technology should be viewed in the context of this system.

Venediktov, who articulated these three goals in his book on international problems of health care (1977), spent several years in the United States (1962–1965) as the medical adviser to the USSR's mission at the United Nations. Upon assuming the post of the deputy minister of health care in the USSR, he actively worked to facilitate international cooperation between the USSR, other countries, and international organizations such as the WHO. In the book, Venedictov elaborates a health-care foreign policy for the USSR in which he suggests cooperating with socialist and developing countries on the basis of "selfless assistance." Capitalist countries would be both rivals and critical partners, in a strictly symmetrical way, to achieve "mutual benefit," and international organizations would be both tools for international cooperation and sites where competition for influence over the developing world took place. In Venediktov's view, the USSR's most valuable contribution to all these fields of international cooperation was disseminating the approach of the Soviet health-care system, which he argued was the most progressive and effective system in the world. Although Venediktov acknowledged that the system was not perfect and was particularly wanting in medical science and technology, he also insisted on its organizational and methodological superiority, which was to be recognized internationally.

The position of Venediktov, who argued for the dissemination of the methodology of the Soviet health-care system throughout the world, can be understood as a case of mixing medicine, including pharmaceutical science and technology, and politics. I demonstrated earlier in this section how the organization of drug R&D in the USSR, being a part of the wider healthcare system, became an articulation of the communist ideals of society. The attempts to disseminate this system therefore can be understood as attempts to disseminate these ideals and, correspondingly, influence the development of other countries to expand the Soviet regime.

Western analysts at the time made no mistake in interpreting this mix of health care, pharmaceutical science and technology, and politics as such. For instance, Mark Field, a prominent analyst of Soviet medicine, argued in his 1967 book:

> Soviet socialized medicine must . . . be considered an important and integral component of [the Soviet] challenge. . . . This challenge is . . . not limited to the political, economic, or even military spheres; it is also part and parcel of Soviet propaganda and of its claim of having, among other things, pioneered and developed an advanced form of "socialized" health service unique in many of its features and possible only under Soviet conditions. The Soviet regime thus seeks to evoke, among its own people, an attitude of gratitude toward itself as the fountainhead of progress and the organizer of medical care; and, by inference perhaps more than by direct statements, the regime tells the people of other countries (particularly the former colonial nations) that only the adoption of a Soviet

or "socialistic" form of government will make it possible for them to provide for their health needs. (cited in Geltzer 2012, 47)

Interestingly, the dominant approach in the United States, the superpower opposing the USSR in the Cold War struggle, was to respond to the communist threat by focusing on pharmaceuticals as a necessary weapon "to win the hearts and minds of the people of underdeveloped and undecided nations in capitalism's fight against communism" (Tobbel 2009, 441). For example, in 1957, Senator Hubert Humphrey argued for employing pharmaceuticals to free people in developing countries from both disease and the communist threat, assigning the American pharmaceutical industry a crucial role in this battle for influence. In his view, the industry was to promote international health by providing drugs such as antibiotics and vaccines to developing countries and to promote the development of pharmaceutical science and technology there that would follow the American commercialized model. In other words, as historian Dominique A. Tobbel wrote, "Humphrey saw the work of American drug firms as a critical vehicle in which the American system of free enterprise could be delivered to those undeveloped and undecided nations in Asia, Africa, and the Middle East" (2009, 442).

Thus, the Soviet pharmaceutical science and technology and a wider health-care system not only allowed articulation of the Soviet vision of society within the country, but also shaped the Soviet foreign policy agenda and became an instrument for pursuing the project of disseminating communist ideals to engage other countries, all being a part of the Soviet national pharmapolitical regime. Altogether, the technoscientific as well as political elements of this regime can be understood as working to pursue Soviet pharmapolitics: strategic use of pharmaceutical science and technology to pursue political goals both internally and in the international arena. Importantly, while the Soviet Union did export pharmaceuticals to developing countries, in addition to other Communist states, throughout the Cold War, it did not rely on pharmaceuticals themselves in the way the United States did to promote the benefits of a Communist vision of society. In fact, Venediktov himself admitted that medical science and technology in the USSR was far from perfect. Rather, the pharmaceutical science and technology were part of the entire package of the Soviet socialized health-care system that was viewed by its Soviet proponents as the most significant and innovative achievement in medicine and one that could transmit the political message of the superiority of the Soviet vision.

Soviet Bioethics: Claiming a Superior Vision of Society

In this final section of the chapter, I attend to some characteristics of the Soviet culture of collecting and evaluating evidence in drug development. These characteristics provide yet another vantage point to reflect on relations between politics and pharmaceutical science and technology in the Soviet pharmapolitical regime. Here I continue to rely on my comparative approach, used in the previous sections, by putting existing narratives on the topic in dialogue and contrasting examples from the USSR and the United States. The country comparator was chosen not only because of political contrasts between the essentially capitalist and socialist states, but also because the US process of drug review and the FDA-developed standards for drug evaluation and clinical trials came to be the basis for current global pharmaceutical regulation (Carpenter 2010).

By 1926, Soviet legislation stipulated that "new drugs are allowed [to be produced] after pharmaceutical and clinical trial of their value."[2] This was rather unusual compared with other countries with a sizable pharmaceutical industry. In the United States, the premarket testing of safety of pharmaceuticals began to be required in 1938 with the Food, Drug and Cosmetic Act. In 1962, when the Kefauver-Harris Amendments to this Act came into force, the FDA gained a legal basis for requiring data on the effectiveness of new drugs before allowing them to reach consumers.

The organization, rules, and practices for testing and evaluating new drugs in the Soviet Union differed significantly from those in Western countries with a strong record of drug innovating.[3] In the USSR, this difference was emphasized and cultivated because Soviet drug development culture was viewed as more efficient, ethical, and scientifically sound. The state was guiding and controlling every step of the Soviet drug-testing system: providing permission for clinical trials, developing specifications for trials of new drugs, appointing institutions where clinical trials would take place, and evaluating results and deciding whether a new drug should be mass-produced. All these tasks were performed by the Pharmaceutical Committee of the MoH, staffed with scientists performing work on this committee as a public service. The absence of private actors and monetary profit interests from this process was viewed as a guarantee of the quality and thoroughness of the review. Much emphasis was also placed on the quality of the experts, who—because they were both highly qualified and safeguarded from the corrupting influences of private industry—would develop reliable methods for drug trials and objectively judge a new drug's safety, efficacy, and comparative advantage.

There are some parallels between the work of the USSR's Pharmaceutical Committee and the United States' FDA in that both relied greatly on the judgments of scientific experts. Scientific expertise was to determine the worthiness of drugs and the best methods to ascertain it. After 1938, the FDA increasingly engaged in developing manuals and standards for collecting reliable pharmaceutical evidence. Moreover, even prior to the enactment of the Kefauver-Harris Amendments, it was not unusual for FDA experts to provide scientific advice to companies on the design and execution of studies. The FDA was gradually projecting its scientific vision of reliable clinical study onto the development practices of pharmaceutical companies, as illustrated, for example, by a 1961 statement of Shelbey Grey, chief of the agency's Bureau of Program Planning and Appraisal:

> The FDA is confronted with the problem of evaluating the efficacy of many new drugs. This can be done only by the conduct of strictly disciplined investigations which have to be initiated and supervised by FDA physicians. (cited in Carpenter 2010, 176)

That is, the FDA too was increasingly involved not only in premarket evaluation of drugs but also in designing drug trials, and after the Kefauver-Harris Amendments its authority grew to include the regulation of trial conduct as well as being able to halt trials for various reasons, including insufficient scientific rigor (Carpenter 2010, 260–61).

While the US' FDA and the USSR's Pharmaceutical Committee did agree on the central role of scientific expertise, their ideas about what constituted reliable evidence of drugs' safety and effectiveness diverged greatly. The three-phase system of clinical trials that was institutionalized by the FDA in the United States in the 1960s and became central for drug development globally was explicitly rejected in the USSR. The Investigational New Drug rules, composed by the FDA in 1963, suggested that clinical trials be structured according to phases. Phase 1 begins when an experimental drug is first introduced to humans (most often these are healthy volunteers) after in vitro and animal studies to determine such parameters as human toxicity, metabolism, absorption, elimination, and safe dosage range; phase 2 typically covers initial trials with a limited number of patients for specific disease control and prophylaxis purposes; and phase 3 assesses the drug's performance in large numbers of patients, typically divided into different groups that follow variations of the same trial protocol. Importantly, the FDA insisted that drug efficacy must be demonstrated with randomized double-blind and well-controlled trials, with the preferable control being placebo comparisons. This entails study protocols in which different subject groups are assigned to receive different interventions, including placebo (no intervention), and in which assignment to groups is random, with neither research participants nor investigators knowing which group participants are assigned to. With time, randomized controlled trials (RCTs) have come to represent the "gold standard" in pharmaceutical evidence, supposedly making drug development rational, systematic, and comprehensive (Timmermans and Berg 2003).

In the United States, and later on in other locations that adopted FDA-designed standards for drug evaluation, research ethics regulations governing studies with human subjects have become heavily influenced by a view of research and treatment as fundamentally different activities (Anderson 2010), a stance that Soviet research ethics rejected. The rationale for differentiating research and treatment in drug trials conduct, as elaborated within an influential strain of predominantly Western bioethics literature, lies in the potential conflict between the treatment aim of enhancing the well-being of an individual patient and the research aim of producing generalizable knowledge to guide the care of future patients (Appelbaum 2010; Belmont Report 1979; Miller 2004; Miller and Brody 2003; Morreim 2005; de Melo-Martín and Ho 2008; de Vries et al. 2011). In this view of the fundamental difference between research and treatment, health-care professionals provide patients with individualized diagnostic procedures and treatments, guided by the patients' best interests. Biomedical research, including RCTs, by contrast exposes participants to uncertain risks for the sake of producing generalizable data. It is argued that some features of RCTs, being necessary to ensure validity and reliability of evidence, do compromise the quality of medical care available to research participants; examples include randomization, placebo controls, restricted flexibility in the dosing of study drugs, restrictions on the use of concomitant treatments, and invasive data-gathering interventions. In the case of phase 1 trials where healthy volunteers tend to be involved, the difference between research and treatment becomes especially pronounced. Because the qualitative difference between research and treatment appears to be inevitable when reliable pharmaceutical science is to be pursued, participants must understand this difference when agreeing to enroll in a trial in order to provide valid informed consent. I would like to note here that while this view has dominated regulations governing biomedical research with human subjects in the United States and other locations, it has also been increasingly criticized recently. Criticisms have come from empirical social science studies demonstrating that clinical trials often allow for various forms of care for research participants (Wadmann and Hoeyer 2014; Timmermans and McKay 2009; Zvonareva et al. 2015) and also from some philosophers arguing that from an epistemological point of view, "clinical research and clinical practice are not sharply distinct but intimately intertwined" (Anderson 2010, 46). Nonetheless, clinical research and treatment have been governed by largely distinct ethical principles in the United States and in other locations with US-inspired systems of drug R&D.

In the USSR, collection and evaluation of evidence on the safety and efficiency of drugs proceeded differently. Eduard Babayan, physician and medical researcher who for thirty-three years worked in the MoH's Board for Implementation of the New Drugs and Medical Technologies, wrote a book that compares the drug development systems in the USSR and the United States in coauthorship with legal scholar Oleg Utkin. In this book, Babayan and Ytkin (1982) wrote that in the USSR, clinical trials of pharmaceuticals were usually performed in two stages. The first stage involved a limited number of adult patients and aimed at evaluating the therapeutic properties, finding early indications of adverse-event risks, and determining dosage ranges. The second stage involved more adult patients to obtain more detailed information about the pharmaceutical, determine its efficacy compared with already existing drugs, and specify dosage and treatment schemes. In the USSR, the regulatory requirements of such organizations as the FDA were considered excessive, unnecessarily prolonging the drug development process and wasting resources. In the absence of private actors driven by self-interest and profit motives rather than societal good, and with the close state oversight, Soviet pharmaceutical science claimed to be capable of producing reliable results without a three-phase trial system that took years and hundreds or thousands of people to implement, and without resorting to the uncaring practices of randomized controlled methodologies. The MoH, with its Pharmaceutical

Committee, itself guided drug trials in specifically chosen state treatment facilities and based its decisions to register new drugs on the documents produced by its own experts. This arrangement was viewed as granting an exceptional objectivity to the Soviet process of collecting and evaluating evidence regarding drug safety and efficacy. Babayan and Utkin (1982) pointed out that in the United States,

> [the FDA assesses] documents (which are aggregated results of a study of a drug) provided in several stages by a producer company itself. On top of that drug research in clinics is carried out based on private relationships between producer companies with specialists, who are paid by the companies. The choice of clinics and specialists for trials is made by a company. The company sets a goal of research, type of tasks, which means the interested party itself has an opportunity to guide the trials' course (102).

Thus, the involvement of private interests in drug development in the United States was viewed in the Soviet Union as introducing a fundamental bias in evidence of drugs' efficacy and giving rise to larger, more prolonged, and more stringent trials with design elements such as placebos that added methodological rigor at the expense of the exploited research participants.

Soviet bioethics formulated another group of objections to involving healthy volunteers in trials and to the use of placebos, randomization, and double-blinding characteristic of the US clinical trials system, which was also becoming entrenched in Europe and Japan at the time. While these characteristics have been viewed by the developers and supporters of the three-phase trial system as safeguarding scientific rigor and ultimately the societal good through ensuring the effectiveness and safety of medicines that circulate in society, a statement from Babayan and Utkin (1982) illustrates an alternative view:

> [in USSR] Clinical trials of pharmaceuticals are carried out only on patients first of all for the sake of their treatment and also for an experimental evaluation of treatment results. In accordance with the procedures set by the USSR Ministry of Health, clinical trials of a new pharmaceutical are carried out on those patients who require treatment with such pharmaceuticals for health reasons. Prescription of the indicated

drug is based on data regarding efficacy and safety obtained during deep experimental research[4] of the studied drug. (60)

Because clinical trials were viewed in the USSR as being performed first of all for the benefit of the patient-participants' health, such elements as placebos, randomization, and double-blinding were seen as inappropriate, in contrast with the dominant research ethics framework in the United States. About placebos, Babayan and Utkin wrote:

> It is important to stress that in the Soviet Union, generally, previously known drugs with effects similar to those of the drug being studied are used instead of placebo. As we do not see it possible to deprive a patient of the necessary treatment as a means of control and give him a placebo in its literal sense, we use a placebo only when it is not dangerous for the patient, for instance when a mosquito repellent is being studied. (1982, 57)

They further added that in "the Soviet Union the law guarantees that for no purpose, for no 'higher' reason will a single patient be deprived of treatment" (101).

Clinical trials of new pharmaceuticals with healthy volunteers were generally prohibited in the USSR, with the exception of those cases when a drug was meant to be used by healthy people. Each case when a drug was to be tried on healthy people required specific approval by the MoH. From a scientific point of view, in the USSR, it was argued that data about the safety of the candidate drug obtained from healthy volunteers (as is typically done in phase 1 trials) were of limited validity because the drug might have a completely different effect on a sick person, whose organism functioned differently because of illness. From an ethical point of view, Babayan and Utkin argued that using healthy volunteers in clinical research is unacceptable because one "cannot consider people who lack medical education, who are not able to assess all possible consequences of medical experimentation, to be truly volunteers" (90). That is, interestingly, they downplayed the issue of informed consent, stipulating that it is experts with in-depth knowledge of pharmaceutical science and medicine who can decide when it is in the best interest of an individual to participate in a clinical trial. Because in this view people without this knowledge cannot provide meaningful informed consent, the only acceptable way to involve them in pharmaceutical trials is when they, as patients, benefit from this participation, with this benefit being ascertained by the experts.

Therefore, the Soviet ethical regulation of drug research, along with the system of drug testing itself, enabled a vivid articulation of Soviet ideals and also made a political claim aimed at highlighting the superiority of the Soviet societal order over others where capitalistic interests appeared to be leading to injustice and exploitation. The less extensive testing of new pharmaceutical agents in the USSR appeared to illustrate the benefits of socialism, where resources were efficiently used and patients who were trial participants were saved from exploitation by the just societal architecture. Thus, together with institutions, pharmaceutical technologies, and socialist political programs, bioethical considerations and drug testing methodologies were also engaged in the Soviet pharmapolitical regime.

Before turning to concluding remarks for this chapter, I reflect on some implications of the culture of collecting and evaluating evidence established in the USSR. On one hand, in line with Soviet claims, scholarly analyses of drug development regulation in the United States clearly document the influence of private business activities. First, the efforts of the FDA to make drug testing and evaluation more stringent that culminated in the Kefauver-Harris Amendments in 1962 were indeed stimulated by some practices of private industry. Companies tended to be less than forthcoming about risks of their products. For instance, Carpenter (2010) notes that in the late 1940s, Abbott Laboratories' sedative Nembutal suppositories induced days of sleep in pediatric patients. The company collected data on adverse events but did not inform the FDA about the problem (147). Prior to the 1962 changes, FDA experts routinely lamented the quality of evidence provided by pharmaceutical companies, which would send "investigational" samples of their drug to physicians, who, in turn, would write "testimonials." In this regard, FDA official Ralph Smith discontentedly remarked in 1952:

> A great difference exists between detailed reports and a short letter in which the investigator states in effect that the drug has been used successfully with no toxic effects, and that he thinks it should be marketed. The latter is merely a testimonial. (cited in Carpenter 2010, 175)

Second, in the United States more generally, the influence on pharmaceutical regulation by the industry, which steadfastly resisted attempts to institutionalize more control over its practices, was also not null. To illustrate this point, originally Kefauver's reform agenda contained revisions of the patent law, including a decreased period of market exclusivity; to increase competition, Kefauver sought to encourage physicians to prescribe drugs by generic name rather than by trade name; and, finally, the FDA was to receive greater authority as a market gatekeeper evaluating drug safety and efficiency and approving advertising claims. Throughout the Kefauver hearings, as Tobbel (2009) shows, the drug industry and its supporters effectively shored up their defenses against measures proposed by the senator, drawing on the rhetoric of the Cold War and presenting the US pharmaceutical industry as a national asset in the struggle against communism. The final provisions of the Kefauver-Harris Amendments were very different from the original regulatory proposal: all measures regarding patents and trade names were gone, and the Amendments did little to challenge drug prices and industry profits, as was originally intended. Tobbel (2009) concludes that the content of the Amendments, like the content of prior US legislation in the field of pharmaceuticals, was significantly determined by the pharmaceutical industry (472).

Nonetheless, one can view the FDA standards for drug evaluation as being driven by other considerations as well, beyond eliminating the bias introduced by corporate profit making. The validity of these considerations, summarized below, was not recognized in the USSR. The regulatory logic behind the expanded premarket research also signaled a departure from the testing model aimed at infectious-diseases medicines that dominated the first three generations of drugs. Pharmaceuticals were increasingly becoming intended for chronic conditions, that is, for long-term use, as exemplified by a statement of an FDA official in the 1950s:

> [I]n recent years there have been developed high blood pressure drugs, anticonvulsant drugs, arthritis preparations, and other drugs that are in the category of "maintenance" drugs, to be used over long periods of time—perhaps for a lifetime. These recently developed drugs are obviously in a different category than the usual drugs of 15–20 years ago, which were expected to be used perhaps only once or twice in the treatment of a particular illness. The need for information on toxicity and the likelihood of chronic toxicity effects obviously become important in the case of drugs that are to be employed continuously or over long periods. Hence the development of requirements for residue data and more animal experimentation in pharmacology. (cited in Carpenter 2010, 140)

That is, regulatory science questions of safety shifted from short-term to long-term use. Also, the questions of effectiveness required new methodologies suitable for application in assessments of medications for chronic conditions, with longer periods of administration.

Moreover, not only chemotherapeutic developments supported the adoption of new methodologies. With the advance of clinical pharmacology, pharmacologists and statisticians came to dominate FDA decision making (Carpenter 2010, 139–46). The medical profession was viewed by the FDA with distrust, because physicians were not expected to have training in statistics, pharmacology, or toxicology, and therefore were not expected to be able to assess the quality and hazards of new drug treatments. Lack of trust in physicians' capacity engendered FDA-enforced precautions such as double-blind designs to account for placebo effects, the psychological "biases" of the doctor-patient relationship, and the dynamic nature of the disease state. That is, the introduction of the three-phase clinical trial system went beyond the need to control for the bias of profit-seeking firms. It was facilitated by the changing landscape of drug types and by pharmacologists' efforts to account for the biases of physicians.

The USSR's system of collecting and evaluating evidence of drugs' efficacy was effectively safeguarded against bias toward economic profit interests and against some charges of exploiting participants in clinical research. However, it relied too much on a nonmarket environment and the central state control warding off private economic interests, while challenges in the assessment of drugs' safety and efficacy are not limited to economic profit motives alone. The fourth generation of medicines that began in the 1960s, when the Soviet drug development system solidified on the basis of earlier practices, was concerned mostly with chronic diseases such as cardiovascular disease, cancer, and central nervous system diseases (Achilladelis and Antonakis 2001). Evaluating the long-term safety and efficacy of drugs for chronic diseases could be more challenging than evaluating those directed toward infectious, parasitic, and viral diseases, on which the Soviet pharmaceutical industry mostly concentrated up until then. The latter often require only a short-term single period of administration that results in full elimination of an infection. Chronic diseases, for example, cardiovascular disease, generally necessitate prolonged, even lifelong, use of drugs that often do not fully eliminate the disease. Rather, those drugs aim at positively influencing different aspects of the human organism to prolong life and enhance its quality. However, Soviet pharmaceutical science did not adapt its practices to this shift in drug landscapes. The use of small samples, the lack of comparison groups, and the observational methodologies common in Soviet pharmaceutical clinical research, which worked well for infectious diseases and prevented emergence of a gap between clinical research and clinical practice, made it difficult to discern and isolate the effects of drugs directed at chronic diseases and meant for long-term use.

Pursuing Pharmapolitics

Pharmaceutical technoscience and politics mutually shaped each other during the Soviet period, forming the national pharmapolitical regime. In this chapter, I focused on three points to delineate this mutual shaping. The first point was the reorganization of the pharmaceutical industry during the early years of the Soviet Union into a centrally managed and planned sector that embodied the aspirations of those who took power in the October 1917 revolution to build a society of ultimate social justice. The Soviet pharmaceutical industry was modeled to reflect an imaginary future society where efficiency and rationality are achieved through excluding private economic profit opportunities, and science and technology are employed to transcend inequalities. It was during this time that the Soviet pharmaceutical industry turned fully to medical chemistry, the field of science that gave rise to most innovative drugs at that time.

The second point was the USSR's drug development system that was designed to prevent the ills of the commercial system of drug development, such as unreasonably high prices for drugs and resource waste. Soviet pharmaceutical science and technology, as an integral part of the wider health-care system, not only enabled articulating the Soviet vision of society within the country, but also shaped the Soviet foreign policy agenda and became instrumental in the project of disseminating communist ideals to engage other countries. The third point was the culture of collecting and evaluating evidence in the USSR's drug development and the bioethical considerations that played a part in it. Particularities of this culture allowed making political claims for the superiority of the Soviet vision of society.

Bringing all three points together characterizes the architecture of the Soviet pharmapolitical regime and its strategies and highlights the workings of coproduction of pharmaceutical science and technology on the one hand and politics on the other. Politics in the newly emerged

Soviet state promoted the race to catch up with the modern scientific drug development methods in countries such as Germany and dictated finding ways to substitute imported drugs with locally produced ones, shaping the development of the local pharmaceutical industry. Later, politics influenced the ways in which pharmaceuticals emerged from an idea to actual medicine and directed the development of drug testing methodologies. At the same time, pharmaceutical science and technology helped to articulate Soviet visions of society and ground them in a material infrastructure of the institutions and pharmaceuticals themselves; it shaped Soviet political ambitions in the international arena and became a tool for political claim making. Working together, politics and pharmaceutical science and technology in the USSR not only underwrote each other's existence, but also produced, rehearsed, and strengthened an imaginary of a future society of a specific kind of social justice. For many decades, this technoscientific imaginary, in turn, animated the Soviet pharmapolitical regime.

In the following chapters, I explore the four processes that together define the shape and functioning of pharmapolitical regimes, using data from the post-Soviet period in Russia. The next chapter focuses specifically on vision-production as the first of these processes and turns to new visions of the nation and its future that arose with the end of the Soviet Union and to the corresponding implications for pharmaceutical science and technology.

Chapter 2

Neoliberal Experiments in the Post-Soviet State

Producing an Alternative Vision of Society

In the decades of the Soviet Union, the pharmaceutical industry in Russia was shaped by aspirations for absolute rationality and efficiency in a larger project of building a socially just society. At the same time, advances in and characteristics of the Soviet pharmaceutical industry were used in political practices of promoting the superiority of communism, as discussed in the previous chapter. When the Soviet Union abruptly ended in 1991, the industry changed dramatically. State-controlled pharmaceutical research and development (R&D), carried out in the planned economy and evaluated by expert scientists—characteristics intended to ensure distributive justice and technoscientific progress without waste or duplication—gave way to a deregulated field dominated by private businesses and structured by the newly arrived clinical trials system. This chapter investigates how changes in the organization and practice of pharmaceutical R&D arose together with shifts in political imagination, and analyzes *vision production* as a process central to pharmapolitics. The arrival and embedding of clinical trials in post-Soviet Russia is discussed separately in chapter 3.

These transformations can be viewed as a part of a wider global trend of economic liberalization. Yet scholars of organizational change in various industries have pointed out that transitions in Eastern European, Asian, and Latin American countries are qualitatively different from industry-specific changes in the long-established market-driven Western economies (Newman 2000). These scholars have argued that market-driven Western economies have never undergone economic reforms of such magnitude as those experienced by many Eastern European, Asian, and Latin American countries. Chittoor and colleagues (2008) specify that major economic liberalization efforts across these latter geographical contexts were initiated in approximately the same time period (the 1990s) and generally can be grouped into three major categories: "a) privatization or change of ownership of key sectors of economy from government to private sector; b) founding and development of market institutions to bring about efficient intermediation in financial, legal, labor and regulatory domains . . . ; and c) improvement in the efficiency levels of market players as well as institutions propelling a movement towards more perfect markets" (253).

In Russia, processes of economic liberalization spanned all three categories and were especially rapid and intense. In the domain of pharmaceuticals, after the end of the USSR, Russia quickly adopted many of the previously rejected elements of pharmaceutical R&D, such as strong involvement of private interests and withdrawal of the state from managing and organizing the sector. What enabled such radical transformation? I approach formulating an answer to this question by turning to the process of *vision production*, which I consider central to pharmapolitics.

This chapter is structured in three parts. First, I trace the emergence and conflict of different visions of the nation and its futures during the initial years of post-Soviet Russia and illustrate how the neoliberal ideal came to and then lost its power. This provides a background for understanding the shifts within the pharmaceutical industry. Second, the chapter attends specifically to the transformations within the pharmaceutical sector and explores both the molding of the sector by neoliberal ideals and the emergence of resistance to them. Third, I elaborate on the failure of the neoliberal vision to take root among groups involved in pharmaceutical research, development, and manufacturing in the country, facilitated by rapid deterioration of local pharmaceutical science and technology. The chapter concludes with a reflection on how national regulatory agendas in the early post-Soviet reforms interacted with technoscientific opportunities and constraints as well as with national historical experiences in a coproductive process that resulted in a wide rejection of the neoliberal vision of the Russian future among those involved in the country's pharmaceutical industry and facilitated the emergence of an alternative vision of an independent and self-sufficient Russia, investigated in chapter 4.

I base my account in this chapter on an analytic reading of existing scholarship related to the post-Soviet transitions in Russia and specifically in the Russian pharmaceutical industry, and on interviews with thirty actors currently involved with pharmaceutical innovations in the country. Some of them were already part of the Russian pharmaceutical industry in the early 1990s and shared their personal experiences. Others who entered the arena later offered their reflections and interpretations of the events in the industry during the early post-Soviet period.

Previous research documents that there are unique models of responding to institutional changes associated with economic liberalization across the most affected geographical contexts of Eastern Europe, Asia, and Latin America, although major liberalization efforts were initiated in the same time period. My analysis of the Russian case adds explanatory depth to existing studies by highlighting the role of meaning making in shaping of the onset, directions, and specific results of economic liberalization in Russia in the domain of pharmaceuticals. Specifically, I suggest that regulatory agendas are being shaped by, and simultaneously contribute to shaping, the state of pharmaceutical science and technology through producing different visions of the nation and its futures.

A Neoliberal Vision of the Nation and its Future

Clash of Visions

On December 25, 1991, after Mikhail Gorbachev resigned as the first and last president of the USSR, the Soviet flag was lowered from the Kremlin and the pre-revolutionary Russian tricolor was raised, symbolically marking the birth of the sovereign state of the Russian Federation. The events preceding this moment can be described as a story of emerging and competing visions of the nation and its futures. In political decision making, visions inspire the emergence and introduction of particular governance practices. These practices, in turn, can strengthen and modify the original visions.

In the years before this moment and after his election as general secretary by the Politburo on March 11, 1985, Gorbachev worked to materialize a vision of the Soviet Union as a more open, liberal, and democratic country. However, this vision failed to become dominant in the country, and by the end of 1991 there were fifteen new states where a world superpower had recently held sway. Prior to these events, Gorbachev and his supporters began what was termed *perestroika* (restructuring), which involved introducing limited competitive elections (the first such elections were held in 1988 for a new central legislature to be called the Congress of People's Deputies). Another element of their work to embed the vision of the reformed Soviet state in society and in political and economic systems was *glasnost* (openness), allowing freedom of speech and increasing freedom of publication. Gorbachev was also in favor of marketization because the Soviet command economy was showing signs of decline and a need for revival. Therefore, he began to gradually introduce elements of a market economy, such as permitting individual enterprise in 1986 and legalizing cooperatives in 1988.

The Gorbachev idea of the reformed Soviet Union was, however, not the only vision of the Soviet nation and its future that existed. Competing with it were perspectives of the conservatives, who were opposed to what they saw as weakening the Soviet state and its highly centralized power structure, and who organized a military coup in August 1991, placing Gorbachev under house arrest. The coup ended on August 21, three days after the beginning of its active phase, having failed to find popular support. The resistance to the coup was led by more radical reformists, first of all Boris Yeltsin, who envisioned the national future as a rapid transition to freedom and the complete end of the communism-building, even if it would mean the disintegration of the USSR into smaller formations. After the coup was defeated, Gorbachev returned from house arrest, resigned the position of general secretary of the Communist Party of the Soviet Union, and dissolved all the party units within the government. By then his position had significantly weakened. In the last quarter of 1991, one Soviet Republic after another declared its independence, and Gorbachev in practice no longer had authority to influence events. Yeltsin, who was elected the president of the Russian Soviet Federative Socialist Republic in June 1991, had criticized the "dictatorship of the center" and proceeded to demand Russian sovereignty and independence from the Soviet Union (despite the fact that Russia had largely dominated the Soviet state). On

December 26, 1991, the day after Gorbachev's resignation from the presidency of the USSR, the Council of Republics issued a formal declaration stating that the Soviet Union had ceased to exist, and Yeltsin became the first president of the new Russian state.

To grasp the specificities of this story of emerging and competing visions of the future, it is helpful to invoke scholarship here on the life cycle of imagination. On this topic, Jasanoff (2015) writes that newly emerging imaginaries of the societal futures often experience moments of resistance, when new conceptions collide with the old ones or when alternative imaginaries compete to establish themselves in the same social terrain:

> Imaginaries move through the realm of resistance in double guise, sometimes raising impediments to the spread of new ideas and at other times crystallizing the dissatisfactions of the present into possibilities for other futures that people would sooner inhabit. Revolutions, whether in science . . . or in social order . . . , can be seen as the overthrow of one no longer sufficient imaginary by another that looks more promising. Key to such complete and radical transformations is a widespread resistance to the status quo that makes the projected alternative appealing, believable and worth attaining, even through immense struggle and sacrifice. (329–30)

Yet at the point of the dissolution of the USSR and the emergence of the Russian Federation, a new vision of the national future that would supersede a clear and stabilized Soviet identity and vision of what the nation stood for was yet to be formulated. Dissatisfaction with the status quo was indeed widespread, and the vision of the Communist state of social justice, opposed to unjust market economies and progressing to human equality through large-scale industrialization and continuous advances in science and technology, was losing its footing. But alternatives were still taking shape, inspired by the idea of "freedom" but conceived and practiced in many different ways and also challenged by the Soviet vision, which did not dissolve completely.

Envisioning Freedom

The rapid process of state disintegration reaching its full momentum in 1991 enabled similarly fast-paced radical governance measures in response to it. Gradual shifts of *glasnost* and *perestroika* initiated by Gorbachev were replaced by "shock therapy," whose main architect was Yegor Gaidar, who rode to power with Yeltsin. Radical reformers, of whom Gaidar was perhaps the main face and voice, envisioned a new Russian state that would make a sharp turn in its development, breaking with the seven prior decades of socialism. Gaidar, who referred often to the works of Adam Smith and Friedrich Hayek as the sources that particularly influenced his view of how the economy and society work, together with other "young reformers" (as this group of politicians was called in Russian, *mladoreformatori*), their teams, and supporters, imagined a liberal state, integrated in the global economy, with entrepreneurship and private initiative driving economic growth and citizens enjoying the benefits of liberty and property ownership. They rushed to release market mechanisms that would remedy the ills of the command economy, including persistent deficits of goods and services and large-scale inefficiency, through lifting price controls, removing restrictions on trade (including foreign trade), inviting foreign investment, and implementing a countrywide privatization program. In contrast to the strong central planning characteristic of Soviet times, the role of the state was to be severely diminished and power was to be decentralized. In this imaginary, a liberal economy would go hand in hand with liberal democracy, with property owners and prospects of prosperity securing the newly found freedom.

This vision of the Russian future developed by the young reformers group became integrated with policy instruments and governance infrastructures from the first days of the new Russia, providing this imaginary with a powerful impetus to take hold at the nationwide level. But in practice the jump start to a market economy and rapid decentralization did not result in a widely shared vision of the new nation and the prospects ahead. These governance measures were accompanied by much chaos and uncertainty and a great diversity of interpretations, practices, and decision-making structures adopted in different regions and spheres. That is, while the vision produced mainly by the young reformers and backed by the power of government was being disseminated by different pathways to become embedded in the country's social fabric, individual and institutional actors on the ground were reinterpreting and reshaping elements of this vision, feeding back these changes into the overall outlook of the nation's present and future. Scholarship on post-socialism has documented a surprising persistence of Soviet-born material structures, bureaucratic organization, and social norms (Collier 2011). These insights suggest a nuanced view of the transformations shaped as much by the project of marketization and state retrenchment as by the existing infrastructures, routines, and norms and by everyday practices spanning both of these planes.

An example from the field of pharmaceuticals is provided by Alexandra Vacroux (2005) in her dissertation on the evolution of pharmaceutical regulation in Russia in 1991–2004 that focused on the distribution and circulation of drugs. She described the uncertainty experienced by the state decision makers in the Russian regions because suddenly they had become "free" from central planning and found divergent ways to do their job in the transforming environment:

> These people were not only ill-equipped to promote reforms under conditions of capitalism and democracy, but in many cases were skeptical, if not actually hostile, about the need for these changes. Russia's transformation from a monolithic communist-run state was overseen by bureaucrats who were either supporters, opponents, or opportunists. Reformers in the small, first category were convinced that Russia had to change in order to survive, and were ready to throw themselves into the implementation of reforms. Opponents (including the majority of officials that I encountered in the privatization agency in 1992 and 1993) were openly resistant to the policies they were supposed to be implementing, and hopeful that the democratic interlude would be short. Opportunists, meanwhile, positioned themselves to profit personally from new economic rules. (67)

While reformers saw the state and its bureaucrats as obstacles to Russia's social and economic development and integration in the world economy, officials on the ground, confronted with decentralization and the opening of drug distribution markets, often had other conceptions of their responsibilities and tasks and the overall role of the state. According to Vacroux (2005), some continued to apply Soviet-era legislation, maintaining centralized medicines purchase and distribution structures within their regions and resisting development of private health care. She describes an instance when "[t]he Marii El official in charge of licensing [of pharmacies] in 1996, Galina Otmakhova, had come to her post as the former director of one of the capital's largest pharmacies (Ioshkar-Ola). She didn't believe in private health care, and tried hard to find problems in the license applications of private pharmacies" (73).

Furthermore, the vision of a liberal democratic country with an open and free market was actively contested on the highest levels as well, fueling sharp conflicts between and within parliament and the presidential apparatus. While it was hardly possible to completely turn back the clock after privatization, decentralization, and market liberalization were set in motion, efforts to challenge the liberal development course were intense. In 1993, the Congress of People's Deputies initiated a countrywide referendum that included the question "Do you support the economic and social policy that has been conducted since 1992 by the President and Government of the Russian Federation?" A year earlier, the Congress already succeeded in pushing Yeltsin to replace the most vocal neoliberal reformer, Gaidar, in his position as prime minister with Victor Chernomyrdin, who appeared to be more moderate.

These developments illustrate the emergence and conflict of different visions that animated shifting and diverging governance practices during the first years of post-Soviet Russia. No stabilized way of looking at the future that would capture the collective imagination was developed. Actors were figuring out in their daily lives and work what it meant to live in a new state and making sense of ongoing, rapid changes. It is in this turbulent and uncertain environment that the Russian pharmaceutical industry was undergoing transformations. The next section details these transformations, tracing connections between politics and pharmaceutical science and technology and the role of vision production in establishing and shaping these connections.

A Neoliberal Vision and Pharmaceutical Industry

Deregulatory Reforms in the Western Pharmaceutical Sectors

The ideas of neoliberalism adopted by Gaidar, the primary architect of market-style reforms in post-Soviet Russia, and his supporters, were first articulated and developed largely in the West. Moreover, these ideas have exercised a significant influence precisely in the pharmaceutical domain in the Western countries. The history of pharmaceutical governance in these settings during recent decades has been interpreted by many scholars as a progressive attack by supporters of neoliberalism on state regulation of the pharmaceutical domain.

While the 1962 Kefauver-Harris Amendments accepted in the United States defined the contemporary global pharmaceutical regulation regime through introducing premarket review of safety and efficacy, the FDA since has been under increasing pressure to adopt a more permissive approach to regulation (Hogarth 2015). More generally, deregulation has been called one of the main trends in the contemporary pharmaceutical regime in the Western settings (Williams et al. 2011). Not only has the American pharmaceutical regulatory agency experienced such pressure, but the same dynamic has been noticeable in Europe in the context of a broad raft of deregulatory reforms peaking after 1980 that have distinctly neoliberal origins. Davis and Abraham (2013) suggest that the entire post-1980 era in the United States and Western Europe can be called "neoliberal"

> because it was and remains a period in which a political project of minimizing state intervention, subjecting the state to competitive tests of "the market," and elevating individual consumer choice above the state as a form of collective decision-making, all came to the fore. This has involved the 'liberalization' of the markets, that is relaxation of government regulations and controls, believed to hamper business activity and the socio-economic signals of consumer demand. (5)

Specifically, pharmaceutical-sector deregulatory reforms in the last three decades included making American and European drug regulatory agencies dependent on funds from the pharmaceutical industry, raising the scope and flexibility of consultations between regulators and companies, reducing the scope and types of evidence necessary to obtain marketing approval, and shortening the review time by regulators (Davis and Abraham 2013). For example, in the early and middle 1980s, the scope of the FDA's review of phase 1 studies was narrowed, and individual case report forms in applications for drug approval were replaced with summary presentation of data (Davis and Abraham 2013, 47–48). These shifts to more permissive regulation are expected to accelerate and increase pharmaceutical innovation, thus ostensibly responding to the interests of patients and public health through enabling faster access to therapeutic advances promised by drug innovations.

The neoliberalism itself, as a set of ideas about knowledge, is traceable to a group of scholars who identified themselves as members of the Mont Pelerin Society, founded in 1947, and those influenced by them. The first president of the society was Friedrich Hayek, an economist who exerted much influence on the young Russian reformer Gaidar. The characteristic belief of this group concerns the epistemic virtues of markets: that the market acts as a method of information processing and conveyance that is more potent than any human mind. The broad neoliberal critique of state reason and, more specifically, regulatory science is based on "a presumed inherent inability of the state—or any person—to comprehend as much as the market" (Nik-Khah 2014, 491).

The era of deregulation in the Western pharmaceutical industry domain has a neoliberal pedigree, as demonstrated, for example, by Nik-Khah (2014) in the case of the United States. He documented how members of the Chicago school of economics, a prominent outpost of the Mont Pelerin Society that included such figures as Milton Friedman and George Stigler, specifically targeted pharmaceutical regulation, attacking the FDA's regulatory authority and opposing the Kefauver-Harris Amendments. In its concerted effort to deregulate the pharmaceutical industry, the Chicago school organized an influential 1972 conference on the introduction of new pharmaceuticals. This conference resulted in the consolidation of a network of FDA critics and the establishment of dedicated think tanks: the Center for the Study of Drug Development and the Center for Health Policy Research at the American Enterprise Institute. They generated critiques of pharmaceutical policy and arguments for industry audit and control over governance bodies, such as the famous "drug lag" thesis: the idea that excessive regulation increases the time needed to introduce valuable new drugs into the US market compared to the time needed in other countries. Neoliberal ideas about the epistemic virtues of markets also spurred calls to substitute large-scale randomized controlled trials with naturalistic marketplace tests, largely moving the study of medicines to the period after they are allowed on the market.

Overall, radical calls, such as those for abandoning the system of clinical trials entirely, were not implemented. But, under pressure from anti-regulation critics, who claimed that excessive drug regulation stifled innovation and acted as an obstacle to patients' access to medicines, increasingly close relationships with the industry and reforms to reduce the regulatory hurdle were adopted by the FDA and its counterparts in Europe.

The Russian Pharmaceutical Industry: Living through Neoliberal Experiments

While in the West governance in general and pharmaceutical regulation in particular have been gradually reshaped by political pressures that are distinctly neoliberal in their origins and effects, Russia in the wake of 1991 went through a sudden, massive experiment of putting ideas that originated from the Mont Pelerin Society straight to practice. A neoliberal vision of a free society, articulated by the young reformers headed by Gaidar, underwrote radical deregulation, decentralization, privatization, and withdrawal of the state from control and planning in research, development, and production. Amid these wider societal changes, those involved in the Russian pharmaceutical industry sector, suddenly finding themselves in drastically changed conditions and exposed to novel opportunities, were determining in practice what making drugs in a free society could look like. Their experiences and the consequences of the early post-Soviet reforms for local pharmaceutical science and technology shaped the further round of pharmaceutical policy making in late 2000s, which was significantly different from the neoliberal experiments under consideration here. I examine this next policy-making round and novel vision of the nation and its future produced during this round in chapter 4.

The Russian pharmaceutical industry underwent a series of transformations after the end of the Soviet Union that accompanied its transition to a market economy, including changes in ownership, price liberalization, and departure from the state monopoly on planning and managing the sector. These transformations were so radical that nearly two decades later my informants still remembered them very vividly, presenting the end of the USSR as a landmark separating different eras; as one of them said, "It is clear that the 1990s are important in that everything broke down then. The whole system built in the USSR, everything collapsed altogether when *perestroika* started and for all those years" (2014, 1VF). Below I map these transformations instigated by neoliberal ideals during their short-lived grip on governance discourses and practices in

Russia, and as an illustration, I use the words of an informant who has profound experience in the Soviet and post-Soviet pharmaceutical industry.

The production sector of the pharmaceutical industry became largely privatized soon after the birth of the independent Russian state. In 1991–1992, new legislation was developed and approved by the government and president of the Russian Federation for enabling and stimulating the privatization of various industries. For example, in 1992, Presidential Decree No. 721, which came to force on July 1, stipulated compulsory privatization of pharmaceutical industry production units by November 1, either through converting them into joint stock companies or through other means, such as selling them through auction or commercial tender. The speed and breadth of the 1992 privatization was similar to that of the 1918–1919 nationalization, when previously private pharmaceutical enterprises became state property, as described in the previous chapter. Because of the generally large size of pharmaceutical enterprises, the leading method of privatization was turning them into joint stock companies. During 1992–1993, twenty-eight previously state-owned factories, which in total were producing about 70 percent of the country's pharmaceutical products, were converted into such companies, including the oldest, Akrikhin, in the Moscow region, Ferrein in Moscow, and Purin in Anzhero-Sudzhensk (Dorofeev 1995). Often, those employed by the factories received significant discounts for buying stock in their enterprise. According to Balashov (2012), in most cases the majority stake came to belong to workers' collectives and regional property funds, and many stocks were also bought by top managers of the privatized enterprises, other private individuals, and a few investment companies (66). This ownership composition suggests that the new pharmaceutical industry enterprise owners generally were not experienced in managing private companies in market conditions, and very few had sufficient funds to invest in the development of their companies.

Furthermore, the new owners faced additional difficulties related to the breakdown of cooperative connections between organizations involved in the local pharmaceutical industry. Within the Soviet Union, production of pharmaceutical substances was mostly concentrated in Russia, while factories producing finished pharmaceutical products were built in other Soviet republics, including Ukraine, Belarus, and the Baltic states. When, with the end of the Soviet Union, the unified system of cooperative relationships between pharmaceutical factories that were now divided between the newly formed states also broke down, Russian units producing pharmaceutical substances faced a serious decline in demand for their products. Concurrently, because of price liberalization, a sharp increase in the costs of raw materials, energy, and transport occurred, driving a corresponding increase in production costs, while pharmaceutical substances manufacturing facilities faced tough competition with cheap substances that now were flowing from China and India. Simultaneously, few facilities for production of finished ready-to-use pharmaceuticals remained in the country after the separation of the former Soviet republics, and these facilities were dealing with the same challenges.

Another set of factors contributing to the difficulties experienced by the Russian pharmaceutical industry soon after the end of the USSR can be discerned in the newly emerged market environment itself. The USSR's Ministry of Medical Industry was abolished, and the Ministry of Health now was tasked with drug registrations, clinical trials permissions, and developing and implementing measures for quality control of pharmaceuticals; that is, some of its departments turned to performing functions similar to those of the United States' FDA. No more was the state involved in decisions regarding quantities and types of drugs to be produced in particular sites or in drug price setting. It was now market forces that the reformers envisioned as animating the pharmaceutical landscape: private companies would be more attentive to demand for certain drugs than a rigid state apparatus, and hence population needs would be more fully met; competition would stimulate innovation and quality improvement, both lagging previously in the Soviet state; and more motivated private ownership would make for more efficient and creative use of resources. Moreover, barriers to international trade were lifted, and mass imports of pharmaceuticals (both drugs and substances) from abroad began, linking Russian and international markets. But, as mentioned above, the new owners of the local pharmaceutical enterprise were not experienced in working in market conditions and found it difficult to compete with newcomers. Consequently, the volume of sales of Russian-manufactured pharmaceutical products decreased by half between 1991 and 1997 (Balashov 2012). The range of drugs still produced also narrowed. In 1994 alone, local production of 156 drugs, including those for oncology, tuberculosis, and cardiovascular disease, was stopped (Iudanov, Volskaia, and Lagunov 1998).

Before 1991 the output of Soviet pharmaceutical industry, including factories located in the Russian Soviet Federative Socialist Republic (SFSR), was increasing for two decades. In 1992 production of pharmaceuticals in Russia dropped drastically and by 1996 decreased almost by half in comparison to 1991:

Table 2.1. Dynamics of pharmaceutical production in Russia (in comparable prices)

Volume of pharmaceutical production	1991	1992	1993	1994	1995	1996
Percent in relation to the previous year	105	84	75	95	95	92
Percent in relation to 1991	100	84	63	60	57	52

Changes in production of specific kinds of drugs are presented in table 2.2. It appears that the largest decrease occurred in production of drugs that were used mostly or only in inpatient conditions, such as drugs for anesthesia and oncology, blood and plasma substitutes, and drugs for cardiovascular diseases in ampules. That is, the decrease was especially notable for those drugs the demand for which is formed by public drug procurement for hospitals.

Table 2.2. Dynamics of pharmaceutical production in Russia according to therapeutic categories

	1990	1995	% change
Drugs for cardiovascular diseases			
Million ampules	334	164	−50.9
Million packs	94.8	145	+53
Drugs for oncology			
Million ampules	11.9	2.6	−78.2
Million packs	31.6	3.3	−89.6
Drugs for neuropsychological disorders			
Million packs	32	30.7	−4.1
Medicines against fever, pain, and inflammation			
Million ampules	39.5	90.7	+129.6
Million packs	441	227	−48.5
Blood and plasma substitutes			
Million ampules	72.4	8.5	−88.3
Million packs	55.8	40	−28.3
Tuberculosis drugs			
Million ampules	93.1	54.8	−41.1
Million packs	7.2	2.5	−65.3
Anti-asthmatic drugs and antihistamines			
Million ampules	211	75.5	−64.2
Million packs	101	47.5	−53

	1990	1995	% change
Anesthesia drugs			
Million packs	1.5	0.3	−80.9
Drugs against eye diseases			
Million packs	29.8	5.8	−80.5
Antibiotics			
Million ampules	191	49.8	−73.9
Million packs	1042	615	−41
Drugs for endocrine and digestive system disorders			
Million ampules	238	93.9	−60.5
Million packs	92.7	31.3	−66.2
Vitamins			
Million ampules	557	355	−36.3
Million packs	489	223	−54.4

Note that the data in table 2.2 present both ready-to-consume pharmaceutical drugs and pharmaceutical substances. But the dynamics of the two are quite different. Volume of production as well as assortment of drugs began a recovery after the described drop in 1997. But production of pharmaceutical substances, which was the specialization of Russia within the collaborative economic system of the USSR and Comecon (Soviet-dominated Council for Mutual Economic Assistance), dropped even more dramatically: by 1996 it decreased to a third of what it was in 1992 and continued to drop. Of 272 substances produced by the pharmaceutical industry in 1992, only 100 remained in production by 1996.

Data presented here were obtained from the following sources: Iudanov, Volskaia, and Lagunov 1998; Dorofeev 1995.

How did those who were working in the pharmaceutical industry view and experience the changes? Some sense of that can be provided by a narrative of one informant, whom I spoke with for the first time in 2013. This informant, who formerly worked in a Soviet state pharmacological research institute and currently heads a private organization that manufactures pharmaceutical substances and provides contract research services, explained in detail how process of economic liberalization initially played out in the post-Soviet setting:

> After the collapse of the USSR the structure of the sector changed. Originally everything was owned by the state. The state was employer, provider, and user. When *perestroika* happened, factories gradually became mostly private property. And then

the state was not obliged anymore to support these factories with its funds. If these are private, they must produce and sell on their own. So the state ceased to support those. . . .

Those factories were provided with the rights for production of certain drugs that were previously registered in the USSR. It was decided that whatever previously was produced by a particular factory could continue to be produced by that factory. In this way, owners received factories with an old nomenclature [assortment of drugs] and continued producing and selling. . . . While new owners of the old factories were producing old nomenclature, they were making profit with this. Usually they got those factories for nothing, so to say. More profit, less profit, but still in the Soviet times they did not have even that money. They did not. Some years passed—money emerged. They did not get that money as a salary, they just got those factories because they were very "creative," so to speak. Because all these factories had been gained basically for nothing, however much profit these factories were making, that was good enough. Also, they did not really know how to manage all of this. Previously, there had been no business. And this was not business, either. They just used to work in this sector. Some previously were red directors (*krasniye directora*); some obtained such factories in other ways. The factories were working, bringing in some money, life was not endless. Maybe these people were in their forties and thought: "Well, I will live for forty more years, equipment is installed in this factory, everything is working, it is enough for me. Who cares what will happen further." No need to think about R&D investments.

Who would invest? What for? The state stopped investing because the need to do so ceased. These were not state factories, why would the state feed someone's else private property with its money? And the new owners did not realize yet that they needed it. At the end they started to think, appetite comes with eating. They began to think, trying to do real business, and noticed their products were of low margin, because everyone could produce it. Registration was done in [the] Soviet Union, so there was a period when anyone could start producing what was Soviet, because it all was registered in USSR, then you could just take a document with requirements specifications and produce. How to compete on the market? Only with dumping. And in fact competition by dumping led to that everyone was trying to economize on everything possible to lower production costs but still have profit. And economizing came to that point that many drugs became of a very low quality. (5BK, 2014)

This narrative paints a picture of a crisis looming in the Russian pharmaceutical industry. The young reformers put their hopes on the market forces, which, however, played out differently than in the neoliberal vision. My informant suggests that after the end of the USSR, private pharmaceutical enterprises, newly emerged through hasty privatization and freed from the close supervision of the state, focused on extracting immediate profits. Competition in such conditions actually resulted in a loss of quality rather than improvement in it. A novel opportunity to gain capital paired with old infrastructure and work cultures translated into very short-term business work strategies incompatible with long and costly innovating in drugs.

In this situation, not only the production of already developed drugs suffered. Pharmaceutical R&D was affected as well, not least because collaborative connections were now severed between drug R&D that remained located in the state institutes and laboratories, on the one hand, and production sites that were now privatized, on the other. That is, in addition to the short-term business strategies mentioned above, the lack of industry capacity to develop new pharmaceuticals was aggravated by the disconnect between the historical centers of pharmaceutical R&D, the so-called applied scientific research institutes, and manufacturing businesses. Those who now owned pharmaceutical companies generally did not have experience with drug R&D, as described by the same informant:

Gradually people started getting smarter, started to understand that the market was opening up, foreign drugs began to arrive. People started to think, how can we do the same? Drugs are expensive, profits are high. So how could we, owners of old plants, also acquire such profits and new drugs? They would command their production and technical department: "make such drugs for me." These departments were mostly staffed with technologists, people with an engineering or pharmacist background. Their understanding of drug development was reduced to taking an existing substance that was registered and making a tablet, a new dosage form. This is how endless generics entered the stage. They did not understand how to work differently and did not know how. Because the owner was saying that sales need to start tomorrow. Today we are making a drug, tomorrow already sales need to begin. And this would mean only generic. It is a very short scheme, it can't be different in such a case. (5BK, 2014)

After privatization, some new companies were formed as well. However, studies of pharmaceutical industry dynamics in the country, for example by Lin, Sokolov, and Slepnev (2013) and Balashov (2012), suggest that initially all Russian companies, both newly created and privatized old factories, generally focused on low added-value production such as packaging or pelletization or production of simple medicines such as infusion solutions, phytochemical ointments, and creams, without engaging in pharmaceutical R&D.

It should be noted that while scientific research institutes and laboratories remained mostly under the authority of the state, many of them were shut down or reorganized, further limiting drug innovation capacities within the country. All surviving elements of the existing R&D infrastructure, including both the applied scientific research institutes that were mentioned above, and the academic scientific research institutes, which worked in basic science, were experiencing hard times. Working relations within and between these institutions and those collaborating with them in R&D, and the means and terms of such collaborations, had to be adjusted to new circumstances brought by the end of the Communist era, as vividly explained by the already-quoted informant:

The state ceased to support those organizations that were developing drugs. This was a potent infrastructure . . . Previously there was no need for different institutes to pay each other for collaboration, everything was owned by state. . . . They were collaborating with other specialized organizations. Everyone lived off the same state money, so if part of work is given to another party, there were no obligations to pay for it. The work corresponded to the topic of the institute that was commissioned and this institute reported [to the state] performing this work. They [the institute] also were co-developers of a drug, but all rights still belonged to the state irrespective of where R&D was performed.

And negotiations were easy. I myself, for instance, was working in an academic *NII* [Russian-language acronym for scientific research institute] heading the laboratory of molecular pharmacology. I could easily negotiate with any other *NII*, if a project fitted their specialization, if they were interested in scientific work on a particular drug, they would respond: "Ok, let's do." Their director would respond: "Yes, it corresponds with our specialization, we are not against this." And we would just sign an agreement that we collaborate together and then considerable parts of work related to a drug development could be performed in other places. And everything was paid for by the state. In fact no one was really counting those moneys. It was just important that a report was produced, which would be in line with an institute's specialization and that's it. Then later an institute, when reporting on its work, would include that they participated in a development of a drug. It also was important. This is how work was accounted for.

When state financing stopped seriously supporting these institutes, it was just enough for survival and a bit for salary, such work was not possible anymore. When you turn to them asking for something to be done, they would say that personnel is still present, equipment is there, but chemical reagents need to be bought, this work needs to be paid for, because this is a separate piece of work. We barely cope with the work we already have with available money they would say. That was the end. Everything began to decay. (5BK, 2014)

The informant indicated that the adjustment to new circumstances was not easy and resulted in a significant loss of R&D potential as researchers and developers were leaving the institutions or having difficulties sustaining themselves, equipment was becoming dated, and further prospects were unclear. The same informant further explained that when after a while local pharmaceutical companies began to realize the need for more R&D work, the *NII*s already could not provide much:

Then they [pharmaceutical business] started to realize that generics are produced by everyone, dated drugs, generics also became low margin. Something innovative was needed. Where could it come from? On one hand, they started to approach different *NII*s, as before, where some few capable people did stay. The younger ones went abroad, because salaries were not paid, they needed to support their families, somehow survive. Some switched to other professions. And specialists were lacking. Older people stayed, who did not want to go anywhere, somehow were living their last years, and social security pays and a small salary was enough for their needs. But money was needed, so directors [of production facilities] were grasping everything they could find. Something was done, in a very fragmented way. (5BK, 2014)

This overview of transformations in the Russian pharmaceutical industry suggests that rapid and unanticipated changes in the area of drug research, development, and production brought on by the end of the USSR and rushed neoliberal experimentation disturbed settled collaborative networks and work habits, threw actors who had worked in the planned economy into an emerging and immature open market environment, and overall paralyzed drug innovation. Some pharmaceutical companies did manage to attract foreign investors and launch joint production of complex pharmaceuticals. For example, Akrichin and Bristol-Myers Squibb began joint production of the cardiovascular drug Capoten in 1992. But overall, the local industry, which was already struggling by the end of the Soviet era, as shown in the previous chapter, moved into a full-scale crisis with the onset of the free market and withdrawal of the state, guided by the neoliberal vision of the reformers.

Rejection

The analysis in the previous section indicates that those involved in the Russian pharmaceutical sector experienced much uncertainty regarding how to operate in the newly emerged market environment, which soon became linked to the international market space, with private property, competition, and no directing hand of the state. This new environment, shaped by the aspirations of the young reformers who viewed freedom as the freedom to own property, to engage in entrepreneurship, and to make profits, appeared chaotic and confusing to many of the actors in the pharmaceutical sector.

To understand the ensuing transformations of the pharmaceutical industry in Russia, we can again view further events from the angle of political imagination. The crisis that the Russian pharmaceutical industry promptly entered into during the first years of reforms, along with a wider deterioration of health care that was commonly felt, contributed heavily to the difficulty for those involved in the early post-Soviet pharmaceutical sector in imagining a market to be a perfect "information processing method" and the route to the nation's prosperity and well-being. The neoliberal vision of the Russian nation and its future put forward by Gaidar, his team, and supporters was disseminated through new laws and institutional infrastructure, but it still failed to take a firm root among groups involved in research, development, and manufacturing of pharmaceuticals in the country. The rapid decline in local pharmaceutical science and technology described underwrote the wide rejection of the neoliberal aspirations among those involved in the sector and the subsequent articulation of another vision centered on the revival of the strong and independent nation-state.

Against the background of the crisis, calls for greater state involvement and control and support for the Russian pharmaceutical industry became more vocal. For example, in 2000 a programmatic article was published in a central Russian pharmaceutical industry journal (*Khimiko-Farmatsevticheskii Zhurnal/Pharmaceutical Chemistry Journal*) arguing for measures that ran contrary to the neoliberal ideal that had animated the early Russian state and governance reforms. By 2010, these measures were actually implemented in an attempt to boost local drug development and production, as discussed in chapter 4. Through a careful reading of this 2000 article, we can glimpse a new direction in relations between politics and pharmaceutical science and technology and a new vision of the national future that came to supersede the short-lived dominance of neoliberalism in the early post-Soviet period.

The article was written by Yoryi Kalinin and his colleagues. Kalinin had been the head of a Russian joint stock company, Biopreparat, the largest state pharmaceutical holding company at the time, with a history of biological weapons development in Soviet times. Beginning in 1995, Kalinin led the association Rosmedprom, which united many local pharmaceutical enterprises; he had also become the head of an influential commission for the pharmaceutical and medical industry of the Russian

Union of Industrialists and Entrepreneurs. In the 2000 article, Kalinin and his colleagues harshly criticized the neoliberal reforms, stating:

> The organization of the production of pharmaceuticals was most detrimentally affected by the results of rapidly executed compulsory privatization of industrial enterprises. Unfortunately, the state interests were not taken into account during privatization of the pharmaceutical plants. The enterprises were left to their own devices and, under these conditions, each plant tried to organize the yield of products most profitable at that time. (52)

That is, in his assessment of the reforms, Kalinin, an industry spokesperson, divorced free market forces from the interests of the state and correspondingly from the people of the country the state represents in this reasoning. While for neoliberals letting the market reign would ultimately ensure that the population's interests are met in the best possible way, for Kalinin such reign meant quite the opposite. Moreover, he brought in the idea of state security, which in his interpretation required erecting barriers to international trade, the same barriers that neoliberal reformers of the early 1990s worked hard to demolish. Having too many foreign-produced pharmaceuticals in the country market was presented here as a threat to both the population and the state:

> From the standpoint of state security, in solving the task of providing the population with medicines, Russia is now dependent on foreign suppliers of pharmaceuticals. (52)

Kalinin et al. (2000) proposed strengthening the role of the state in coordination and planning, as they doubted that the industry's performance could be improved by "the management of plants without the aid of governmental bodies" (510); relying on the government to provide resources for industry support measures; and aiming for independence from imported pharmaceutical substances and drugs:

> In order to eliminate the dependence of the country on the import of pharmaceuticals, ensure stable operation of enterprises during economic instabilities, and use the potentials of this country, it is necessary to coordinate the effort of specialists

of the Ministry of Public Health of the Russian Federation, the Ministry of Economy of the Russian Federation, research institutions, commercial enterprises, and public organizations in elaborating a program for development of the scientific, technological, and industrial potential capable of solving the task of ensuring guaranteed production of vital and most important medicines. (54)

The program articulated by Kalinin et al. (2000) can be understood as a case of pharmapolitics. On the one hand, these authors presented political goals, including those of the return of the strong state, of restraining the economic liberalization, and of confining and controlling markets. On the other hand, this articulation of political goals was made possible by the state of pharmaceutical science and technology. That is, not only did local pharmaceutical science and technology and the crisis in them enable this articulation, but they also shaped and strengthened it by grounding it in concrete and tangible realities of drug development and production infrastructures. In the process of this interaction between science, technology, and politics, a new vision of the nation and its future began to be produced, that of an independent and self-sufficient Russia with a strong guiding state.

I have used the article by Kalinin et al. (2000) to characterize the new, post-neoliberal round of relations between politics and pharmaceutical science and technology in Russia. This article can be viewed as an expression of a wider sentiment among those involved with pharmaceuticals in the country that arose and consolidated in the process of mutual shaping of pharmaceutical technoscience and politics in the early post-Soviet period. In the pharmaceutical field, it is precisely the deterioration of technology, including the termination of drugs and pharmaceutical substances production and an inefficient R&D system, that facilitated the revival of the idea of the strong state. Simultaneously, the abundance of foreign-produced drugs and pharmaceutical substances in the country market enabled the rise of the national security ideal that was mentioned by Kalinin et al. (2000) and later became central to the country's political landscape. The ideas of a strong state and of the nation's security became elements of the new vision of the nation and its future that were being produced and fed back into the Russian pharmaceutical field and its governance, consolidating in the form of the government's strategy Pharma-2020, which is investigated in chapter 4.

Search for Alternatives

The rapid transformation of the pharmaceutical industry in Russia was enabled by the powerful entry of the neoliberal imaginary of society carried into governance decisions by the young reformers group and disseminated throughout the country in new directives and procedures. In a short time, the backbone of the Soviet pharmaceutical research, development, and production—central state management and planning, and primacy of scientific expertise in pharmaceutical regulation—was gone. Instead came an open market environment, deregulation, and private enterprise. But the Russian pharmaceutical industry, already troubled by the time of the Soviet Union's collapse, not only failed to thrive in the new environment, but quickly deteriorated into a condition of full-fledged crisis.

Chittoor et al. (2008), who studied organizational change in the pharmaceutical industry in emerging economies during economic liberalization, singled out several factors influencing successful adaptation of organizations in the industry. Discussing the example of the Indian pharmaceutical industry's accomplishments, these authors show that it has developed in a mixed economy; that is, "India has not carried out significant privatization so far, but focused more on opening all sectors of the economy to private players, both local and foreign" (264) for decades following independence from Britain in 1947. Moreover, the Indian economic liberalization program has been distinguished by the gradual pace of reforms, proceeding in a cautious manner. Organizational studies scholars stress that there is a limit to the environmental uncertainty and institutional upheaval that organizations can withstand (Newman 2000). In the words of Chittoor et al. (2008), "If the pace of economic reforms exceeds the pace at which organizations can adopt appropriate strategies, those organizations would not be able to survive even if they have the potential to do so otherwise." Consequently, in the conditions described, India's pharmaceutical organizations, already having had some experience with private sector and international pharmaceutical companies, had time to develop and adopt appropriate strategies to survive and grow.

In light of the analysis by Chittoor et al. (2008), it can be seen that the rapid pace of the severe reforms in the context of economic liberalization in Russia inhibited adaptation by the local pharmaceutical industry organizations. In this situation, Russian pharmaceutical companies overwhelmingly either exited the market by divesting the business, failed, or adopted a defensive strategy, trying to protect their positions in the domestic market in the same product niches they had occupied previously. Against the background of this rapid deterioration, actors in the Russian pharmaceutical industry did not become convinced adopters of the neoliberal imaginary of the society and of the corresponding practices and forms of organization. Rather, they, including business actors, began suggesting more state involvement in supporting and guiding local industry as well as shielding it from foreign competitors, thus inviting a comeback of the strong state to protect the national market, which indeed materialized by the beginning of the 2010s. The process of the mutual shaping of pharmaceutical science and technology and politics in the early years of post-Soviet Russia delineated in this chapter contributed to rejecting a neoliberal vision of the nation and its future and producing an alternative.

The Russian Pharmaceutical Industry and Market in 1996 at a Glance

Number of active licenses for production of pharmaceuticals in the country: 287. This number includes former state factories, research institutes involved in small-batch production, and manufacturing sites for which pharmaceuticals is not the main business area (for example, this list of 287 licensed production sites includes nine beef and dairy factories).

Volume of the Russian pharmaceutical market: $3.5 billion. It quickly shrank between 1991 and 1993 and began increasing in 1994.

Russian market composition in terms of purchaser: commercial sector: $1.6 billion (46%) and public sector (hospital purchases and drug coverage programs): $1.9 (54%).

Top-ten Russian pharmaceutical producing companies in 1996:

Table 2.3. Top ten Russian pharmaceutical producing companies in 1996

	Company name	Sales volume in million $
1	Biosintez	95
2	Ferrein (Bryntsalov)	94
3	Biophimik	75
4	Moskhimfarmpreparati named after N.A. Semashko	73
5	Sintez	63
6	Akrikhin	45
7	Krasnoyarskmedpreparati	44
8	Oktyabr	41
9	Tomsk Khimpharmzavod	35
10	Belvitamini	34

The overall share of locally produced drugs in the country market constituted 42 percent in value terms. It is estimated that in the late USSR, pharmaceuticals produced in the Russian SFSR represented 50 to 55 percent of what was consumed in Russia and that the remainder came from other Soviet states and member-countries of Comecon (such as East Germany, Hungary, and Poland). Then the share of Russian-produced drugs in value terms dropped with the collapse of the Soviet system of economic cooperation to about 30 percent in 1994, but during 1995 and 1996 this share shot up again. The reason for this rapid increase likely was the equally rapid rise of prices for pharmaceutical drugs produced in Russia. While locally produced drugs originally were sold for very low prices in the newly formed market environment, after 1994, Russian producers increased prices to levels that were previously unheard of (between 1994 and 1996, prices for Russian pharmaceuticals increased by 63 percent in US dollars). This is why, despite the catastrophic decrease in pharmaceutical production, the share of locally produced drugs in value terms nearly recovered.

Data presented here were obtained from the following sources: Iudanov, Volskaia, and Lagunov 1998; Dorofeev 1995.

Chapter 3

The Arrival of Commercial Clinical Trials in Russia

Generating Multiple Value

The question of value is of central importance in pharmapolitical processes. This is because development and production of drugs entangles the prospects of improving the lives of patients, soaring profits for industry, and opportunities to advance both scientific knowledge and state interests. Correspondingly, questions loom large about what kind of value is being generated and for whom in the drug development and production systems. In this chapter, I use the case of international commercial clinical trial conduct in Russia to investigate *value generation* as another process that, together with vision production (chapter 2), problem definition (chapter 4), and collaboration (chapter 5), shapes pharmapolitical nexus.

Since the second half of the twentieth century, clinical trials have gained much authority—first in the United States, then in Western Europe, and later in other locations—in establishing the safety and efficacy of drugs. In the current regulatory environment of major drug markets such as the United States and Canada, the European Union, Japan, and increasingly other countries as well, medical interventions are allowed to move from bench to bedside only after a series of trials. In recent decades, along with the rise in numbers,[1] clinical trials have been moving outside the regions of their conception, Europe and North America, to other settings, including post-Soviet Russia, and have become a truly global enterprise (Karlberg 2011, 2008). The drivers of this movement of medical experiments include possibilities for cost cutting, expedited participant recruitment, access to therapeutically naive populations, and also humanitarian efforts to address historically neglected health issues. Scientific and regulatory requirements for larger and diverse samples for robust results have also indirectly supported the geographical expansion of trials because such expansion allows for assembling large multisite trials with thousands of people in different countries (Glickman et al. 2009).

Globally, the development of new drugs continues to be largely concentrated in the commercial pharmaceutical sector, and the end of the public drug development system of the Soviet Union reinforced this situation. Sariola and colleagues (2015) write that when "pharmaceutical companies outsource trials in search of new markets and treatment-naïve patients, they transform the existing pharmaceutical sector, harmonising it to resemble more closely international or 'Big Pharma'" (240). Therefore, the trend of globalizing clinical trials can be viewed as a part of "big pharmaceuticalisation." Sariola et al. (2015) argue that in India, for instance, big pharmaceuticalization denotes "how Randomised Controlled Trials (RCTs) become central to a particular form of knowledge production, and begin to displace preexisting generic drug production regimes" (240). These authors further note that while big pharmaceuticalization is a process whereby new locations such as India become more like the international pharmaceutical sector, Big Pharma, this resemblance is not perfect. Returning to the example of India, Sariola et al. (2015) demonstrate that by now the big-pharmaceuticalization process in India has introduced new regulatory practices and methodologies, skills, and ideas from the international pharmaceutical sector into the country. These, however, served primarily as a vehicle for generating universal data for Big Pharma and facilitating its access to the Indian market, rather than being a driver for developing the capacity of the local industry to compete with Big Pharma companies. This illustrates that clinical trials can generate multiple kinds of value, and what kinds of value and for whom are actually generated in various contexts is a question of politics just as much as it is a question of science and technology.

This chapter originates in an academic research center in Moscow that was one of the first institutions in Russia to join the commercial clinical trials enterprise at the beginning of the 1990s. I did fieldwork at this center for four months in 2013 and conducted several follow-up visits in 2014. Drawing on interviews with seventeen research participants and five investigators and observations of trials work at the center, I analyze how trials have come to be integrated in the Russian environment and with what effects. I also interviewed five investigators from other clinical research sites to solicit their perspectives on the issues that transpired during my fieldwork at the center. In what follows, I first provide background on the debate on the value of clinical trials. Further, I sketch the situation in Russia and at a specific research center during the 1990s, when international commercial clinical trials began to arrive there. Then I analyze how center investigators connect the academic and corporate domains, translating clinical trials into academic capacity building and development of local medical expertise. I focus on how investigators and research participants relate to each other to entwine medical experimentation with health-care provision. In conclusion, I reflect on the implications of these processes of value multiplication for governing the globalizing conduct of clinical trials and on the significance of value generation for pharmapolitics.

Value of Medical Experimentation

The issue of the value of clinical trials is controversial. On one hand, trials are an important stage of therapeutic research and development (R&D) meant to prevent the circulation of dangerous medications. Their value therefore can be understood in terms of contributing to the future well-being of patients and society at large. On the other, studies of the political economy of trials highlight the centrality of the logic of profit in the contemporary global pharmaceutical arena. Globalization of the clinical trials enterprise, being a part of a free movement of capital and commodities, is shaped by global health inequalities, with people living in situations of health crisis often coming to sustain medical research, the results of which are mainly used by more affluent populations (Petryna 2009). The value of clinical trials, then, can also be understood in terms of profit generation against the backdrop of the capitalist economy. Thus, pharmaceutical R&D appears to be struggling with a divide between meeting people's health needs through developing relevant and accessible drugs and generating profit.

This divide, where health often becomes a resource for wealth, is not new. For example, to recruit participants for testing new pharmaceutical products, the industry in the United States has long capitalized on the political and economic conditions that disadvantage certain populations, such as migrants, the uninsured, and, until the late 1970s, prisoners (Fisher

2015). Now, as international commercial clinical trials arrive in new locations, outside Europe and North America, conflicts between economic and therapeutic value production processes reappear in a stark light.

Offering a reading of clinical trials as a stage in the production of bioeconomic value and using the example of China, Cooper (2008) proposes treating clinical trial participation as a highly precarious service labor with a trial site performing the same function as an export processing zone and capitalizing on the labor of the poor and uninsured. Sunder Rajan (2010) also stresses the dominance of market rationales in drug development processes, but locates the problem not only in a lack of recognition of experimental subjects' labor in producing value in a strictly economic sense. Instead, using an example from clinical trials in India, he problematizes uncoupling "experimental subjectivity from therapeutic access" (72) when trial participants contribute to wealth by making themselves available for experimentation, but this is not linked to either their own health or the health of other populations in India. This problematization suggests that while clinical trial practices are overdetermined by capital, the value of the trial-produced knowledge need not be reduced to the logic of profit and can be rethought to be more closely linked to the production of social value.

The issue of social value generated by globalizing clinical trial conduct has been actively discussed in bioethical literature. Authors such as Emanuel et al. (Emanuel et al. 2004) suggest that social value of clinical research can be enhanced if research participants and their communities receive benefits from the conduct and results of research through dissemination of knowledge, product development, long-term research collaboration, and/or health system improvements (931). In a similar vein, the fair benefits framework (Participants in the 2001 Conference on Ethical Aspect of Research in Developing Countries 2004; Schroeder and Gefenas 2012) highlights diversity of possible clinical research benefits, including the construction of health-care facilities, development of public health programs, and health services provision, and also emphasizes public participation by suggesting that host populations themselves point to the benefits that are of value for them and are fair. Generation of social value thus is closely tied to mechanisms of collaborative partnerships (Lairumbi et al. 2008) and community engagement (Marsh et al. 2008) and is thought to bring the realms of corporate profits and research populations' well-being closer together.

Realization of benefit sharing and maximizing social value of trials in practice is complicated. Even in the context of international humanitarian health research, local actors often have few opportunities to attune the agenda for research conducted in their communities to existing health needs, and structures to link research, policy, and practice can be weak or nonexistent in lower-income settings, as Lairumbi et al. (2008) showed in Kenya. In the context of commercial clinical trials, benefits derived by local actors involved in conducting them are generally incidental and haphazard. For example, Petryna (2015) documented how Ukrainian physicians in the mid- to late 1990s were anxious to engage with commercial trials because of both the lack of opportunities to treat patients and deterioration of the scientific infrastructures without public funding. In this case, there was no benefit-sharing framework envisioned, and trials were initiated by the industry, intending to capture new segments of pharmaceutical markets. At the same time, trials were being employed by physicians to provide treatment and to support the academic work in a situation of crisis, illustrating that clinical trials may produce other kinds of value beyond an economic one even in situations where sponsors do not intend them to.

The approaches to the analysis of trials discussed above—the one focusing on political economy and the one inviting attention to social value—to some extent separate the social and economic dimensions of clinical trials. In this chapter, I follow an approach offered by Kelly and Geissler (2012), who suggest considering normative and sociological questions of medical research not separately from, but together with, political and economic analysis by exploring ethnographically the value generated in clinical research. This approach enables transcending the dichotomies between market valuation and population welfare and accounting for how research value is configured in therapeutic, social, and economic landscapes in post-Soviet Russia, where commercial clinical trials have come to be uneasily inserted in ongoing conflicts over market reforms and the role of public institutions.

Joining the Global Clinical Trials Enterprise

The research center on which this chapter focuses was founded in the era of the Soviet Union. From the time of its inception, the work of this state institution has focused on cardiovascular disease (CVD). Studies conducted in the center in Soviet times generally could not be sponsored by for-profit organizations and did not involve randomized controlled trials (RCTs) of pharmaceuticals. Research focused on the epidemiological situation in the country and risk factors and prevention of CVD, relying on cohort and other nonrandomized studies. Center activities were not confined to the borders of the USSR. The staff published English-language articles in international journals, attended international conferences, and communicated with colleagues abroad.

In chapter 2, I described the state of crisis experienced by the Russian pharmaceutical industry after the end of the USSR. Times of hardship fell upon the center as well. State financing was in decline, many research programs had to be terminated, and scientific work was undermined by a lack of resources. These disruptions led to decreased scientific output and the center's diminished presence in the international scientific community. It was not only scientific work that stagnated. The center's specialized in- and outpatient clinic where patients with life-threatening diseases, including coronary heart disease, received medical care was also affected. The end of the USSR brought much disorder throughout the entire health-care system, including delays in salary payment to personnel and absence of drugs and supplies. Subsequently, providing adequate medical services became more difficult (Schecter 1992; Brown and Rusinova 1997).

People working at the center began looking for ways to allow the institution to survive through the turmoil, continue providing care for patients, and secure resources to support themselves. Biomedical research institutions throughout the country found themselves in a similar position, facing uncertainty and a lack of resources. They used a range of strategies to continue working, including pleading with officials for support, requesting aid and assistance grants from the international community, participating in international research projects, and, finally, joining commercial clinical trials (for analysis of transformations in the research systems in the post-Soviet territories see Balázs, Faulkner, and Schimank 1995; Gaponenko 1995).

Foreign-sponsored clinical trials were not conducted in the Soviet Union until their arrival in Russia in the early 1990s. Around this time, trial sponsors began to explore Russia's and the post-Soviet regions' potential, originally focusing on supplemental enrollment of participants for international studies where the number of patients recruited was lower than expected. Among the sponsors, Russia quickly earned a reputation as a location where eligible and often treatment-naive patients could be easily identified and quickly enrolled because of a highly centralized health-care system. For example, in some therapeutic research areas, Russia's patient recruitment rates have been reported to be ten times quicker than in the United States and Western Europe (Stefanov 2007). Additionally, low drop-out rates, the presence of skilled local researchers, and, initially, the lower costs of clinical trial conduct contributed to an increase in the number of foreign-sponsored clinical trials in the Russian Federation. Furthermore, pharmaceutical corporations were eager to take advantage of the potential for profits held by the country's large market (for views on Russia's potential as a clinical trial region and pharmaceutical market, see articles written by representatives of industry, such as Anokina and Meshkov 2007; Stefanov and Tverdokhleb 2008; and Stefanov 2008). Numbers of foreign-sponsored, multicenter, commercial clinical trials conducted in accordance with the three-phase trial system, with RCTs as the gold standard of evidence, grew exponentially by the beginning of the 2000s. While in 1992 there were fewer than twenty such trials approved to be conducted in Russia (Varshavsky 2002), by 2004 the number of approvals had increased to 252 (Association of Clinical Trials Organizations 2010). In the following years, this number fluctuated, and in 2016 the landscape was the following: 302 international multicenter clinical trials were approved to be conducted, with the top three sponsors being Novartis, Merck & Co., and GlaxoSmithKline. In addition, the numbers of foreign-sponsored trials conducted only in Russia, without sites in other countries, and foreign-sponsored studies of bioequivalence of one pharmaceutical product to another became substantial: 82 and 146, respectively, in 2016 (Association of Clinical Trials Organizations 2016).

However, a view of the clinical research arena in Russia only as a neoliberal exploitative use of Russian populations as guinea pigs by rapacious multinational companies does not do justice to the complexity involved. Sunder Rajan makes a similar argument with regard to the arrival of international clinical research in India, stating that "the scenario is more complicated than one in which Western multinational companies are trying to tear the door down to exploit cheap Indian populations" (2010). For example, the Russian legislative infrastructure itself has come to encourage the inflow of clinical trials by requiring data from Russian-based trials for the registration of new pharmaceuticals, in order to allow them into the country's market—in part to stimulate acquisition of profits and capacity building among local actors.

Originally, once liberal reforms were set in motion in newly independent Russia, foreign-sponsored clinical trials were proceeding haphazardly in the absence of comprehensive legislation and mechanisms that would govern the production of commercial pharmaceutical knowledge. One of the first developments was the introduction in 1992 of a regulation that legalized phase I trials with healthy volunteers "in order to create a modern system of clinical trials."[2] Law No. 5487 of July 22, 1993, "On Fundamentals of Russian Federation Legislation on Public Health Care," reaffirmed that the federal government is responsible for licensing and certification of medicines and clinical trials (statute 5) and permitted creation of ethics committees (statute 16). However, as details of the regulatory infrastructure were yet to be worked out, the actual practices of clinical trial conduct were largely shaped by the foreign pharmaceutical companies.

Pharmaceutical companies first found contacts with those few large scientific research institutions that had experience participating in international academic collaborative studies. Concurrently, local clinical research organizations (CROs) were being formed, easing connections between international pharmaceutical business and local research sites. About the clinical trials environment in Russia in the 1990s, Sergey Varshavsky, founder of one of the first Russian CROs,[3] writes:

> Besides the lack of GCP [good clinical practice] standards, clinical trials were not governed by any regulations at all. Anyone could do anything. . . . Not a word about informed consent, no ethics committees, nothing. The time needed to obtain study approvals from the State Pharmacological Committee was unpredictable and took up to two months—depending on nobody knows what. No customs regulations were in place—any drug could be imported. It was up to each customs house officer to decide what could cross the border. (Varshavsky 2002, 74)

In this situation, foreign trial sponsors were working to ensure through trainings and monitoring that trial conduct in Russia observed good clinical practice standards (GCP) in trial protocols. GCP standards were first published in the United States by the FDA in 1978. In the late 1980s, a similar set of standards was accepted in France, the Scandinavian countries, and Japan, and in 1991 in the European Union. Adherence to GCP in the course of clinical trials is key for trial data to be recognized as reliable evidence of drug safety and efficacy by regulators in the countries and regions that accepted these standards. Starting in 1992, the International

Conference on Harmonization (ICH), already mentioned in the introduction, was preparing harmonized GCP standards for the European Union, United States, and Japan. In 1996, the ICH's GCP was finalized. In 1999, the Russian-language version of the ICH GCP was accepted as an industry standard,[4] and in 2006 a more extensive version of this document with definitions and clarification prepared under the lead of the Association of International Pharmaceutical Manufacturers (AIPM) was put in force as a national standard.[5]

The international pharmaceutical industry was also a leading force behind the establishment of the first research ethics committees (RECs), because local review of international trials came to be seen as increasingly desirable to satisfy publishing and regulatory requirements in the regions of origin of Big Pharma, as well as because of public opinion. Drawing on his own experience, neuroscientist and medical journalist Boleslav Lichterman (2002) questioned operations of the ethics committees of the 1990s, which generally were self-assembled:

> How independent and competent are such committees? Recently I was visiting a director of a medical school. Next door to his office was a room for the ethics committee headed by a deputy director. Fourteen out of fifteen committee members are employees of that institution. Many of them are university professors who are involved in clinical trials. The lay public is represented by one orthodox priest. In some research institutions the functions of ethics committees rest upon scientific boards [*uchenye sovety*]. There is no list of ethics committees for hospitals and research institutions. Generally such committees are established for legalizing clinical trials. For example, it was decided to conduct a trial for a new drug in a Moscow clinic. When a hospital director was asked for permission to start the trial he replied: "That is okay but just in case please protect me." So, an ethics committee was established for his "protection." (384)

Only in 1998 did the Federal Law No. 86 "On Drugs" lay the foundation for establishment of the local RECs, and the detailed regulations on how to establish RECs and how they were to function followed after 2000. Overall, the development of regulatory infrastructure for commercial clinical trials was slow and fragmented, and during the first years of the market economy, trials-related decision making and practices were mostly informal and shaped by the international pharmaceutical industry.

The research center where this chapter originated was quick to join the global clinical trials enterprise, largely because of its modern equipment, qualified staff, and prior professional links with the West. Much-needed resources began to arrive through international RCT channels, contributing to the center's ongoing operation, the staff members' livelihoods, and health care for patients, many of whom became research participants. The center in turn began to produce data that were given to industry for analysis and, together with the data from trial sites in other locations all over the globe, contributed to establishing the value of novel drugs and securing market profits.

Value for Investigators and Academia

Since the early 1990s, the research center has become a well-known trial facility in the pharmaceutical industry and has acquired the reputation of being a reliable trial site. Gradually, support through state funding resumed, and the center began returning to its own scientific work while continuing its involvement with commercial clinical trials. It has become a part of a larger state organization that is also involved in the provision of health-care services and advanced training for physicians. Health care here is delivered in a specialized clinic, where consultations and complex medical procedures such as coronary stenting are performed. The organizational structure of the clinic is not designed to ensure routine, long-term health care, which is to be provided in polyclinics;[6] rather, its focus is on highly specialized medical services, which are provided free to those patients who are referred by their polyclinic doctors. The center itself now comprises about forty research staff members, who are mostly physician-scientists specializing in cardiology, alongside clinical and administrative personnel. The majority of research staff are involved in both academic and industry research as well as treating patients. At the time of my fieldwork in 2013 and 2014, several concurrent long-term trials involving patients were being conducted.

The center, as one of the Russian institutions with the longest history of involvement in commercial clinical trials, presently receives many "feasibilities" from pharmaceutical companies and CROs. The term feasibility is used to refer to a document that contains information about a particular trial protocol and also a request for information about the center's infrastructure, quality, and participant recruitment and retention potential. The feasibility instrument aids in the multisite trial planning process by helping CROs and pharmaceutical companies decide whether to work with a particular clinical site. At the same time, the center's investigators use feasibilities to screen out trials that do not correspond to their scientific interests and specialization. For example, the center tends to avoid entering into trials unrelated to CVD. After the center responds favorably to feasibilities that are in line with its priorities and seem to be possible in terms of recruitment and equipment requirements, several correspondence exchanges follow, possibly a site visit, and then the CRO/sponsor decides whether it intends to work with the center. Investigators explain that responding to a feasibility request does not necessarily guarantee a trial will come to the center. As one investigator stated, "It is not always that responding to a feasibility results in a start of a clinical trial. Out of four feasibilities, one project may actually work out." Sponsors may prefer a demographic of patients different from the ones the center typically works with. Sometimes sponsors want more patients per clinical site than the center plans to enroll. Investigators explain that the center "is not chasing huge enrollment numbers," because staff members need to balance conducting trials with other scientific and clinical work.

Investigators work closely with the CRO and/or sponsor upon a trial's commencement. The CRO/sponsor's focus is on ensuring that the trial protocol is followed diligently; therefore, continuous, detailed reporting on progress, unusual events, and changes in patients' drug regimens is required from investigators. This information is usually provided through electronic report forms that are sent to the data management division of the company. The sponsor or CRO representative(s) regularly monitors trial conduct by performing documentation reviews, auditing stocks of experimental medications, observing experimental pharmaceuticals administration, and following up on cases of adverse events. The results of the monitoring visits are documented in standardized site visit reports.

After the end of a trial, the primary investigators may be gathered to hear about the results, but such meetings are rarely arranged. Trial results can also be sent to participating research sites, but most often the center investigators learn about trial outcomes from publications and clinical trials registries such as clinicaltrials.gov. At the stage of planning a new trial, companies that have already worked with the center are likely to send another feasibility request.

Information Needs of Investigators and Academic Work

As previously described, originally, during the 1990s, funds from trial conduct were used by the staff as one of the ways to support the existence of the center in the conditions of severe lack of state financing. Gradually, the situation in the country changed, and the center's existence was no longer dependent on industry resources. However, international commercial trials have continued serving the information and practice needs of investigators.

First, investigators both at the center and in other organizations that conduct clinical trials mention that through involvement in trials, they obtain new information about state-of-the-art approaches to diagnostics and treatments and also access to and experience with novel drugs and devices. As one investigator explained:

> Trials are very helpful. We learn about new technologies, new treatment methods, new interventions. We are able to make this first step of trying a new drug that may soon enter the market. And it is not only about drugs, it could be experience with new stents, for instance, these devices are evolving very rapidly nowadays. So basically we can be among the first ones to learn and try new things. This concerns not only treatments, but diagnostics as well: trial protocols allow us to learn about and use more up-to-date diagnostic methods. (PI1 2014)

Clinical trial value is thus being configured as a means to access information and obtain experience with new treatments, diagnostics, and approaches. It is grounded, on the one hand, in the widely recognized delay with which innovative drugs reach the Russian market. During a press lunch in October 2013 in Moscow, Frank R. Lichtenberg presented data showing that drugs used in Russia on average are fifteen years older than the ones used in the United States, and only 1 percent of drugs used in the country in 2009 were developed after 1990.[7] These data correspond to impressions of market insiders, as stated by the CEO of a company that manages two large Russian governmental projects in drug R&D in an interview by one of the country's major professional journals:

> Innovative drugs arrive in the Russian market 4–5 years after they are approved either by the American FDA or European EMEA. This is an important time, because access to a new, more effective drug could be a really a matter of life and death for some. Also not all these [innovative] drugs ever reach the Russian market. (*Pharmvestnik* 2013)[8]

On the other hand, the value of trials as a source of information and experience is also related to the delay in translation, adaptation, and dissemination of the recent and updated clinical practice guidelines and recommendations among physicians in the country. Therefore, clinical trials sometimes perform an almost educational function to develop local medical expertise, albeit information provided is filtered by the industry, as described by one investigator:

> Clinical trials organize the work of clinician. . . . For example, the process of treatment selection and adjustment could be described in much detail in some protocols. More clarity, more precision and detail in working with patients, and this then is gradually transferred into a physician's clinical practice. For instance, there could be a clear-cut definition of some condition, say, angina, you read it ten times in some trials, understand it, and use it further with your own patients. Or, for instance, this and this are contraindications when such and such drugs are prescribed. Again, you read it ten times and remember indications and contraindications. And this is disciplining the doctor. . . . So this may be educational, I think. (PI2 2014)

Second, the influx of industry resources into the publicly owned research center serves as support for the scientific work of the center itself. Surplus funds of the center are channeled into acquisition of various facilities and the support of the center's own activities, as explained by one investigator:

> The payments for working in clinical trials are generally going into salaries for physicians and investigators. Part of it is going to the center itself and the center decides what to do with these funds: maybe some equipment can be bought, maybe

some materials, maybe again salaries. . . . It is not enough to fully fund large scientific research programs, but is helpful, it gives us more freedom in our everyday work. We can support ourselves, allow trips, buy some, not very large, things we need. (PI2 2014)

Participation in commercial clinical trials provides investigators and their institution with more freedom in their academic research work. For example, the center investigators conduct pharmaco-epidemiological research, including studies of the utilization and effects of drugs in large numbers of people in actual clinical practice in Russia, where little is known about which medications are used, how, and with what results. This is because the use of electronic medical records allowing thorough postmarketing surveillance of pharmaceuticals' and medications' use is not widely adopted in the country. (See news articles reporting on electronic medical records implementation in Russia in Markina 2013; Zingerman 2013). The center's investigators assemble regional registries of CVD patients to complement highly standardized data obtained through clinical trials with information about real-life effects and dynamics. Investigators often view such studies, conducted on their own, as being more valuable for their scientific careers than participation in commercial trials and also crucially important for improving treatment in the country. Thus, the value of trials is also being configured as a contribution to local academic capacity building, with the center's own scientific work, which brings the recognition of academic peers and also is attuned to the local health-care needs and conditions, being partially supported by resources obtained through involvement in commercial trials.

Entwining the Academic and the Corporate

In scholarly and public debate, collaborations between physicians and industry have often been associated with concerns about the production of biased medical information that generates unneeded therapies and invalid scientific results (Moynihan, Heath, and Henry 2002; Law 2006). That is, "corporate" and "academic" are often presumed to be easily distinguishable domains that must be kept separate to avoid corruption, because it is economic interests that are depicted as a main driver of physician-industry collaboration (Fisher 2009).

At the same time, industry and academia or public and private cannot always be easily disentangled. Lakoff (2004) argues that in some settings in Argentina, relations between physicians and pharmaceutical companies can be viewed as involving a "reciprocal access to guarded resources" rather than direct transfer of goods (265). For companies, these relations enabled access to patients as subjects in trials or drug consumers, while for Argentinian doctors, such resources as computer equipment and travel to professional congresses that were supplied by the pharmaceutical industry enabled engagement with the latest medical knowledge and greater professional authority. This illustrates how private interests become closely entwined with public service and medical expertise in a relationship characterized by blurred boundaries and a complex web of resource transfers.

Physician-investigators at the Russian research center actively bridge the academic and corporate spheres, collecting evidence for future industry profits while simultaneously absorbing industry-provided information about new drugs, treatment approaches, and diagnostic procedures and translating it into their medical practice with local CVD patients. Industry resources coming to the center also gain value through their investment in the center's own research, which both advances academic science and holds relevance for local health care with its specifics shaped by the Russian economic, regulatory, and infrastructural contexts. That is, commercial clinical research comes to facilitate development work, linking corporate operations with public science and medical services. This process encompasses the circulation of various kinds of documents such as feasibilities and reports; data channeled through electronic forms; and samples as well as protocols, drugs, and devices, thereby producing overlapping clinical, scientific, and economic value. Recognition of this kind of value multiplication in clinical trial conduct on the ground can facilitate more systematic action to maximize distribution of research benefits; at the same time, it can help to overcome the undoubtedly important, but narrow, focus on the conflict of interest thesis in discussions of physician-industry relations. As Wadman (2014) suggested, when the problem of physician-industry collaboration is defined as one of conflict of interest arising from economic motives, "it directs attention to financial relationships per se and attributes (too much) explanatory power to economic interests as the main driver—and the main danger—of physician–industry collaboration" (547), which may dampen discussion of wider issues, such as that of more systemic yet subtler influences of industry on biomedical knowledge production and also that of benefit sharing in for-profit international clinical research.

Beyond such value generated through clinical trials as new medicines, monetary profits, and the enhancement of local academic research capacity as described above, the practice of trial conduct also allows filling some gaps in local health-care provision, potentially generating more immediate benefits for local well-being, as described in the next section.

Value for Patients

Of all the actors involved in clinical trials, research center investigators engage most closely with research participants. The process of involving patients in a clinical trial is built around formal inclusion/exclusion criteria predefined by the trial protocol. However, in practice it develops into a lengthy individualized process. Physician-investigators review the databases of their current and former patients and screen out patients who do not meet formal inclusion criteria. They then carefully examine the medical files of patients who do meet the inclusion criteria, looking for anything unusual, such as comorbidities, previous complications, or uncommon progression of disease or symptoms. Investigators often exclude patients whose medical history "raises suspicions," that is, contains indications that patients may have a higher chance of adverse reactions. As one center investigator explained: "Sometimes we exclude those who do meet the inclusion criteria, in some cases we try to be on a safe side, [choosing patients] is not an automatic process" (PI2 2013). Sometimes center investigators refer to external physicians, usually those working in polyclinics, for help with recruitment, and then take extra care to ensure that there are no "red flags" for the external patients' participation.

At the center, research work with patients does not involve trial coordinators or recruitment officers. In contrast to the situation described by Fisher (2009) in the United States, where trials are often executed by nurses and supported by coordinators, at this center and at many other Russian trial sites, work related to inviting patients, signing informed consent forms, answering questions, responding to concerns developed during the course of trial, and much more is done by the investigators. Because investigators are the ones primarily engaged with the trial participants, they look for "reliable" participants with whom they can "work and communicate," who would keep agreements, stay in touch, and report accurately about their health. Investigators explain that sometimes the patients they invite to participate in a clinical trial reply indignantly, "How can you offer me such a thing?!" or get noticeably uncomfortable with the idea of being experimented upon. In such cases, investigators prefer to refrain from persuading and insisting. They note that such a person can drop out at any time after hearing "horror stories" from the media or a friend. Terminating participation in a clinical trial is routine practice for investigators when it is due to adverse reactions, negative dynamics in the health parameters being monitored (which may not fall under the criteria of adverse reaction, but are seen as threatening by cautious investigators), or life circumstances precluding regular visits. At the same time, investigators try to avoid dropouts for other reasons and, correspondingly, often invite "experienced" patients first, those with whom they have already worked in trials.

The center investigators invest time and effort in their relations with the research participants they work with. For instance, clinical trial protocols traditionally require CVD patients to be on a stable suitable drug therapy for at least several months before entering a clinical trial. At the same time, when patients are referred by outside physicians for participation, it sometimes turns out that the patients do not follow a stable or suitable drug regimen. Then center investigators do the work of polyclinics in the state health-care system. They diagnose, prescribe drugs, observe, and then, when a drug regimen is chosen and has been stable for several months, enroll a patient in a trial. Investigators meet with all research participants regularly over the course of trials. They provide available results from trial test procedures, explain the results, and give individualized recommendations. They become medical care providers for those participants who have not been receiving adequate care in the state health-care system. Investigators are available by phone for questions or concerns. They also provide consultations for non-trial-related issues and find ways to do additional tests if they feel it is necessary for a research participant's condition.

When a trial is over, former research participants can still call investigators with health-related questions and ask for advice. Investigators explain that upon trial completion, their relationships with the patients enrolled in a trial are not finished: "We cannot say ok, done, I do not know you anymore." In this way, investigators continue to be in contact with participants, supporting them, while simultaneously easing the recruitment process for later trials. Overall, investigators go far beyond trial protocol in their communication and relations with trial participants, and it is largely through this invisible relational work that clinical trials are continuously conducted at the center, which contrasts with a situation of detachment observed by, for instance, Petryna (2007) in a US trial site where, during visits, research participants were separated from an investigator by a glass partition.

Patients involved in a trial appreciate and contribute to supportive relationships with investigators. They also acquire skills valuable for trial participation, making them more reliable and competent allies for investigators. They describe learning "to be more attuned to one's body." As one participant said: ". . . in the course of research you learn more about yourself, your body," which helps patients to accurately and timely report all changes in how they feel. Such reporting is important for clinical trial conduct, and with time participants learn to perform this better. Another important skill that makes patients more reliable as trial participants is their habit of taking their drugs regularly. Research participants state that while being involved in the center's trials, they get used to consistently taking drugs according to the prescribed regimens, which facilitates adhering to the trial protocol. Research participants also learn new techniques, for example how to check their pulse, assess their current health state, and use and report the information obtained to investigators. As one participant narrated:

> There was a trial, when I started taking one more drug, there my pulse became 46. I woke up in the morning, something strange, 46–50. I called [the center], they immediately cancelled it [the experimental drug]. Here there is such direct connection. If I feel sick, I call. I have very good contact with X [investigator], I was her first patient when she just came here. We have such continuous contact, if there are problems: a phone call, she would explain something to me, give advice. I don't worry, it is a reliable protection. (RP8 2013)

If this participant had been less prepared to monitor his state and less disciplined in reporting, the negative dynamic in pulse rate described might have been detected later, or the nature of the drug side effects he was experiencing might have been blurred. In these ways, participants become skilled contributors to clinical trial work. Furthermore, the above statement regarding close contact with an investigator is reflective of relational ties developed and cultivated by both participants and investigators as central to day-to-day trial conduct. After the involvement of this participant in this trial was canceled, his relations with the investigative team continued, and later he was invited to enroll in another trial.

Through participation in clinical trials and continuous contact with investigators, some participants come to see themselves as members of the research team, appropriating scientific work being done at the center and feeling committed to performing this work in the best way possible. As one research participant put it:

> I do not view them as doctors. When you come to the polyclinic, there is a doctor. Here there is a partner with whom you are doing common work. I already got into this, this is important needed work. [The same participant further described a case when he and other participants in one trial] all received a device that automatically documented certain changes in the body and then at a particular time of a day we were supposed to forward this information through the satellite. [The instructions for how to use that device were unclear, and he and other participants experienced problems in using it. He suggested changes in the instructions, which were later adopted for the entire trial.] So they changed the instructions, in a week it was approved and there were no more problems . . . I think everything is fine here, in terms of collaboration. (RP8 2013)

That is, investigators, while working for pharmaceutical companies, continue having concerns and care for patient-participants' well-being. At the same time, participants also care about the research process and results, while their self-interest lies in accessing health care, as described below.

Ways to Live with Chronic Disease

Many of the research participants are continuously involved in clinical trials at the center, translating trial participation into a way of living with their chronic diseases. The continuous contact of research participants and investigators is facilitated by the world of the state health-care system. By law, every Russian citizen is entitled to free health care. For patients with CVD, obtaining medical care is supposed to work in the following manner:

a patient with complaints comes to a general practitioner in a polyclinic, and the general practitioner recognizes the nature of complaints and refers the patient to a cardiologist in a polyclinic. A cardiologist investigates the patient's condition, makes a diagnosis, refers him or her to a hospital if necessary, and may meet with the patient for treatment modifications. The general practitioner is the one who monitors the condition of a patient, renews drug prescriptions, and provides routine medical care required for a chronically ill person, consulting the cardiologist when needed. Patients who are of a certain age or have an officially registered disability or low income are entitled to receive certain drugs for free. If the path of a patient with CVD begins in a hospital, for example with a sudden CVD event, a cardiologist in a polyclinic is the specialist whom the patient is supposed to see after leaving the hospital.

This scheme envisioned corresponds with actual medical practice to varying degrees. Research participants convey that they generally are not satisfied with medical help in polyclinics, mentioning difficulties in accessing doctors (both general practitioners and cardiologists) and the complicated bureaucratic organization of service provision, the lack of time doctors have for patients, and the high turnover rate of doctors as being among the factors that complicate adequate treatment. As one research participant explained:

> They always change there and every time I come I see a new person. And even if polyclinic doctors really want to be interested in me and give me their full attention, they can't: there are crowds in waiting room[s], much pressure from polyclinic management, doctors are quite young. . . . In a word, they are in [a] difficult position, so one can't expect much from them. (RP9 2013)

The center investigators agree that such situations occur. They add that the turnover of clinicians precludes establishing a therapeutic alliance between the doctor and patient, and patients often have no personal doctor who would provide long-term medical care to them. One common strategy Russian patients with CVD reportedly use is trying to be admitted to a hospital as often as possible to gain access to physicians and receive their attention. The patients who participate in the center's clinical trials have found another way to establish a long-term connection with medical specialists that is necessary to manage their chronic illness. Research participants are not inclined to expect medical benefits from a trial per se, nor do they confuse research with treatment, which would constitute a therapeutic misconception (Appelbaum, Lidz, and Grisso 2004; Appelbaum 2010). Rather, they emphasize long-term, close relations with center investigators that involve monitoring and treatment, as well as connection and support, as illustrated by the statement of one participant:

> Polyclinic doctors are overworked, they just give me something and send me away. But here we have regular meetings, the doctor understands who I am, my body, change of drugs, change of dosage, all that. (RP22 2013)

At the center, clinical trials provide an opportunity to reach a new level of loyalty between investigator-clinicians and research participant-patients and to form a relatively stable work group. Investigators develop and preserve access to skilled and reliable research participants, ensuring timely trial recruitment and completion, through which they obtain resources used, for example, for conducting their own research. Participants, in turn, incorporate trial participation into their health condition management through receiving continuous attention and support from competent medical specialists who choose and adjust their treatment regimens and monitor their condition:

> They won't let you down, they are always around. If you feel worse—call, it will be checked. If there are questions—no problem, come, we will see. If some tests are urgently needed, these are organized. (RP6 2013)

Investigators as well view trial participation as beneficial for chronically ill patients with CVD, stating that clinical trials allow for providing health care often superior to that generally seen in state primary health-care facilities:

> Well, I know our contemporary free health care. Here [in a trial site] one comes, is being completely checked, undergoes such tests that are almost completely unavailable in polyclinics. Then one is being advised by specialists who are, so to say, head and shoulders above doctors in polyclinics. And who, consequently, select and prescribe more adequate therapy. (PI3 2013)

Here the value of trials is being configured as a long-term relationship with medical professionals, enabling provision of health services in a situation of limited access in the state-supported health-care system.

Bridging Research and Treatment

At the center, commercial trial conduct and health-care provision have come to be mutually enabling practices. This appears contrary to an influential strain of bioethics literature that has significantly impacted regulations governing studies with human subjects. This literature stipulates a fundamental difference between research and treatment (Anderson 2010) as highlighted in chapter 1. However, categorical demarcation of research from treatment does not do justice to entwinements of research and treatment in the practice of trial conduct described in this chapter. Furthermore, strict demarcation of research and treatment risks dismissing the moral concerns and convictions among actors on the ground and attenuate the responsibilities of trial organizers, sponsors, and investigators toward research participants and their communities (Kimmelman 2007). In recognition of this risk and of profound health disparities permeating globalizing clinical trial conduct, debate in bioethics has shifted now to include calls for trialists to find ways to increase their impact on local health and well-being, and, as this chapter suggests, day-to-day clinical trial practice can be a resource in enhancing and distributing the social value of research.

The process of trial conduct at the center, bridging commercial research and public health care through reconfiguring trial value in terms of therapeutic access, is an imperfect substitute for health care. However, it still facilitates both the provision of health care, such as diagnosis, treatment prescription, monitoring, and emotional support for some patients, and the collecting of scientific data for industry. Interestingly, while medical professionals in some other settings also tend to consider care for research participants to be a moral imperative (see, for example, Wadmann and Hoeyer 2014), physicians in Russia may be especially inclined to work to preserve their duty to act in their patients' best interests even in the situation of clinical trial conduct, because Soviet research ethics were formulated and practiced largely with an emphasis on the primacy of the individual interests of the research participant. In a volume devoted to pharmaceutical research regulations in the USSR, already mentioned in chapter 1, Babayan and Utkin write: "Clinical trials of pharmaceuticals are carried out only on patients first of all for the sake of their treatment and also for an experimental evaluation of treatment results" (Babayan and Ytkin 1982). Later in the text they proclaim: "In the Soviet Union the law guarantees that for no purpose, for no 'higher' reason will a single patient be deprived of treatment" (101). Correspondingly, long-established work ethics among medical professionals could continue to exert subtle influence on the ways in which many of them approach running clinical trials.

Overall, currently it is personal relationships between participants and investigators and the willingness of the latter to go beyond trial protocols that facilitate the production of health benefits in trials. However, recognition that day-to-day investigative work can provide a powerful means of promoting social value (Kelly et al. 2010) may become a starting point for extending and streamlining via formal regulatory change the contributions of commercial research to local public health.

Boundary Process

Clinical trials have been moving outside the locations where they were historically concentrated—Western Europe and North America—and are becoming a truly global enterprise. Global trials are carried out in the context of profound health and resource inequalities, where situations of economic and health crisis systematically make disadvantaged population groups available for experimentation. In other words, the risks faced by research participants often exceed the risks associated with isolated trial protocols. Against this background, the long-standing bioethical focus on securing individual informed consent has been augmented by wider attention to interests of research populations so that "the ethical dimensions of research protocols are increasingly assessed in terms of their investment in local public health or scientific capacity" (Kelly et al. 2010, 1917). The reason for this is an evident and in many respects growing disconnect between pharmaceutical innovation and the alleviation of suffering, despite the latter being generally envisioned to be a result of the former. This chapter therefore focused on value generation as a central dimension of pharmapolitics, drawing on an example of clinical trial conduct as a particular mode of pharmapolitics.

This chapter has highlighted how clinical trial conduct mediates economic profits and local well-being through generating multiple kinds of value in a particular setting. Thus, I suggest viewing trial conduct as a boundary process that operates in between, and connects the realms of, health and wealth and potentially can contribute to bringing them closer together. The idea of a boundary process builds on the concept of the boundary object (Star and Griesemer 1989; Fujimura 1992; Star 1989)—a thing that exists at junctures "where varied social worlds meet in an arena of mutual concern" (Clarke and Star 2008). Here I take a boundary process to be a process that enables interaction of different and potentially conflicting value-producing practices, for example profit making, health-care provision, and knowledge generation. Through such interaction, clinical trial conduct is being transformed to fit diverse needs and circumstances, while still maintaining a common, recognizable identity across the different social groups involved. Through multiplication of value, clinical trial conduct bridges the corporate and the public, the worlds of industry and academia and health care, and in this sense can be viewed as a boundary process extending through the lifetime of a single trial and beyond.

It is necessary to note limitations of clinical trials in terms of their capacity to produce social value. Both investigators and participants involved in clinical trials at the research center in Moscow conceived of commercial trials as presenting beneficial opportunities to them in terms of both health-care provision and academic capacity building. At the same time, their views should be considered against the problematic structural background that largely motivates them to engage with trials, including a lack of public funding for scientific research, few opportunities for developing medical expertise, and difficulties in the functioning of the health-care system. Moreover, incoming trials could have disequalizing effects by forming an additional layer of haves and have-nots. Clinical trial sites are concentrated in big cities in Russia, the top-three locations being Moscow, Saint-Petersburg, and Novosibirsk (Stefanov 2007). Therefore, the opportunity to join the trial enterprise is available only to those living and working in these locations, whereas the options of those who live in rural areas are more limited. At the point of trial enrollment, preference tends to be given to those with the fewest comorbidities and least history of exacerbations, and often the younger ones. Patients with more complex health conditions, the elderly, and those who require much medical attention are left out of the clinical trial track to health care. Also, the industry gives preference to those trial sites that already have experience in carrying out commercial research and possess trained personnel and up-to-date equipment. Therefore, the sites that may have the greatest need of capacity-building opportunities and resources are sidelined. Thus, clinical trials can provide a much-needed opportunity for quality treatment and research and health-care infrastructure development, but this opportunity is open only to a few patients, researchers, and institutions. Others are left to deal with unresponsive public health-care and research governance systems. Correspondingly, work to ameliorate such structural conditions that motivate those in Russia who have no better alternatives than to engage with clinical trials must become a priority. Too much reliance on clinical trials for health-care delivery and academic infrastructure development is risky, not least because this option is volatile, as trials arrive irregularly and create new forms of exclusion.

Even with the limitations of clinical trials, recognition that research value not only is brought about in the form of profits resulting from the research product, but also emerges in the process of trial conduct, is still important. This recognition can aid in rethinking the international clinical research enterprise to make it more responsive to the interests of local actors and to employ it in actually addressing structural problems in health care and academia that form the problematic background of the involvement in commercial clinical trials in Russia. Currently, commercial clinical trials in Russia are barely connected to improvements in population health not least because, while market mechanisms do bring some newly developed medicines back into the country, prices put these medicines out of reach for many patients who need them. It is some investigators and research participants who personally engage in the work of translating trials into academic capacity building and developing local medical expertise and public health benefits and, thus, value multiplication. Because the benefits trials can bring into local settings are potentially significant, I suggest that more systematic attention now needs to be given to questions of how to extend and institutionally ascertain these benefits and how to develop what Petryna called "a different sort of market-oriented pharmaceutical contract" globally (2015, 218). Such attention, in line with the current move in bioethics from a narrow focus on individuals and isolated clinical trials to a wider and more structurally oriented debate, is necessary for attempts to maximize the social value of clinical research to actually contribute to public health rather than make local conditions and populations even more amenable for experimentation.

When value generation is considered as central to pharmapolitics, it becomes apparent that value in pharmaceutical science and technology is not a given, but rather it is multiply configured in the clinical, scientific, and economic domains. How and which kinds of value are being generated depends on how priorities of more powerful actors shape pharmaceutical governance, how R&D practices actually proceed on the ground, and what kinds of technologies and knowledge circulate through networks where new drugs emerge. In the most basic terms, this means that, while rhetoric of improving public health is central in the pharmapolitical arena, public health benefits do not follow automatically from developments in national or international pharmaceutical science and technology. Rather, they require targeted efforts by regulators and others involved to link these developments with people's health concerns. At the same time, the ways in which current outcomes of drug R&D are appreciated and the ways in which value of future outcomes is imagined feed into shaping the operation of pharmapolitics. Consequently, the pharmapolitical developments may turn attention away from meeting the health needs of populations and tie pharmaceutical science and technology primarily to other goals, as also highlighted in chapter 4 in regard to the recent attempts to boost local drug development in Russia.

Chapter 4

Pharma-2020 Policy

Defining the Problems of the Russian Pharmaceutical Industry

In 2009, the Strategy for the Development of the Pharmaceutical Industry in the Russian Federation to 2020 (Pharma-2020) was adopted by Russia's Ministry of Industry and Trade (Minpromtorg 2009), followed in 2012 by a dedicated state program, "Development of the Pharmaceutical and Medical Industry for 2013-2020" (Minpromtorg 2012), that specified the actions to follow. The development of the program was led by the same ministry. The Strategy aims to ensure the "innovative development of the Russian pharmaceutical industry" with one of its primary objectives being the "fostering of research, development and production of innovative drugs."

The adoption of the Pharma-2020 Strategy has been accompanied by media and professional discussions of the crisis in the Russian pharmaceutical industry. The difficult situation encountered by the local pharmaceutical industry upon the disintegration of the Soviet Union was outlined in chapter 2. As described there, many pharmaceutical manufacturing sites stopped operations, the country system of drug research and development disintegrated, and the science base deteriorated as well. Academic staff left the institutions, and state funding to support research was lacking. Even though the situation in Russia gradually stabilized by the end of the 1990s, the local Russian industry has not managed to make a comeback and become an important player in the national or international markets. One sign of the prolonged local pharmaceutical industry crisis that often has been featured in the media and professional materials is the fact that drugs produced by the Russian companies constitute only about 20 percent of the value of the country market (DSM group 2006). Moreover, this share consists mostly of cheap generic drugs (DSM group 2006), indicating a low innovation activity of local producers, who appear to generally focus on imitating long-existing, technologically simple medicines. The Pharma-2020 document compares the national pharmaceutical industry and the US and EU producers and states that more than half of the production portfolio of the latter consists of innovative medicines, in this way illustrating the weakness of the Russian pharmaceutical sector.

In this chapter, I consider these attempts to boost local drug development and production in Russia as a technopolitical process, in which pharmaceutical technologies are strategically employed to constitute, embody, and enact political goals, to paraphrase Hecht (2001). Specifically, I attend to the centrality of *problem definition* to pharmapolitics, using the set of Pharma-2020 policies as an example.

My account in this chapter is complementary to a set of innovation studies literature that has extensively studied differences between nations in terms of industrial development and technological innovation performance. This body of literature generally argues that such differences are due to the combinations of institutions involved and their interactions. However, innovation studies literature has been less productive in explaining why particular combinations of institutions and their interactions emerge in specific settings. My reading of the efforts to boost drug development and production in Russia as a case of technopolitics and attention to the problem definition processes involved in it open up an opportunity to approach this question in the Russian setting.

I base my account on document and media analysis and thirty interviews with academic, business, and state actors involved in drug innovation in Russia. In what follows, I first introduce the scholarly debates on variations in innovative performance across countries. Then I outline the content of the Pharma-2020 strategy and analyze how problems it aims to solve are framed and what kinds of future(s) are being envisioned in formulating this policy. Then I explore how actors on the ground interpret and relate to Pharma-2020 and highlight how a particular kind of imaginary—that of a "pharmaceutically secure," self-sufficient, and independent Russian nation—gained dominance in the Russian local pharmaceutical arena. I conclude by reflecting on the significance of problem definition as a dimension of pharmapolitics and of studying meaning making for understanding innovation trajectories.

Cross-National Differences in Innovative Performance

The project of boosting drug development and production in Russia can be considered congruent with a globally prominent view that scientific and technological advances are a driver of economic and social development (Gibbons et al. 1994). The focus on innovation has been replacing another influential development paradigm, the so-called Washington consensus. The Washington consensus refers to a package of policies prescribed by the US government and such powerful international bodies as the International Monetary Fund (IMF) and the World Bank as the path to economic growth and hence the improved well-being of various societies. This policy package is based on the three pillars of liberalization, privatization, and deregulation and promotes neoliberal globalization, doing so especially forcefully in the 1980s and 1990s. More recently, in the aftermath of the limited success of these policies in closing the gaps between rich and poor societies, another view on development has gained popularity, one that suggests that developing economies and societies are the ones that innovate.[1]

This view has prompted a wide adoption of policies and an influx of state funds aimed at stimulating advances in science and technology and translating them into enhanced innovation in many countries (Gibbons et al. 1994). Substantiating the necessity of this, economists and innovation studies scholars Metcalfe and Ramlogan (2008) give the example of Latin America. There, trade liberalization has facilitated restructuring of local economies to exploit comparative advantages based on resources such as steel, soya, and low-skilled intensive labor, which often become elements in global supply chains. While there was some success in macromanagement and stabilization of the investment climate, without work to build local innovation capacity, this pattern risks locking Latin America into unfavorable trade terms and out of opportunities to capitalize on techno-scientific advances. The authors conclude that the "danger of a low (tech) road to development is manifested in this constellation of practices" (434).

A large body of literature addresses the process of innovation at the national and also regional and sectorial levels, seeking to explain differences in innovative performance across countries and thus equip policy makers with knowledge of how to stimulate their countries' capacities to innovate. This literature, originating primarily in economics and innovation studies, invokes the notion of national innovation systems to explain the differences.

One of the popular definitions of a national innovation system is that it is "the system of interacting private and public firms (either large or small), universities and government agencies, aiming at the production of science and technology within national borders. Interaction among those units may be technical, commercial, legal, social and financial, inasmuch as the goal of the interaction is the development, protection, financing or regulation of new science and technology" (Niosi et al. 1993). Proponents of the concept argue that differences in innovation and hence economic performance across countries are due to the combinations of institutions involved and their interactions. The latter point is important, because national innovation system literature does not limit the institutional environment to the "hardware" of the formal structures, as illustrated by the statement of an Organization for Economic Cooperation and Development (OECD) policy paper: "The overall innovation performance of an economy depends not so much on how specific formal institutions (firms, research institutes, universities, etc.) perform, but on how they interact with each other as elements of a collective system of knowledge creation and use, and on their interplay with social institutions (such as values, norms, and legal frameworks)" (OECD 1994). In other words, variation in national innovative performance is attributed in this body of scholarship to "institutional differences in the mode of importing, improving, developing and diffusing new technologies, products and processes" (Freeman 1995).

The scientific and policy literature mentioned above has significantly advanced our understanding of variations between countries in innovative performance. Nonetheless, the problem of difference in sociotechnical outcomes across nations is not fully accounted for by the analytic tools available in this tradition. For example, how do differences arise that lack obvious grounding in natural, economic, or social disparities in the institutional environments? Or why do "social institutions (such as values, norms, and legal frameworks)," important for national innovation systems and cited in the above-mentioned OECD paper, diverge even among liberal democracies that seem to share fundamental aspirations and commitments? (Jasanoff 2005). I suggest that innovation systems literature lacks analytical tools geared toward discerning meaning-making processes and, consequently, could not fully answer these questions without input from Science and Technology Studies (STS).

Here is an example of how innovation systems literature can be complemented by STS insights. To explain the emergence and development trajectories of innovation systems, some innovation studies scholars put forward a functional approach. Tether and Metcalfe (2004) argue that economic activities are organized to respond to specific needs or problems. When the current set of activities becomes inadequate to respond to existing problems, activities are reorganized, that is, the institutional environment is reformed. Consoli and Mina (2008), in a similar vein, suggest that "systems of innovation . . . emerge and develop in a functional fashion as a response to specific problems whose solutions draw on different forms of specialization and depend on their effective coordination" (306). However, what is considered to be a specific problem and the best way to solve it is, to a large extent, a result of meaning-making processes. Therefore, in interrogating the differences in sociotechnical outcomes across nations, we need to analyze not only how systems of innovations respond to particular problems. We also need to study the processes of defining problems that apparently trigger change in the institutional environments of innovation systems.

To do so, more attention is warranted to the collectively enacted hopes and expectations, and the processes of meaning-making, which together with policy formulation do not proceed in a homogenous way on the global scale. Against this background, below I analyze how the processes of *problem definition* frame the goals and trajectories of drug innovation, simultaneously describing and prescribing (national) futures in Russia, which is how pharmapolitics is pursued.

Market and National Security

Both my informants and the media accounts analyzed describe the crisis experienced by drug research and development (R&D) and production in Russia after the USSR's collapse as unprecedented and prolonged. Strategy Pharma-2020 was meant to change the situation through ensuring "innovative development of the Russian pharmaceutical industry" by 2020. It lists seven goals, which, however, receive different degrees of attention in the further text of, and measures proposed by, the Strategy and also in the Strategy implementation efforts, as shown below. These differences point to a particular definition of the problem that the Strategy seeks to address and delineate futures that are being constructed. The goals of the Strategy are specified as follows (2–3):

1. improvement of the supply of the Russian population, health-care institutions, the defense sector, and other federal services with nationally produced lifesaving and essential drugs and drugs for rare diseases;

2. improvement of the competitiveness of the national pharmaceutical industry through harmonization with international good practice requirements;

3. support for research and development of innovative medicines and support of the export of Russian drugs;

4. protection of the internal market against unfair competition and leveling out market access requirements for national and foreign producers;

5. technological upgrade of the Russian pharmaceutical industry;

6. improvement of quality control and removal of excessive bureaucratic registration barriers; and

7. improvement of specialized education, including creation of training programs according to international standards.

In the Strategy, the problem to be addressed through development and implementation of this policy is defined as that of market. This definition is evident in that, first, the Strategy suggests that local producers fail to take advantage of the country market, which has grown considerably since its inception at the beginning of the 1990s. It is foreign pharmaceutical companies that reap the benefits. A diagram at the beginning of the Strategy document depicts the value shares of Russian and foreign producers in the country market in 2007 (20 percent and 80 percent, respectively) and those expected in 2020 (50 percent and 50 percent, respectively). Graphics depicting current not-balanced market shares of the local and foreign pharmaceutical industry and the envisioned equal shares have been featured in many media and professional publications. Second, the Strategy specifies that local Russian producers also miss the profits of the international market, pointing out that export of Russian drugs constituted less than 0.04 percent of the value of the pharmaceuticals sold globally in 2006.

Another component of the market problem constructed in the Strategy is the composition of the internal market in terms of generics and original drugs. The text of Pharma-2020 compares the Russian market structure with that of "developed countries," concludes that the core difference is a significant prevalence of generic drugs in the Russian market, and stresses that Russian innovative drugs occupy only 1 percent of the entire Russian market, something that ought to be changed. This composition of the market is seen as problematic for several reasons. First, very few new drugs (i.e., "original" ones) are present in the country market, meaning that patients are being treated with dated pharmaceuticals, and newer, potentially safer and more effective drugs as well as drugs developed for previously untreatable conditions are not available. Second, original drugs are the most profitable. Because the vast majority of the new drugs that are available on the Russian market have been developed by foreign companies, it is foreign companies that obtain these profits, while the Russian generic-focused industry settles for low added value and correspondingly meager returns. This situation adversely affects the development prospects of the local industry, as summarized in the text of the state program that followed the publication of the Pharma-2020 strategy:

> Currently the Russian pharmaceutical industry loses to foreign companies in terms of development level, technoscientific potential, production volume, and assortment in competition for the Russian market. Profits made by local drug producers are insufficient for financing research and development work for development of highly profitable innovative drugs. In such conditions they have to adapt outdated low-profit drugs to market competition, while foreign pharmaceutical producers devote significant resources to scientific research and assemble their product portfolios in such a way that more than half of these portfolios are formed by highly profitable innovative drugs. (61)

This market composition is problematized widely in the country's governance circles, beyond Pharma-2020 and related policy texts. For example, on November 21, 2013, Minister of Health Veronika Skvortsova alarmed the government by announcing that the proportion of generics on the Russian market is 77 percent, giving Russia third place in the world after China and India in the market share of generics. She stressed the need to support local drug innovation to increase access of the population to newer, good quality, and more effective drugs and to enable Russian industry to exploit the potential of the country market. Pharma-2020 explicitly states that even focusing on development of modern, high-quality generics would not be enough. According to this policy, if such development were set as a target of the current state efforts, then the industry's development capacity would be exhausted once Russian industry achieved a dominant position in the generics sector of the local market. Rather, the Strategy aspires to the Russian pharmaceutical industry developing and producing "high-tech" innovative drugs and "successfully competing with foreign producers in internal and external markets" (29).

Thus, the problem to be addressed by Pharma-2020 is framed in economic terms as that of market. This formulation of the problem is also evident in the expected results of the Pharma-2020 implementation, which are also vocal in delineating a desired future (6–7):

- increase in the share of locally produced drugs to 50 percent (in value terms) on the internal market by 2020;
- increase in the share of innovative drugs to 60 percent (in value terms) in the portfolios of local producers;
- increase in pharmaceutical products export by eight times over 2008;
- ensuring of the pharmaceutical security of Russia according to the list of strategically important medications and vaccines; and
- establishment of pharmaceutical substances production sites in Russia for the output of 50 percent of finished substances (in value terms), sufficient for production of no less than 85 percent of the strategically important drugs list.

Importantly, while the first articulated goal of the Strategy is "improvement of the supply of the Russian population . . . with nationally produced lifesaving and essential drugs and drugs for rare diseases," the actions foreseen by the Strategy focus largely on the market and its regulation, capacity building for local industry, and investments in R&D. The Strategy states that innovative development of the Russian pharmaceutical industry will lead to a "general increase of the drugs supply for those who need them up to the average European level in quality and quantity indicators" (10). However, measures to ensure that the population actually will have improved access to relevant drugs and that population health needs will be met in a better way receive much less attention. It is assumed that such improvements will happen more or less automatically and with the support of existing regulatory mechanisms such as subsidized drug coverage once measures to support the innovative development of the industry are realized.

The Pharma-2020 Strategy does mention one new mechanism to link the industry development measures with the health needs of citizens—a list of strategically important drugs whose full production cycle must be organized in the Russian Federation. This list, consisting of fifty-seven drugs currently not produced in Russia, was developed by the Ministry of Industry and Trade together with the Ministry of Health (in 2010 it was called the Ministry of Health and Social Development) and approved by Government Decree No. 1141-r in July 2010. However, Pharma-2020 does not provide details about how to ensure that all strategically important drugs from this list are actually being locally produced in sufficient quantities and are accessible.[2] Also left out of the picture is the development and updating of the strategic drugs instrument itself to ensure that it corresponded with the changing health needs of people and the state of the pharmaceutical science and technology.

Furthermore, the state program "Development of the Pharmaceutical and Medical Industry for 2013-2020," which followed the Strategy in 2012 and is meant to specify the details and budgets of the actions foreseen by the Strategy, contains only industry-focused goals and economic indicators. An exception, to some extent, is the final indicator, which concerns "the proportion of locally produced drugs from the list of strategically important drugs and from the list of lifesaving and essential drugs" (3). The latter list was not mentioned in the Strategy and first appeared in the program after the Strategy was already approved as another tool in addition to the strategically important drugs list to link pharmaceutical industry development with local health needs. This list of lifesaving and essential drugs was developed and is regularly updated by the Ministry of Health, and includes drugs whose prices are regulated by the government. However, it is mentioned in the program as an indicator only, and both lists are retrospective in that they mention which drugs already available in Russian market appear to be most important for people's health according to the opinions of the Ministry's experts, rather than looking at overall health needs, some of which may not have an optimal solution currently available in Russia or globally.

Overall, the market formulation of the problem to be addressed by the Pharma-2020 Strategy and the corresponding program of development lead to the market- and industry-focused solutions offered by these policy documents. The reasoning connecting market- and industry-focused solutions to people's health is illustrated in a statement from Pharma-2020: "Localization of production of essential drugs, development, testing, and production of innovative drugs on the Russian territory, and innovative development and functioning of the Russian pharmaceutical industry, will ensure significant growth of Russian drugs production and a corresponding growth of their consumption by the population of the Russian Federation" (36). Growth in local drug production becomes synonymous with growth in drug consumption, which, in turn, is taken to be equivalent of "lowering morbidity, alleviation of suffering, and lowering mortality" (37).

Priority is given to solving the problem of the inability of the local industry to dominate the sizeable local market and harvest profits from it as well as from the international marketplace. It is expected that once research, development, and production capacities of the local industry are enhanced through investments in infrastructure (such as industrial parks), distribution of funding for pharmaceutical R&D, and reforms in regulations (such as allowing preferential purchasing of local drugs through state contracts), the people's health will automatically be affected positively.

Importantly, one of the main expected results of the implementation of the Strategy is ensuring pharmaceutical security of Russia. Pharmaceutical security is the core concept of the Pharma-2020 strategy and the associated program of development. Appeals to national security in the policy texts justify the active involvement of state and large public investments in pharmaceutical industry development. For example, the program states: "In the current situation in the Russian Federation, participation of the state is required to solve key problems in pharmaceutical industry development to ensure national security in the health care and health of the nation" (61). Against this background, a paramount risk appears to be perceived in "increasing dependency of consumer market on imported products" (Minpromtorg 2012, 5), that is, foreign-developed and -produced drugs. Associated risks mentioned include foreign exchange risks and external macroeconomic shifts such as global financial crisis.

It is expected that it is through achieving self-sufficiency that national pharmaceutical security can be guaranteed. This expectation is evident, for example, in the emphasis placed by the policy texts on the need to have the full production cycle of drugs, especially of the strategically important and other "essential drugs," within the country. Measures to support organization of the full production cycle within the country involve a revival of the pharmaceutical substances manufacturing that drastically declined after the USSR's collapse (between 1992 and 2008, the output of pharmaceutical substances produced in Russia declined by about twenty times, as suggested in Pharma-2020, 17). Producing pharmaceutical substances locally is nonetheless seen as important to ensure independence of the national pharmaceutical industry from foreign pharmaceutical substances producers, because currently even those drugs that local industry does produce are manufactured using mostly imported substances.

Who Is to Benefit?

The discourse of self-sufficiency and the problem of dominance of the foreign pharmaceutical companies in the country market articulated by the Pharma-2020 Strategy and related programs were reflected in the views and experiences of the actors involved in drug research, development, and production in Russia whom I spoke to. From their point of view, the perceived risks of dependence on foreign manufacturers support the vision of self-sufficiency, as put forward by a biomedical scientist who is also a member of a relevant government working group:

> I think that this program [Pharma-2020] is very timely in a sense that . . . we see the kind of political situation developing around Russia, and it is very good that someone in our government or circles close to government is so farsighted that they thought of the issues of national security. . . . It will raise our confidence for tomorrow, from the point of provision of medicines. If the situation deteriorates somehow at least we will be producing essential medicines here. . . . I think it is clear that against the background of the current events, such strategy should be spread to other sectors like agriculture, mechanical engineering, and the chemical industry. We have to produce something ourselves. The development of China shows that the more you produce yourself, the more your weight is in the world and not only economically but also politically. It is clear. (9PM 2014)

Similar worries regarding national security were voiced by a director of a large private pharmaceutical company, who connected ideas about security with the Pharma-2020 program:

> The goal of this program [Pharma-2020] is to create an advantage, to saturate the market, create a certain domination and, ultimately, a certain security for Russia in terms of import substitution and everything else. As I understand, the situation, based on the current collisions, may dramatically speed up. (22BK 2014)

When asked how national security should be understood in this case, the same respondent explained:

> It should be understood as an absence of strategically important drugs that are not produced on Russian territory, which are lifesaving medications. This is one of the foundational parts of a state security. . . . Naturally, a task of a head of a state is to . . . create all conditions that Russian scientific and production pharma is maximally prepared to produce what is not being imported. And this is happening. (22BK 2014)

Thus, according to many, Pharma-2020 and other initiatives to boost drug development are contributing to building a stronger, independent, and self-sufficient nation and state. Self-sufficiency in developing new drugs as well as producing known lifesaving ones becomes perceived as necessary for the country to have weight in the international political arena.

At the same time, relations between the envisioned state of pharmaceutical self-sufficiency and the well-being and health of individual citizens is far from straightforward, not only in the policy papers but also in the perceptions of many actors involved. While the last-quoted respondent made a reference to ensuring availability of essential drugs to country patients when talking about pharmaceutical security, a biomedical scientist involved in a Pharma-2020 working group could not see a direct link between Pharma-2020 and national security on the one hand and population health on the other:

> I think these things [Pharma-2020 and health of the population] are completely unrelated. Quality of life is not directly

dependent on realization of Pharma-2020, because Pharma-2020 is aiming not at increasing quality of life, but at improving the condition of pharmaceutical sector and production of pharmaceuticals and medical devices. This will have positive influence, of course, but very indirect. (9pm 2014)

Another example is the elaboration of a biomedical scientist who also works in a countrywide state project for supporting development and production of drugs and medical devices. This scientist explained his understanding of relations between the state initiatives discussed and population health (which agrees with the reasoning of the previous respondent):

[Pharma-2020 and public health] are related somewhat indirectly. In Russia there are some targets specified by the MoH: to increase life expectancy, lower death rates, something else. These targets are specified in numbers. It is clear that to meet these targets directly, it would be easier to buy quality pharmaceuticals and directly distribute them. Then success would be more noticeable. Clearly, implementation of such programs [as Pharma-2020] is directed not only and not exactly at human health. Probably, this is also what is called pharmaceutical security, innovative development, creation of jobs, competitiveness, scientific potential, etc. So we probably cannot say that this will have direct impact on health . . . while at the same time, it is simple human logic, that if someone somewhere starts to live better, where more quality things are produced, probably this can influence somehow. (7IR 2014)

The way in which these and many other actors whom I spoke to conceptualize pharmaceutical security of the country is in agreement with the economic framing of the problem and the corresponding solutions articulated in Pharma-2020 and the related documents. They view national security also in economic terms, as the presence of a mighty industry able to develop and produce various drugs from locally produced substances. However, this development of industry capacities appears to lead directly to the pharmaceutical security of the state and not exactly that of the citizens, in the interpretation of these actors.

While many informants spoke of national pharmaceutical security when reflecting on the significance of the attempts to boost Russian drug development and production through Pharma-2020, few actually made links between ensuring national security and meeting basic drug needs of the Russian population. For example, the director of a Russian clinical research organization (CRO) elaborated on what Pharma-2020 could have looked like had it been connected to the health sphere and stressed that only in that case could national pharmaceutical security be truly achieved:

> A strategy with a title like "assuring drug security of Russia" . . . has to firstly contain prospective treatment standards. . . . In my opinion, from the beginning treatment standards should have been the starting point. To understand, which products should be used for treatment of which nosology in a particular time perspective, realizing that these are unlikely to be breakthrough innovative products created in Russia. What can be used for treatment of arterial hypertension in 5–7 years? . . . Only based on an understanding of what the state needs in 5–7 years to treat its citizens, a support strategy should have been built so that in 5–7 years what can be used to treat patients would be obtained for state money.
>
> From my point of view, the process turned another way. I am not saying that this is completely absent, but I have never noticed in talks, or in publications, or during conferences, never heard from anyone that the state has a concrete strategy of treatment, particular standards that we are supposed to reach. Therefore now, when money is being provided to pharmaceutical companies, this is stimulating single growth points to some extent, but it is not a formation of a coherent system of Russian pharmaceutical industry that would allow meeting the needs of the Russian Federation in Russian-made drugs. (23CT 2014)

This informant stated that pharmaceutical security in terms of supplying the Russian population with needed drugs is unlikely to be achieved by the current Pharma-2020 implementation. He further elaborated that, in his view, public health benefit should be the ultimate goal of the state efforts to boost drug development and production in the country, which is not addressed by the current innovation support policies. This issue of boosting drug development and production to improve the stance of the Russian pharmaceutical industry rather than improve public health is illustrative of the discussion regarding value generation in the previous chapter: how the value of developments in pharmaceutical science and technology is generated and for whom is an uncertain and highly political process.

Overall, most informants did not draw a direct connection between public health in Russia and the implementation of Pharma-2020 and related initiatives. The architecture of these state-supported measures does not appear to support this link either. Importantly, despite the pervasive rhetoric of national security surrounding Pharma-2020, this policy and the mode of implementing it do not necessarily mean national security in terms of meeting the essential drug needs of the population, despite meeting these needs being one of the declared aims of this policy. A conceptualization of pharmaceutical security as ensuring that the Russian population has access to needed drugs did not become prominent.

It can be argued that while Pharma-2020 and related state initiatives focus largely on the industry itself, on increasing its capacity and ultimately the profits acquired by it, there are other actors and state programs that address health directly, for example, the government-developed Reimbursement Drug List. At the same time, focus on the pharmaceutical industry's development in both policy and many actors' conceptualizations can be understood as a particular characteristic of the sociotechnical imaginary of the Russian nation, where images of mighty local industry overshadow individual citizens' health needs. Their health needs are expected to be addressed somehow in the process of erecting a self-sufficient pharmaceutical economy or by other means, while the state acquires political weight in the international arena and power becomes more concentrated within the country as well.

However, without specific measures linking pharmaceutical industry development with citizens' health, efforts to boost local drug development and production in Russia may result in no improvements in people's access to medicines and in their health. Innovation studies scholars Reid and Ramani (2012) make a similar argument with regard to the efforts of the Indian government to develop biotechnology in that country: "Despite the confirmation of continued State support for capacity building in biotechnology, it is of utmost concern that there does not seem to be any focused effort to bring out biotechnology innovations that will impact the poor in a major way. . . . The reigning premise seems to be that supporting the accumulation of industrial capabilities in the biotechnology sectors is sufficient and positive results will percolate in some measure to the poorer masses on their own. Clearly, this may not happen (652).

Relations with the World

The economic problem definition and corresponding aspirations for independence and for having all facilities and capacities available within the country reaffirm the importance of the borders of the nation-state. These aspirations give shape not only to the corresponding state programs but also to business practices and, first of all, inhibit internationalization. For example, the head of a small company reflected in the following way on the opportunities to enter markets abroad:

> And a second moment, how to make your way in this market? There is established pharma there, which is pressing everyone quite heavily. And our [people] can come there only, as I understand, maybe I am wrong, only if you sell a controlling stake of your company to European pharma, they allow you in that market. Generally from the point of view of business, it is somewhat good. You sold a share in a company, obtained money. But from the point of view of a state, it is an erosion of capital (funds drain). Ok, today he bought shares, paid you for these shares and invested in a company, but this is a single inflow today. While if we look at a future, when a company begins to bring profits, then profits are going there and there it is capitalizing. Not in Russia, but there. (18SK 2014)

The seeming apprehension of working internationally expressed by some respondents is also related to the self-sufficiency ideal. The dream of self-sufficiency implies that all national developments in innovative drug development and production are contained "inside," within the country. When the drug industry is branching out abroad, it means that there is less left inside, which creates risks to national security.

Several informants provided historical narratives illustrating the dangers of trading and engaging with foreign entities. The head of a large company that provided drug development and testing services and developed active substances described how drug candidates were unfairly bought out by "former countrymen":

> All this time [after the USSR's collapse] the country was being cleaned out by foreign "walkers," who were bartering old ideas for basically beads and shells. The Soviet Union was very productive, there were many interesting substances.

They were taking out everything possible. Those scientists who were working on these projects, ideas, they mostly were people with the old mentality. They did not understand what business is and how they are being fooled, tricked. I watched it multiple times. And intellectual property was flowing away like a landslide. (5BK 2014)

Such past experiences of unfair exchanges by actors unfamiliar with the new market environment may be contributing to the ongoing apprehension regarding working internationally. Overall, there was a noticeable discomfort among many informants about Russian drugs, businesses, and other resources leaving the country and also about relying on foreign-produced resources, including pharmaceutical substances.

At the same time, a few informants doubted the rhetoric of self-sufficiency that calls for closing down. One of the managers of a large state pharmaceutical company favored the idea of going beyond national borders and recommended avoiding focusing on "national" drugs in a way that implies complete self-sufficiency and lack of interest in foreign markets. When asked about the relationship between going beyond borders and national security, this manager explained:

> In pharmaceutical security, just as in any other form of security, the prevailing word is independence. If any country in any market depends on adjacent and other countries in some key aspects of a product development cycle or cycle of a product's added value, it means that at some point a country can find itself in a difficult situation. This applies to drugs. On another hand, the best drugs that were invented by humankind are penicillin and aspirin, which can be produced by anyone, anywhere, any time. If a situation of a global embargo arises, everyone goes to their own corners, everyone lives in their own corner, then a solution can be always found. Nonetheless, from the position of international integration, the more weight, the more capitalization. The more Russian developers, venture companies, and venture capitalists are working outside of Russia, it also has security aspects. In these ways we begin to make those markets depend on our conditions. (24BK 2014)

That is, this informant views the foundation of national pharmaceutical security in international interdependence, rather than in self-sufficiency in developing and producing drugs. He suggests that while there is a view locating pharmaceutical security in self-sufficiency and independence from foreign drug and substance producers, an alternative is possible. This alternative is based on the proposition that most basic drugs essential for the health of the population, such as penicillin, can by now be produced "by anyone, anywhere, any time." Against this background, this respondent suggests, further drug innovation work can rely on the interdependence of drug markets, where countries rely on each other in development and production of new drugs. This interdependence, in this view, ensures national pharmaceutical security, because, being mutually dependent, countries would avoid compromising each other's interests.

Overall, however, the aspirations for self-sufficiency articulated in Pharma-2020 resonate with many actors' hesitations about engaging with the pharmaceutical market outside the country. Pharma-2020 does establish goals related to increasing exports and the presence of Russian drugs in foreign markets. That is, the policy documents themselves do not necessarily dictate the closing-down strategy. However, the policy problem definition focused on the inability of the local Russian pharmaceutical industry to dominate the internal country market, the very slow implementation of measures directed at integrating the Russian pharmaceutical industry into the international space, and a strong emphasis on the national security idea indirectly facilitate such closing down. Moreover, the lack of positive experiences of working internationally among local actors reinforces the dominance of the closing-down strategy in the country. This is not to say that there are no alternative views of national security. The reflection of the last-quoted expert represents such an alternative, one that, however, has not gained much support.

Viewing this situation from the angle of innovation studies literature, we can see a possible implication of the dominance of the closing-down strategy. Insights from this literature suggest that the focus on self-sufficiency in the efforts to boost drug development and production in Russia can actually inhibit innovative development of the local pharmaceutical industry. Contemporary life sciences, as well as drug development, especially when it comes to innovation, is a highly networked, distributed activity (Consoli and Mina 2009; Consoli and Ramlogan 2008). Drug developers tend to be in touch with scientific groups in various locations and to work with equipment, materials, and substances from various sources. Engaging in pharmaceutical innovation requires access to and use of a diverse range of materials and resources because of the essentially unpredictable nature of innovation: one cannot have everything that is needed to innovate in drugs in one setting simply because it is not possible to know in advance what will be needed. Therefore, the focus on self-sufficiency as it is generally framed in the sociotechnical imaginary of a pharmaceutically secure Russia can be at odds with the goal of the innovative development of the local pharmaceutical industry.

An illustration of this argument can be derived from the work of innovation studies scholars Chittoor and colleagues (2008) on the growth of the Indian pharmaceutical industry. These authors argue that the recent rapid development of the Indian pharmaceutical industry has been enabled by its active internationalization. They demonstrate how Indian pharmaceutical firms took advantage of economic liberalization, which proceeded in India at much slower pace there than in Russia, by acquiring modern technology, businesses, and other resources ("inputs") abroad, while simultaneously internationalizing their product ("outputs") markets. Internationalization of both "inputs" and "outputs" has proceeded in a reciprocal fashion, resulting in the development of new capabilities in the Indian pharmaceutical industry that have enabled it to successfully operate on the global market. Chittoor et al. (2008) concluded that for emerging market firms, "internationalization is a mode to access new resources . . . needed to compete effectively against global rivals at home and abroad" and leads to "capability development and competitive advantage" (263). This illustrates that focus on self-sufficiency in the Russian efforts to boost innovative drug development and production risks inhibiting the development of the innovative capabilities of the local industry.

Independence and Self-Sufficiency

This chapter demonstrates the central role of *problem definition* in shaping workings of pharmapolitics. In Russia, the lack of locally developed and produced drugs has been predominantly defined as a paramount threat to national security in both policy documents and the reflections of actors involved. The country's dependence on foreign companies in delivering medicines and the current failure of local companies to harvest profits from the growing Russian market have been defined as long-term risk factors. Consequently, the problem to be addressed by the set of Pharma-2020 policies has been defined in economic terms, as that of market. That is, the research, development, and production capacities of the Russian pharmaceutical industry must be enhanced to solve the current problem of the inability of the local industry to dominate the sizeable local market and harvest profits from it. This problem definition, itself rooted in specific characteristics of the Russian companies and in internationalization anxieties, has exercised significant impact on the practices and organization of drug development in the country, while at the same time provided a leverage to steer the political action toward security and independence.

As I suggested in the previous chapters, pharmapolitics proceeds through a coproductive dynamic, where technologies become sites and objects of politics, while political ambitions and agendas interact with technological opportunities and constraints and are shaped in the process of such interaction. But this general dynamic needs to be scrutinized further to explain particular directions of pharmapolitical processes. Attention to how problems to be solved with the use of pharmaceutical science and technology are defined, as well as to the kinds of visions of the future produced (chapter 2), value generated (chapter 3), and relationships constituted in the drug development arena (chapter 5), helps to understand the shaping of pharmapolitical trajectories in different settings.

One more question arises from analysis presented in this chapter. How are we to understand the visions of the nation and the national futures encoded in Pharma-2020? Is it a case of a preexisting and widely shared sociotechnical imaginary shaping pharmaceutical policies? Or is it an attempt by political elites to disseminate their vision through policy making? I suggest another option. We can trace the preexisting elements of the vision of an independent and self-sufficient Russian nation, but Pharma-2020 is not simply a manifestation of this vision. Through bringing together and articulating these elements, Pharma-2020 on the one hand reformulated them, giving them a concrete form, expression, and grounding in the pharmaceutical research, development, and production system. On the other hand, it strengthened the resulting vision through rehearsing, disseminating, and publicly enacting it.

First, the sociotechnical imaginary of the pharmaceutically secure and independent Russian nation articulated by Pharma-2020 points to what is perceived as the achievements of the Soviet pharmaceutical sector. The USSR's drug industry was far from being perfect both in terms of innovation and making essential drugs available and accessible for the entire population, as was discussed in chapter 1. However, in the aftermath of the large-scale deterioration of the local industry in the 1990s, the Soviet pharmaceutical industry appeared to many to be strong, well developed, and importantly, together with factories in other Comecon (Soviet-dominated Council for Mutual Economic Assistance) countries independently producing drugs for the entire country, without relying on imports of either pharmaceutical substances or already manufactured drugs, while also exporting pharmaceutical substances and even some drugs. Many of my informants praised the Soviet drug development and production sector for being self-sufficient:

> In Soviet times a clear and understandable structure and system of implementation of new drugs was built. And if we remember (you probably can't remember those times, but I can), if we remember Soviet pharmacies, most drugs there were local Soviet drugs. (19SKSE 2014)

Second, Pharma-2020 integrates new, more recent elements into the imaginary of a pharmaceutically independent and self-sufficient nation. These elements are market and innovation. The ideas of market forcefully infiltrated Russian society at the beginning of the 1990s, brought in by the wave of neoliberal reforms described in chapter 2. In the same chapter, it becomes clear that the neoliberal ideal of society, however, failed to take root in the country's social fabric. Therefore, in the technoscientific imaginary of the nation articulated by Pharma-2020, market is not the powerful information-processing mechanism and a form of collective decision making that should be free from the state's interference, as neoliberal thinkers considered market to be. Rather, it is a space where profits can be made, and the state is to control and arrange this space within the country to make it exploitable to the national advantage and to facilitate extraction of resources from markets outside the country. The barriers to international trade that in the neoliberal view must be eliminated on the way to achieving a level playing field in the global market are being erected here, and market is meant to strengthen the country borders. Innovation in Pharma-2020 is also interpreted largely to fit a closed-up imaginary of an independent and self-sufficient Russia. Pharmaceutical innovation is a tool to achieve national control over the internal market and a prominent position in the external market.

It must be noted that in the text of the program that followed the Pharma-2020 strategy, the need for integration of the national pharmaceutical industry into "international chains of development and production of pharmaceutical and medical products" (10) is mentioned several times. This view of the national pharmaceutical future as integration in the global pharmaceutical arena diverges from the discourse of national security as articulated in Pharma-2020 and can be viewed as an element of an alternative sociotechnical imaginary, where pharmaceuticals become a vehicle for expanding sociotechnical networks. While it appears that those writing Pharma-2020 and related policy papers tried to reconcile the closing-down dynamic of reaching pharmaceutical independence and self-sufficiency with the opening-up trajectory of concurrent integration into the global pharmaceutical arena, the two development directions appear to be too different. The closing-down direction, rooted in the perceived reliability of the self-sufficient Soviet pharmaceutical industry and animated by the generally negative experiences of the Russian pharmaceutical industry upon meeting the market, appear to outweigh aspirations for international integration, as can be seen in the Pharma-2020 implementation plan. The measures that were supposed to ensure progress in the integration, such as harmonization of the Russian regulatory sphere with the international one (for example, mutual acceptance of clinical trials results and compliance of Russian drug manufacturing sites with the international Good Manufacturing Practices [GMP]), largely were not realized. Rather, the emphasis was placed on measures to jump-start development and production of local drugs on the way to self-sufficiency.

Finally, Pharma-2020 has grounded the vision of an independent and self-sufficient Russian nation in the system of pharmaceutical research, development, and production. Pharmaceutical science and technology have a special significance and everyday relevance for many of the country's citizens. Therefore, the discourse of national pharmaceutical security that appears to hold promise of responding to the health needs of people can resonate with their hopes, further contributing to the strengthening and persistence of the vision described. For those active in the local pharmaceutical arena, such as scientists, developers, and industry representatives, the importance of the national security concern means the active return of the strong state that disappeared with the end of the Soviet Union, and of the associated support and clarity. For political actors, articulation of a technoscientific imaginary of a self-sufficient Russian nation provides an opportunity to earn more support for the political agenda of the concentration of power and strengthening state control over various aspects of societal life. Thus, Pharma-2020 became a reformulation of a particular vision of the Russian nation, one that was rehearsed in the policy texts and in the media and professional discussions of Pharma-2020 and publicly performed through Pharma-2020 implementation efforts. This initiative also grounded this vision in a pharmaceutical technoscientific system, granting it more strength and immediate relevance for different groups of actors. Consequently, this vision came to be commonly adopted and a full-fledged sociotechnical imaginary.

This vision of a self-sufficient and independent Russia is expected to be realized through pharmaceutical industry development, securing the dominant position in the local market and strengthening Russia's position in the international market under the lead of the state. That is, pharmaceutical security that involves having essential drugs of good quality, including new and innovative ones, is also being framed in predominantly economic terms with the state taking the responsibility of boosting drug R&D and production and expecting these measures to trickle down more or less on their own to meet the Russian population's drug needs. While it appears that pharmaceutical security, as an expert commentator from the foundation Open Economy put it, "will serve to provide the country with pharmaceutical drugs in case of an emergency" (Gordeev 2009), Pharma-2020 does not give much attention to measures for ensuring the actual satisfaction of people's health needs, be there an emergency or not. The Russian population and its health needs are thus being implicated in the vision of self-sufficient nation-state, with the nation's struggle for a potent national industry, economic independence, and strong international standing taking precedence over them.

This chapter adds to the existing research on national technoscientific development trajectories and innovative performance through advancing our understanding of how institutional environments pertinent to innovations develop. A prolific field of innovation studies has documented how institutional differences account for differences between nations in terms of innovative performance. Insights from the study of pharmapolitics and its constituent processes, including problem definition, offer resources to understand why national institutional environments, which matter so much for innovation, come to be shaped in particular ways. The next chapter focuses explicitly on how interactions between the key actors in the Russian institutional environment pertinent to pharmaceutical innovations have been changing together with the nation-building efforts analyzed here.

Contemporary Russian Pharmaceutical Industry and Market at Glance

Data are provided for the year 2016. Where necessary to illustrate the dynamic of changes, data for several years prior to 2016 are presented.

Number of active licenses for production of pharmaceuticals in the country: 527

Number of manufacturing sites: 566

85 percent of the overall Russian pharmaceutical producers' sales revenue is earned by the leading thirty companies, making the production highly concentrated. The top five of these companies are Pharmstandart, established in 2003; Valenta Pharm, established in 1997; the more-than-eighty-year-old Akrichin that survived the 1990s and presently produces about 200 different pharmaceutical products; biotechnology-focused Biokad, established in 2001; and Sotex, established in 1999.

The ranking of the top-twenty companies in the Russian market in sales revenue includes two Russian companies: Pharmstandart and OTC Pharm, a daughter company of Pharmstandart (see table 4.1 below). Together, the top twenty companies account for 47 percent of the Russian pharmaceutical market.

Table 4.1. Top twenty producers in sales revenue on the Russian pharmaceutical market in 2016

# in 2016	Company	Sales revenue in 2016, ₽B	Share
1	SANOFI	45,318.7	4.1%
2	NOVARTIS	42,183.9	3.9%
3	BAYER	40,261.0	3.7%
4	JOHNSON & JOHNSON	32,507.6	3.0%
5	GLAXOSMITHKLINE	28,572.2	2.6%
6	TAKEDA	27,593.6	2.5%
7	SERVIER	26,041.3	2.4%
8	TEVA	25,874.3	2.4%
9	ОТИСИФАРМ (OTC PHARM)	25,617.0	2.3%
10	PFIZER	24,989.7	2.3%
11	STADA	22,324.2	2.0%
12	BERLIN-CHEMIE	22,110.4	2.0%
13	MERCK	21,982.2	2.0%

# in 2016	Company	Sales revenue in 2016, ₽B	Share
14	GEDEON RICHTER	20,218.6	1.8%
15	ABBOTT	19,129.2	1.7%
16	ASTELLAS	18,813.3	1.7%
17	KRKA	18,628.0	1.7%
18	ASTRAZENECA	18,182.8	1.7%
19	ФАРМСТАНДАРТ (PHARMSTANDART)	16,867.1	1.5%
20	F. HOFFMANN-LA ROCHE	16,744.2	1.5%

The overall share of locally produced drugs in the country market constitutes 29.4 percent in value terms and 60.5 percent in number of actual packages. This share has slowly increased: in 2015 it was 27.2 percent and 58 percent, and in 2014 23 percent and 56 percent. Note that assessments of the share of locally produced drugs include products of multinational companies' subsidiaries that manufacture pharmaceuticals in Russia, such as Servier and Stada.

The Russian pharmaceutical market is the fourteenth largest market in the world; its volume in rubles estimated at 1510 billion ($23B) in 2016.

Composition of the Russian pharmaceutical market: its largest part is the commercial segment at ₽1.110 billion, with the rest covered by state drug purchases (see figure 4.1).

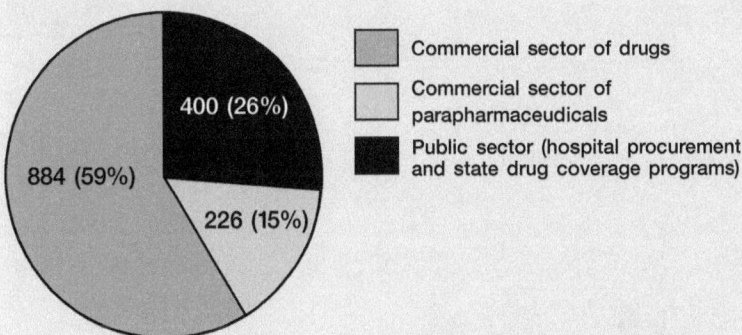

Figure 4.1. Russian market composition in billion rubles in 2016.

Export: Russian companies' volume of export is estimated to be $635 million. Post-Soviet countries such as Kazakhstan, Belarus, and Uzbekistan are the major export markets, accounting for 86 percent of the total exports.

Data presented here were obtained from the following sources: Livanskii 2017; Romanova 2017; DSM 2017, 2018; Deloitte 2017.

Chapter 5

Innovation Environment

Collaborating in Drug Development and Production

As described in the previous chapter, the Strategy for the Development of the Pharmaceutical Industry in the Russian Federation to 2020 (Pharma-2020) was adopted in 2009 by the country's Ministry of Industry and Trade and soon followed by other associated initiatives. One important focus of these state-led efforts to support "innovative development of the Russian pharmaceutical industry" is stimulating collaborative links between various actors in the Russian pharmaceutical arena. Pharma-2020 and the associated initiatives acknowledge the existence of gaps between these actors as a risk to achieving the results envisioned and offer multiple measures to stimulate interaction and attain a more collaborative environment. Such measures include a cofinancing requirement, in which grants for drug development are provided with the condition that state funding is matched by nonstate funding. Another measure is the development of pharmaceutical clusters, in which groups of interconnected organizations, such as pharmaceutical and biotechnology firms, service providers, research labs, and university departments, are colocated to complement each other. This chapter studies how these efforts to build a collaborative environment are actually perceived and acted upon by those working in academia, industry, and state agencies—the three key actor groups involved in the field of pharmaceutical science and technology in Russia—and to what ends, and explores *collaboration* as the fourth process that shapes pharmapolitical constellations in addition to vision production (chapter 2), value generation (chapter 3), and problem definition (chapter 4).

Innovation studies literature has long highlighted the importance of interaction between different actors, disciplines, and sectors in innovation processes in various areas. Innovation studies scholars suggest that through such interactions, skills and capabilities are brought together that are rarely found embodied in the same institution, organizations obtain access to external knowledge, and resource-sharing arrangements can be made. Specifically, innovation in medicine and pharmaceuticals draws on the close communication and collaboration between universities, hospitals, dedicated research institutes, governmental departments, and firms. One of the numerous illustrations of this thesis can be derived from the work of Ramlogan et al. (2007), who showed how a successful North American biotech company, Centocor, organizes its work in close collaboration with research hospitals, which are sites that combine academic and health-care functions, and other firms that possess complementary resources and expertise. That is, innovation studies scholarship endorses the crucial importance of the efforts of Russian policy makers in stimulating the development of collaborative ties between different actors working in the country pharmaceutical arena for the success of the project of boosting local drug development and production.

There is, however, an important lacuna that innovation studies literature largely has yet to address. Innovation studies scholarship has been actively promoting an "interactive model of the innovation process" (Martin 2012), that is, a view of innovation as driven and shaped by the multitude of dynamic connections between various actors, context, and technology. This work has critically moved the innovation research beyond focusing on user-producer interaction to analyze wider interactive processes and systems. Yet the field has been less productive in analyzing the fine details of how exactly these dynamic connections develop or fail to develop in practice. One notable exception is the work by Höyssä, Bruun, and Hukkinen (2004), who studied the emergence of biotechnology in Turku, Finland. They argued that in the study of innovation, attention needed to be given both to innovation systems, encompassing (as detailed in the previous chapter) institutions and interactions between them, and to the social processes that animate these interactions. The field of innovation studies has advanced sophisticated quantitative methods of mapping collaborative networks, but it largely lacks analytic tools to study quality and dynamics of relations within and across innovation systems, as elaborated in more detail in the next section. Höyssä, Bruun, and Hukkinen (2004) linked insights from innovations studies and Science and Technology Studies (STS) literature, which enabled them to comprehensively study the emergence of biotechnology in Turku and detail the "significance of [both] innovation systems and social processes" (770). Following this analytic approach, I study in this chapter the connections of actors in the pharmaceutical arena in Russia through the dual lens of the interactive model of innovation advanced by innovation studies and an STS-inspired approach that pays attention to relations animating these interactions.

This chapter highlights *collaboration* as yet another process central to pharmapolitics. To understand this dimension, paying attention to what is called "political culture" is important. Jasanoff (2005) elaborates that political culture "encompasses institutionally sanctioned modes of action such as litigiousness in the United States, but also the myriad unwritten codes and practices with which a polity supplements its formal methods of assuring accountability and legitimacy in political decision making. Political culture in contemporary knowledge societies includes the tacit, but nonetheless powerful, routines by which collective knowledge is produced and validated" (21). I investigate ways in which political culture matters for relations that animate the interactions within innovation systems.

In what follows, I review scholarship on connections between collaboration and innovation and outline the composition of networks in which pharmaceutical innovations proceed. Next, I provide an analysis of the state of collaboration between business and academic actors, who are considered in Pharma-2020 and related policies to be central in innovative drug development and production, followed by an exploration of the role of the state actors in the Russian innovation environment. In conclusion, I trace ways in which collaborations in the Russian pharmaceutical arena are influenced by the local political culture and how, conversely, implementation of the national pharmapolitical agendas is being affected by ways in which actors on the ground choose to engage with each other.

This chapter draws on thirty interviews with academic, business, and state actors involved in drug innovation in Russia and two group discussions with these actors. I also attended several events devoted to developing innovative drugs organized by Skolkovo Foundation (a large, state-supported organization that comprises a high-tech business area, a technopark, a research and education institute and schools, and five divisions providing grants and research and development (R&D) infrastructure for start-ups and innovation companies, and scientific research institutes.

Additionally, I wrote a Russian-language report that summarized the findings and shared it with the individuals who participated in the interviews and group discussions. They then provided feedback, clarifications, and additional perspectives, adding to my account and interpretations.

Collaboration and Innovation

As contemporary economies become increasingly knowledge based, with science and technology playing central roles, consensus has formed in scholarship that well-performing and competitive industries are innovating ones. This scholarly focus on innovation-based competitiveness is also generally congruent with the actual practice of governments across the world, many of which adopt policies and invest state funds to stimulate advances in science and technology and their translation into enhanced innovation (Gibbons et al. 1994). Against this background, a large body of research has investigated what contributes to the innovative productivity of industries. One important insight from this research is that the performance of industries depends not only on what happens within the organizations constituting an industry, but also very much on the environment in which they operate (Lundvall 1992, 2002; Nelson 1993). On the one hand, such factors as good transportation and communication infrastructures and a highly skilled workforce have been identified as enhancing operational environments and positively affecting the performance of organizations. These kinds of tangible and quantifiable characteristics of the environment have been extensively researched. On the other hand, such hard-to-define and hard-to-study characteristics as "collaborative spirit" also appear to be important ingredients of environments that are conducive to innovation, as was suggested by Höyssä et al. (2004).

Indeed, as innovating in modern, complex technologies has been shown to proceed in networks (Rycroft and Kash 1999), innovation studies scholars did address the questions of collaborative connections. They have studied which organizations and actor groups interact, using such methods as network analysis complemented by various visualization techniques to map patterns of collaboration and change in them over time. For such analysis, bibliometric data on scientific publications and coauthorships can be used to deduce which types of organizations and geographical locations work together in particular subject fields (Consoli and Mina 2009). Data from collaborative agreement databases also can be used, as was done by

Gay and Dousset (2005) to map the composition and types of alliances in particular industries. Such maps provide a picture of visible connections in a particular subject field or industry and compare the differences in the distribution and intensity of such connections by periods of time. But questions of how these interactions emerge, develop, are sustained, and are terminated, and how to understand such environmental characteristics as "collaborative spirit," remain difficult to address.

It should be noted that at the same time, there is a widely shared recognition in the innovation studies field that innovation systems generally are just as social as they are technological (Kash and Rycoft 2000). Therefore, some studies do consider such issues as trust when investigating the functioning of networks and innovation systems. Cohen and Fields (2000), for example, argue that in Silicon Valley, trust is generated by good company performance, which creates a trustworthy reputation and enables and strengthens the formation of innovation networks. Kash and Rycoft (2000) suggest that reciprocity and a history of not behaving in opportunistic ways as norms of appropriate behavior facilitate cooperation and thus facilitate the generation of "social capital . . . e.g., a stock of collective learning that only can be created when a group of organizations develops the ability to work together for mutual gain" (p. 821). The importance of social relations for the collaborative connections necessary for innovating is highlighted in the work of economic sociologist Mark Granovetter. In 1985, discussing whether collaborative interaction among economic actors is facilitated by personal ties or more formal institutional hierarchies, Granovetter argued that formal institutional structures are insufficient to explain why firms, other organizations, and individuals cooperate (Granovetter 1985). For him, it is through social relations and the processes by which these relations become stabilized over time that economic actors learn to and come to work together.

Then how to study relations in innovation systems? In their book on collaboration in life sciences, Parker, Vermeulen, and Penders (2010) note the relative lack of qualitative studies of collaboration in various sectors. However, they argue, it is qualitative approaches that can attend to such features as the reasons for and the internal workings of collaborative connections. This chapter adds to the emerging body of qualitative studies of collaboration through in-depth consideration of the dynamics of relations between key actors in the Russian pharmaceutical arena and of the effects of the recent state efforts to boost local drug R&D with regard to these dynamics.

Who Works Together in Medical Innovation?

Before proceeding to the next section, I first attend to existing literature on what kinds of actors collaborate in innovation and in medical innovation specifically. One way of characterizing the key actors in the innovation sphere and the relationships between them is developed in the work on the Triple Helix by Etzkowitz and Leydesdorff (2000). In it, the relationships central to innovation are between the institutional spheres of the university, industry, and government. Here universities are seen as playing a more central role in the knowledge economy, while the national innovation systems literature introduced in the previous chapter tends to allocate the leading role in innovation to the firm. Another, less structurally defined analytic framework of Mode 2 knowledge production (Gibbons et al. 1994) also focuses on the ongoing transformations of the ways in which knowledge is produced and used in contemporary societies. The new production of knowledge—the so-called Mode 2—is characterized as generated in the context of the application of knowledge and in greatly diverse sites, transdisciplinary, reflexive, and having novel forms of quality control. That is, with the contemporary rise of Mode 2 knowledge production, actors with diverse scientific and technological expertise increasingly come to work together on innovating, as well as in partnerships with various users of the innovations, regulators, and decision makers. This broad arena where knowledge is produced is called agora by Nowotny et al.; they add that it "is populated not only by arrays of competing 'experts' and the organizations and institutions through which knowledge is generated and traded but also variously jostling 'publics.'" A common thread among the Triple Helix, national innovation systems, and Mode 2 knowledge production frameworks is their view of innovation as nonlinear and of innovation environments as continuously transforming with the evolution of technologies and the dynamics of interactions of their diverse elements.

Specifically in the field of health and medicine, researchers have found rich ecologies of actors who are interacting in the development of innovations, with close relations that emerge between entrepreneurs, clinicians, and academic scientists (Gelijns and Rosenberg 1994). Networks engaged in medical innovating often involve universities, hospitals, independent research institutes, foundations, government departments, and firms (Ramlogan et al. 2007). Importantly, these networks are not limited by national borders; rather, R&D efforts are distributed across countries.

Innovation studies literature specifically highlights the interconnected roles of hospitals, specialized university departments, and firms in medical innovations environments. Existing studies stress the importance of feedback from clinical practice for advances in medical science and technology. The close connection between the provision and use of new treatments, with feedback from intermediate users (clinicians) and end users (patients), is essential in shaping the innovation process (Ramlogan et al. 2007; Consoli and Mina 2009; Consoli and Ramlogan 2008). Therefore, hospitals comprise a fundamental component in medical innovation environments because they are centers of clinical practice. It is in clinical practice that the full range of the effects of new treatments is shown, including unforeseen drawbacks. Also, observations and experiences accumulate in clinical practice that are central for identifying unaddressed medical needs and formulating new ideas for treatments. Several authors note that research hospitals (and research foundations or research institutes where clinical services are also delivered) are especially important players (Consoli and Mina 2009). This is because, on the one hand, they tend to perform teaching roles and in this way are integral parts of academic institutions, connecting academia to clinical practice and facilitating intergenerational diffusion of knowledge. On the other hand, research hospitals provide the organizational links between the basic science that is mostly but not exclusively produced by universities and the applied research, for example, clinical trials of new pharmaceuticals, which are often driven by firms. Also, university departments such as pharmacology, biology, and genetics have been shown to not only advance basic science but often share the recognition for product discovery with the firms as well as be involved in further product modification and sometimes even manufacturing (Gelijns et al. 2001). Finally, firms are known to be top investors in new product development in medicine and have distinctive capabilities not only in product discovery and development but also in the management of the regulatory process for the approval of new drugs and devices and the marketing and distribution of innovations.

Overall, interactions involved in medical innovating can be characterized as occurring between patients and practitioners in the health-care delivery system domain; between the health-care delivery system domain and the science and technology domain; and between both of these domains and the governance system (Consoli and Mina 2009). This scheme is very general and is derived from empirical studies performed mostly in long-industrialized Western countries. Nonetheless, it provides a useful starting point for an investigation of relations between various actors in the pharmaceutical arena in Russia and the effects of the recent state efforts to boost local drug R&D, which is presented in the following sections.

Challenges for Working Together: Business and Academia

Innovative development of a sector and a society at large necessitates new and intensified interactions as elaborated in various ways by the Triple Helix, innovation systems, and Mode 2 knowledge production bodies of literature. While efforts to boost innovative drug development and production in Russia include measures to intensify interaction between different actors and create more spaces where exchange can occur, once clearly partitioned systems do not open up easily. In this section, I analyze the state of collaboration between business and academic actors, who are considered in Pharma-2020 and related policies to be central in innovative drug development and production.

Business

All business actors with whom I spoke recognized the need to work closely with academia and the potential benefits of this but acknowledged multiple associated difficulties. The director of a small start-up company that develops a biotechnological candidate molecule explained that, first, a lack of modern equipment in Russian academic institutions limits collaborative possibilities:

> This connection [between business and academia] is an uneasy one. When we are conducting preclinical studies, when we are researching the biology of a disease, preclinical models, how it is working in vitro, on animals, definitely this should be done in collaboration with academia. But interaction with academia in Russia is quite difficult, because experimental facilities do not allow conducting experiments at an adequate level. (21SK 2014)

Therefore, this company interacted with academia generally only by staying in touch with developments in its field of interest and continually scanning the scientific landscape for discoveries and inventions that could be of use to it. From the beginning of its existence, this company has pursued the idea of bringing its drug to international markets, which explains why the most up-to-date equipment was so crucial to it.

The director of another small company, which for the time being had targeted the local market, reported working closely with academia by outsourcing development tasks to research groups and institutes. However, this director explained that while the company works closely with academia, there are still challenges related to blurred responsibilities and lack of results orientation on the part of academics:

> We are looking for them [scientists] in Novosibirsk, in Moscow, when we find them, we commission a piece of work for a particular price, necessarily putting limits, financial limits: here is the work, here is what needs to be done. . . . We have many outsourced works and generally it is problematic to have a contract with an institute. You won't find out who is responsible for what. Money will be spent generally in vain. So, for instance, the responsible person is a director. Works are supposed to be executed by, for instance, a laboratory head. Possibly this lab head won't even see that money. . . . Even if he does get something [money], he still can write: "We tried this and that but nothing came of it." And the director will be just shrugging his shoulders. Responsibility is eroded. So we have direct contracts with institutes only if we are confident that we will get the result we need. . . . Generally we try to find a particular person, negotiate with him, and sign an agreement based on which he is performing particular task. (18SK 2014)

One of the managers of a large state pharmaceutical company that is involved in technology transfers and investments in drug development noted that differences in working cultures between business and academia exist globally, not only in Russia, and make cooperation between the two difficult everywhere:

> It is not easy for pharma to work with academia. It takes much time, it is another subculture. Pharma is a business, it is cynicism to some extent, speed, clear goals. Academia lives with completely another rhythm, there are other goals, other priorities. . . . Take note that on a global scale we can't say that

> pharma is interacting with academia. Pharma creates special settling reservoirs in the form of special foundations, which then communicate with academia because pharma itself cannot do it. (24BK 2014)

This same manager proceeded to describe the challenges in drug development faced by business actors when working specifically with Russian academia. According to him, Russian academics are not accustomed to operating in a market environment and lack focus in developing an actual product as well as understanding of patenting mechanisms:

> If some drug development project is undertaken in a Russian university, they have a budget, they live according to some cost estimation, they do not have a budget that would be oriented towards a result, with some rare exceptions. They are developing something. At some point the moment comes when it should be patented before it moves to a next stage. But a university cannot assess the quality of the drug being developed, its investment potential, and limits itself in the scale of patenting, in development of a corresponding program, and protocols of the further research to minimize expenditures. The moment this project becomes interesting to anyone, it turns out to be not protected properly. (24BK 2014)

Overall, business actors in Russia described difficulties in working with local academia. They viewed the roots of these difficulties in what was perceived as a lack of efficiency and ability to understand and protect the commercial value of candidate drugs among academic actors. Academic actors, in turn, also mostly describe distant and troubled relations with the industry (they generally spoke of local pharmaceutical industry, as collaborations with foreign industry are even rarer). However, academic actors see the roots of difficulties in building collaborative relationships in what was perceived as a lack of capacity and interest in innovating among local pharmaceutical business, as elaborated below.

Academia

Most of the academic actors with whom I spoke viewed the link with business actors as an uneasy one. A large part of the resources used by academic actors for drug development presently comes from the Pharma-2020 program, which stipulates that funding received should be complemented with some "extrabudgetary" funds (15 percent to 30 percent of the final amount), that is, funds not from Pharma-2020. This stipulation is intended to encourage actors in academia to look for commercial partners and stimulate connections between academia and business. Also, funding from Pharma-2020 is not enough to cover a full cycle of clinical trials, something that is also supposed to stimulate collaboration between academia and business, at least in the advanced, that is, most expensive, stages of drug development. These measures and the necessity of dealing with commercial entities are often framed by academic actors as something forced and involuntary. Their reluctance to engage with business could in part be explained by the deeply ingrained habit of Russian academics to take the lead in bringing their candidate molecules through the development and registration stages, which comes from the time of the Soviet planned economy when there were no business actors to whom to hand over the advanced stages of drug development.

Furthermore, academic actors describe experiencing difficulties in liaising with industry when they do attempt to do so. For example, the following exchange took place during my interview with two actors from academia: a scientist involved in health-care foresight and a biomedical scientist who is a part of a team developing a new drug financed by Pharma-2020:

> *Foresight scientist*: It is a compulsory condition that to receive Pharma-2020 money, 30 percent of the sum should be attracted from elsewhere. . . . *Interviewer*: And how does it happen, collaboration between different sectors? *Biomedical scientist*: Our project leaders have some agreements with other groups in our overall organization [medical university]. There are some other parties mentioned [in the application], but additional money is usually our own money [institutional funds]. *Interviewer*: Is business eager to invest? *Biomedical scientist*: No, honestly speaking they are just listed in the application. The work is being done by our structures and that is it. Maximum of what is possible, they [business partners] could do some samples analysis or something else, some support, but they don't invest money. . . . *Foresight scientist*: Write this down, it is difficult to work. It is necessary to force [industry] to innovate. You see

the situation. We can create something, invent, but we cannot make the producer interested, make potential investors interested. It is very difficult to find them. (16FS 2014)

While the cofinancing stipulation has been envisioned as encouraging collaboration of industry and academia, academic actors applying for Pharma-2020, on the one hand, may be reluctant to engage with business, and, on the other hand, when they do try to establish links, they find potential business partners not very enthusiastic. Therefore, academics use the strategy of listing industry actors in their funding applications to satisfy requirements, but look for cofunding in their own institutions. In such situations, industry actors play a formal role and engage minimally in collaborative drug development with academic applicants.

Many academic actors lament what they perceive as disinterest on the side of business and attribute the responsibility for suboptimal drug development rates in the country to business. A scientist working on drug development in a pharmacology institute elaborated, with some bitterness, on the role of business in the current drug development situation in the country:

> I think that the problem is in the manufacturers. Even when we are writing grant applications it is difficult to find them. Or even in the final stage. There are several completed drugs lying on our benches. We work with the Far East region, people with high positions in a Far East university are among the authors of our drug. They tried to find a manufacturer, prove, tell, seduce in all possible ways. We have such a big problem here, from my point of view this is a manufacturer who is the weakest link. (8SD 2014)

Following the criticism of this scientist from a pharmacology institute, a biomedical scientist involved in foresight activities reflected on the reasons for the perceived passivity of the industry:

> As I understand it, Russian business is either generics, or pelleting substances, generally without an early stage. Simply speaking, the one who packages skims the cream off. Classics. So why bother? . . . As practice shows, the first wave passed, funds are used, while results are almost nonexistent. Reports

are produced, while manufacturers who could take this forward are absent. . . . Why are big plants, companies not interested in innovations? Because they already have some range of products, which occupies some part of the market, so to invest money in something new, it is . . . Here people are wary of that. (16FS 2014)

The dominant attitude among academic actors can be described as critical of local industry, its capacities, and its interest in innovation. At the same time, most academic actors mentioned systemic problems experienced by academia as well, including, first of all, chronic underfunding of science. Their responses in the aggregate point to a vicious circle being formed by the presumably weak pharmaceutical industry in the country, unwilling to support innovations, which contributes to underfunded academic drug developers coming up with ideas that are not of a "good level," as formulated by one academic respondent:

Our center is a scientific one, and we cannot reach the level that corresponds with the level of real innovation, such innovation that allows business to access the market, be competitive on the international level, on one hand. On the other hand they [business] do not have money to invest in such things, in long risky projects. This innovations machinery needs to spin up as a whole. But this process will take a long time. I am skeptical in this regard. (4SD 2014)

Overall, the relations between academia and business in Russia described by the informants are characterized by strong boundaries separating the two. This separation is in part rooted in the model of drug innovation that long existed in the USSR, in which academia was responsible for the entire trajectory of pharmaceutical R&D analyzed in chapter 1. When reflecting on the state of the pharmaceutical sector in Russia more generally, representatives of these actor groups tended to blame each other for the lack of cooperation necessary for the innovative development of the industry as a whole. The necessity of collaboration in the new market environment was understood by both academic and business actors, and is even made urgent for academic actors by the conditions of Pharma-2020. However, such collaboration is hindered, and in the next subsection I elaborate on how divergent understandings of the product development trajectories and of the value of candidate drugs contribute to this situation.

Definitions and Trajectories of Innovation

First, actors from academia and the business worlds appear to have conflicting ideas about the origins of new drugs in Russia and also of the number of such drugs in the country pipeline. Some actors, mainly representatives of business organizations, suggested that there are few innovative drugs being currently developed in Russia, most of which originate abroad and some in the Soviet past. A respondent who heads a small company that develops a biotechnological drug stated:

> I think in this area there are three main processes. The first process, which attracts the most activity in terms of numbers of prospective drugs and the most money, is transfer of candidate drugs from foreign companies. Meaning that people get a license for some candidate drug or for a drug that is already approved for use in Western markets and conduct part of the clinical trials here. In this way companies can bring innovative drug[s] to the Russian market in a short time. This is the mainstream innovative drug development in Russia. . . . The second process is a return of some projects from Soviet time, ones that did not make their way to market or just were left. Here we talk about few, in my opinion. If transfer programs have some dozens of molecules, from Soviet storage some few are coming. And the third process is the development of really new drugs from scratch, this is what we are doing. There are very few such projects. If we are talking about molecules that reached the clinical trials stage, there are just several of them. (21SK 2014)

The comments of many business actors resonated with this opinion, highlighting that the transfer of candidate molecules in the process of development from foreign companies is how pharmaceutical innovation has been developing in Russia and indicating that drugs whose development ended with the USSR's end are now reappearing.

However, not all informants agreed with the emphasis on the role of transfers and the prevalence of old Soviet molecules in the Russian innovative drug pipeline. Some, mainly those working in academic institutions, felt that there was an abundance of local domestic innovation candidates who should be supported. The scientific director of a pharmacology research institute stated:

> In relation to bought or our own grown substances, Pharma-2020 practices show that there is enough of our own original molecules. . . . Also our own molecules should be a priority. We cannot say that all our new molecules are coming from elsewhere. Or we are taking old ones . . . About foreign ideas . . . we can even say that it is happening vice versa: not so long ago we know that there were organizations that were searching for molecules and transferring them abroad. Substances were bought from our chemists for some pocket money. So the process is rather reverse. Possibly because of this the reserves of our chemists were depleted, but still there are good chemistry institutes, they are multiple and strong. So I think there is a future. Also there is nothing bad, in my opinion, in that old Soviet experience of past times being utilized. This is one of the ways of innovative drugs development, change of existing ones. This is improvement. It is not a negative thing. (6SD 2014)

For these informants and also for some academics involved in relevant working groups and expert committees, local academic institutions are the birthplaces of innovative drug candidates in Russia.

There is an overall agreement among all informants that the appearance of all innovative drugs in general is enabled by developments in basic science, which is located in academia. But when it comes to specific molecules that later become drug candidates in Russia, there is a strong division of opinion, mainly focused on whether or not local academic actors are capable of providing such molecules. In this conflict of opinion, academic actors, including those working in government committees and groups devoted to Pharma-2020, tend to have confidence that Russian academia will and already is supplying sufficient numbers of molecules and agents that are on the way to becoming innovative drugs. These informants emphasized the domestic molecules (of different degrees of novelty) offered by various state academic institutions, saw an abundance of them in the pipeline, and actually suggested that these candidate drugs should be given preference. But those mainly from the business sector emphasized transfers from foreign companies, disregarded much of what is being offered by local academic institutions, and stated that only very few truly innovative drugs are being developed from scratch in Russia, mostly by business.

How to explain these differences? Interests invested in the drug development processes may shape perspectives articulated by the respondents. Actors, interested in streamlining funding in a particular direction, securing support for themselves, and ensuring preference from the state, articulate perspectives that highlight the necessity of supporting precisely their work. At the same time, divergent understandings of what drug innovation is and what purpose(s) it serves also contribute to the discrepancies between the positions of the informants from the two actor groups as well. I suggest that divergent understandings of pharmaceutical innovation and its value, as analyzed below, find expression in the conflicting views on drug development trajectories and complicate collaboration between academia and business.

When asked about what an innovative drug means to them, all respondents referred to both completely new molecules (radical innovation) and already known molecules that have been modified (incremental innovation). Also, the requirement of patentability featured prominently in the descriptions of what an innovative drug is. However, respondents from academia and regulators focused largely on the definitions used in grant distribution procedures and criteria related to the properties of the molecules themselves, for example: "A drug can be called new if at least one of these characteristics is present: higher effectiveness, lower toxicity, fundamentally new effect, possibility of combining with others, qualitatively new indicators, and also the question of cost" (4SD). Another scientist, who is involved in a governmental Pharma-2020 working group, explained what an innovative drug means in a similar way:

> This is a very difficult question. Here I can speak as a secretary of a working group in the Ministry of Education and Science; for the realization of these activities, preclinical studies of innovative drugs, we have a working group. And of course, prior to beginning the project selection, we had to define what we understand under this term, innovative drugs. From our point of view these are fundamentally new molecules, chemical structures not described earlier. Or if we are talking about

peptides, polypeptides, large proteins, then they must have essentially different physical-chemical characteristics, which would allow us to patent them in Russia and will make them competitive. If we talk about chemical synthesis, this must be essentially new structure.

The second aspect of innovativeness is a fundamentally new target. So far we have not had situations when a known existing structure has a completely new mode of action. Usually [in such cases] it is about widening therapeutic indications. We try to avoid including such drugs, while there are innovations in terms of chemical structures.

Third, it can be a modified known chemical agent, but it was modified in such a way that substantially changes its characteristics [gives an example of interferons for hepatitis C: taking them daily or once a week]. This is very important for treating infectious diseases. (9pm 2014)

The definition of drug innovation preferred by academic actors can then be characterized as a "procedural" one, tailored to the requirements of academic practices.

At the same time, actors more involved in business activities tended to switch their focus from the procedural characteristics of innovative drugs to what could be called the impact side of drug innovation. This different focus gives grounds to describe current candidate drugs that are being developed and brought to market in Russia as being not very innovative:

> Most products that are positioned in Russia as innovative are not really innovative. These are either generics, or analogs, or somewhat modified molecules of the products that are already on the market. I would not call the majority of these products innovative. From my point of view there are two criteria of innovativeness: a patent and sales volume, international acknowledgement of a product. First in the absence of the second (and vice versa) does not allow considering a product innovative under current conditions. . . . If you have a patent and a drug isn't sold anywhere, then it is conditionally innovative and nobody needs it. . . . Furthermore in the modern international pharmaceutical market successful products are being sold in almost all countries of the world. If this product

is really outstanding in comparison to those products that are already on the market then its commercialization is not a problem, but only if it is really innovative and everything is ok with the patent.

Against this background over the course of all this time I haven't come across any product born in Russia that would meet these criteria. While the largest part of the products being developed with the state support within the Pharma-2020 program are somewhat innovative according to the first criteria, if they are going to be created and sold only in Russia it would not mean that they are really innovative from the point of view of the modern pharmaceutical market. (23CT 2014)

The definition of drug innovation favored by business actors therefore can be characterized as an "impact" definition, tailored to the requirements of market success.

Business cannot prioritize procedural innovativeness because return on investment is essential, and for return an innovative drug must make an impact, that is, be successful in the market by being widely used in medical practice. As one scientist described it:

It is always easier to work for the state in this regard. Pharma-2020 is state money. The state does not demand such returns as business would demand . . . this money. (4SD 2014)

Therefore, state-supported scientists and developers can focus on procedural innovativeness, fulfill the requirements set by the funder, and produce the final report; if a drug is not mass produced and is not in high demand, it is not their responsibility. But if this occurs in a business structure, then it is a problem because investors need returns, and market impact is a crucial component of drug innovation for them.

Divergences in estimations of numbers of local innovative candidate drugs in Russia and therefore divergent expectations regarding the ultimate results of Pharma-2020 can be understood as grounded in different ideas of what an innovative drug is, which, in turn, are shaped to a significant extent by specificities of work practices. Those who see multiple promising drug candidates being developed in Russia currently, mainly academic actors, expect that the share of local innovative drugs will increase substantially by 2020, with this share consisting predominantly of their "own" molecules developed completely by Russian actors from the very beginning. Those who are more reserved in their assessments of the number of promising potential drugs being developed in the country, mainly business actors, expect more modest results, mostly from transferred molecules and molecules obtained through collaborative development. The relationships between these expectations and understandings of innovation are depicted in figure 5.1 below.

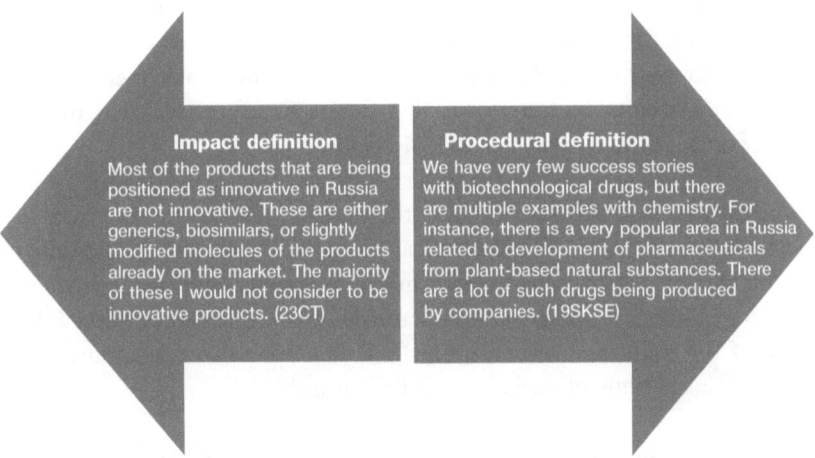

Figure 5.1. Divergent definitions of innovation.

Before concluding this section, I would like to mention an interesting particularity of the Russian pharmaceutical innovation system. As described in the introduction to this chapter, a group of actors and organizations that previous research on mostly Western medical innovation environments has shown to be important is physicians and hospitals. Physicians and hospitals are a crucial source of feedback for advancement in pharmaceutical science and technology (Ramlogan et al. 2007). However, according to the informants in this study, the link between drug development and clinical practice in Russia is rather weak. This is not to say that it does not exist at all. For example, some academic and business drug developers may themselves be not only scientists but also physicians, as was the case with several of my informants. Also, some firms do have close collaborations with physicians to ascertain the relevance of drugs being developed, as explained by the head of a small start-up company:

> I think this is a key point. We, the developers, are chemists, we do not have medical expertise. We can only theorize about whether there will be a demand for a drug, based on

pathophysiological mechanisms of a disease, how we could treat a disease that has been untreatable up to now, and how we will be competing with other developers. But this is not enough for use and we bring in external medical expertise for those projects that are on the stage of preclinical studies. Clinicians who are not only treating patients, but also conduct clinical research, tell us about how their therapeutic area is set up, what they need and what they don't need. In our case this is external expertise. Big companies have their own medical departments that perform this function, of course also in contact with physicians. (21SK 2014)

Nonetheless, interactions between the clinical practice setting and key actors of the Russian pharmaceutical innovation environment appear to be incidental, which constitutes a major difference from the innovation systems in Western industrialized countries (see Consoli and Mina 2009). One of the managers of a venture fund that specializes in biomedicine shared his cautious observations in this regard:

Indeed an important problem in all this process that I see here is a large gap between academia, those who originally develop drugs, and end users. I am not talking about patients here, I am talking about physicians. We have many drugs that are promoted, pushed through, developed, consume resources. Then people come for serious investments to conduct clinical trials, we evaluate all this and understand that this is completely not interesting. Because there is something more interesting in the pipeline or in general, or standards of care are such that this is not needed. There could be various different reasons, but the essence is such that an unneeded drug [for clinical practice] is being developed from the beginning. It happens very often. (1IF 2014)

Overall, business actors do not view multiple drug candidates originating in Russian scientific and academic institutions as innovative in the sense that these molecules could make a pronounced impact on the market. Academics, on the other hand, with some exceptions, tend to see molecules developed locally in their institutions as much more innovative in the sense of corresponding to procedural criteria of innovativeness.

This divergence can in part be explained by the interest of actors in attracting state funding to support their work. At the same time, this divergence can also be understood as supported by the different understandings of innovation favored by the two groups that focus on either the market impact or the procedural side of innovation. Work conditions encourage scientist-developers to focus more on the procedural side of drug innovation, activities such as meeting funding criteria and fulfilling grant conditions, while business actors' environment encourages them to ensure returns on the investments, which is possible only with a noticeable impact of an innovation on the market. These conflicting views on drug innovation and its value underpin differences in understandings of drug development trajectories in Russia between academic and business actors. This further complicates collaboration between them, already made difficult by the historically ingrained lack of connections and interaction between the two worlds. As elaborated in the rest of this chapter, I also suggest that specifics of local political culture actually work to inhibit interaction between actors involved in pharmaceutical science and technology, whereas such interaction is necessary for reaching understanding and bridging their conflicting opinions described in this section. This is despite the Pharma-2020 policies' having declared the necessity of building a collaborative environment for the development of pharmaceutical innovations.

Continuous Change and Lack of Transparency: State

While academic and business actors had divergent understandings of drug development trajectories in Russia, of drug innovation and its value, and tended to blame each other for the lack of collaboration, both groups also generally perceived the third axis of the Triple Helix—the state—similarly. Many informants mentioned a lack of transparency and dialogue as one of the central characteristics of their interactions with state actors. Most such assessments were made in relation to the policy makers, funding decision makers, and especially the federal state budgetary institution, the Scientific Center for Expertise of Medical Application Products of the Ministry of Health (Center for Expertise).

The Center for Expertise is a key regulatory actor in Russia. It assesses applications for conducting clinical trials with humans, and most importantly it assesses dossiers of drugs to be registered for circulation on the Russian market. Based on the assessment by the Center for Expertise, the Ministry of Health grants or withholds permission for trial conduct and drug registration. Many developers explained that because of continuous change in legislation and decision-making practices by the Center for Expertise and perceived lack of communication, the processes and requirements for new drug registration and for clinical trial permissions are not clear to them. Moreover, such lack of clarity facilitates the circulation of rumors and speculation regarding regulatory procedures, as illustrated by a statement of a biomedical scientist:

> Drug registration is not transparent. Usually it is a case-law approach. Legislation does not state anything concrete. Rumors are circulating. For instance, that a comparative study is required with two groups with thirty individuals in each. Previously drug registration was performed by RosZdravNadzor, now it is again done by the Ministry of Health. People are changing continually, procedures are not transparent, everything is happening like in a black box. (2SE 2014)

This lack of transparency and insight on what is going on in the "black box" of the Center for Expertise and, more widely, other governance structures and initiatives gives rise to worries and uncertainty among drug developers. Especially lamented is a lack of opportunity to consult experts from the Center regarding the design of clinical studies before submitting trial protocols or drug registration dossiers for approval, as another biomedical scientist explained:

> The system of going through the Pharm Committee is very bureaucratized. We also have not gone through this yet. I feel they have no interest in drugs coming through. Their business is to find some formal reasons. It would have been ideal if we worked together as partners, that they would be interested in these drugs. For example, I come to you and bring the pack with these documents. They say, "Guys, it would be good if you redo this and that." Now they have review time. They can return the document, saying that comma is not in the right place. And your review time starts all over. It can last forever. This system is not thought through. Now, as I understand it, we are doing many interesting projects in the preclinical stage. How it all will be going through clinical stage and registra-

tion, this is what I am afraid of the most. Maybe these are just fears . . . [M]y competence so far is the preclinical stage, so these are my assumptions, maybe my fears are unfounded. (10SD 2014)

As this statement illustrates, this scientist did not yet have experience in interacting with the regulators in the pharmaceutical arena, but had already acquired the anxiety and anticipation of mistreatment by the authorities that are characteristic of the general atmosphere in the Russian pharmaceutical arena. The absence of opportunity to ask questions and receive advice on protocols and applications contributes to the persistence of this atmosphere. An important rationale for prohibiting contacts between the Center for Expertise and drug developers is to prevent corruption. However, most informants insisted that consultation opportunities are necessary for streamlining and facilitating the drug development process. They also indicated that the current arrangement actually facilitates a covert form of corruption, that is, the existence of the multitude of small, semilegal firms that offer help to applicants unfamiliar with the bureaucratic requirements of the Center for Expertise. An informant representing a venture fund provided an anecdote from his own experience that illustrates the situation regarding drug registration application assessment by the Center, communication of the regulators with the drug R&D community, and the market of such firms:

When we talk about drug registration, about how it happens in reality, I will just quote our former director of Drugs Registration Department,[1] as our interview is being recorded. During the conference in Petersburg in summer 2011, when the Federal Law 61 had just come into force, there were many problems, many questions. And he was presenting at that conference, was telling us how everything will be perfect. And he was asked, "So what should we do? Nothing is clear." And he, without the slightest doubt, in front of many people, says: "You know, now there are many companies which provide consultancy services in the area of registration. You can refer to them." (1IF 2014)

Furthermore, many drug developers feel not only disoriented but also not heard and not included in discussions of the wider matters shaping their work. The issue of lack of dialogue was emphasized, for example, by an academic drug developer who is also a part of a working group within the Ministry of Science and Education. He gave an example of a grant application assessment procedure to illustrate his point:

> I don't like this structure. I told you, for instance the expert axed the project, someone praised it, and someone axed. First of all, expertise needs to be democratized. The ultimate truth cannot be affiliated with a particular person, or two, four, or five persons. There needs to be an opportunity for a wide discussion, moving it from the level of popularization to a level of serious science with critical analysis of your abilities as a scientist, as a group of scientists. . . . In Russia everything works in such a way that control must be present, but this control needs to be mutual. There needs to be a dialogue, a meeting at least. But when an expert says "bullshit," you can't just jump above his head. (14SD 2014)

This general atmosphere of disorientation and uncertainty experienced by drug developers, both in academia and business, due to the continually changing and only partially transparent regulatory environment and also funding distribution mechanisms, has consequences for how the developers plan and implement their work and therefore for the success of state efforts to boost drug development and production in the country. A director of a regional biomedical cluster described how developers, lacking a clear understanding of their opportunities and what these opportunities entail, tend to just try their luck with funding without planning long-term initiatives:

> The problem is that there is a lack of projects and the system is so to say not really adjusted, smooth and running yet, in the minds of people. There is no understanding of how all this way is being built. There is no understanding of the end result, so that everything is done in a way of pass/fail. And if in some stage it did not happen, well, sorry, it did not happen. (15IF 2014)

Overall, the business and academic actors involved in drug development with whom I spoke expressed an attitude of generalized distrust of reforms, regulations, regulators, and to some extent also each other. While new funding and infrastructural opportunities are welcomed, developers are not confident that procedures and requirements will be fair to them and that legislative initiatives are meticulously thought through and will open up new opportunities for them rather than inhibiting and complicating their work. Additionally, an expectation (based on prior experience) that written rules do not necessarily correspond with an actual decision-making practice with regard to funding, permission granting, and new drug registration adds to the confusion. For example, the head of a small company shared his hopes that policy makers would not require full compliance with the policies they are making:

> So the legislation related to drugs here is based on FL [Federal Law] 61, produced quite recently, and on federal standards that are based on the European GMP. Probably there was a lot of rush. Meaning that there are many discrepancies in terminology. . . . Federal standards are also cut down, terminology does not correspond with methodological guidelines, so that guidelines are apart, laws are apart, federal standards are apart. . . . This is why we are delaying our human work [working on drugs for humans] further and further and are trying to work in the veterinary area, while there are still the same problems there. . . . Previously, when we worked according to GosZdrav requirements, our manufacturers were trying to meet them. Veterinaries were living according to their own rules. And now, with this FL 61 all drugs are in essence like for humans. The same manufacturing conditions. Everything. So the only hope is that our legislators after producing this pile of laws will just turn a blind eye to them and we will continue living like previously. (18SK 2014)

While initiatives like Pharma-2020 and new development institutes are appreciated by those involved in drug development in Russia, these initiatives arrive in a particular environment, where actors, especially those working far from Moscow, obtain delayed and fragmented information because of the way the regulatory system works. Furthermore, they do not necessarily trust new information about rules, initiatives, and opportunities, expecting that actual practice will deviate from the formal descriptions. They also do not expect their opinions to be heard or that particularities of their practices will be taken into account, and they lament the extremely limited opportunities for dialogue with policy and decision makers. In this environment, many of those involved in drug development suspect that the new initiatives will not be implemented in the way that is promised, that personal connections are needed to be successful, and that decision makers may not be interested in their actual work.

Opportunities to solicit views of the policy makers on the issues raised by the informants from business and academia proved to be limited for me. Because it was nearly impossible to have an interview with anyone apart from scientists who became a part of relevant ministerial working committees, I also studied the regulatory world through analyzing policies and policy changes, examining officials' public statements and observing (in person and through video recordings) the events in which policy makers participated. These data informed parts of this book and suggest that Russian policy makers themselves have been working in a rushed manner and under serious pressure to adapt to the radically transforming economic and political situation within and outside the country. In such circumstances, regulators and decision makers have limited time to obtain feedback, to align all of the new initiatives, and to fine-tune their working mechanisms.

Against this background, we can interpret an observation I made during a 2014 workshop, "Bringing drugs to the market in Russia: from preclinical stage to registration." There Elena Telnova, a former head of the regulatory organization RosZdravNadzor, gave a presentation in which she clearly explained the steps in the new drug registration process as it was arranged at the time of the presentation and substantiated these steps with concrete laws and regulations. However, one needs to take into account that, for example, one of the most important laws in the field of pharmaceuticals in Russia, 61-FZ "On medicines circulation," also cited by Telnova, was changed three times during 2010 alone, the year it was accepted. That is, policy and decision makers are almost continuously adapting the pharmaceutical governance field and coping with the implications of existing regulations adopted previously in a similarly hasty way. They may find regulatory frameworks to be clear and understandable, but as these frameworks keep transforming, actors on the ground—in business and academia—face serious difficulties in adapting when new regulatory initiatives come one after one. One possible conclusion is that the pace of change is too great for working out optimal regulations responsive to the current actual conditions and challenges and for establishing opportunities for feedback, leading to confusion and suspicion among those affected.

This situation is indicative of particular characteristics of the local political culture pertinent to pharmaceutical innovations. This political culture can be understood as characterized by a changing and nontransparent regulatory environment and a lack of opportunities for dialogue between actors working on drug development and regulation. These characteristics contribute to the general atmosphere of disorientation and uncertainty, which inhibits opportunities for interaction and collaboration between actors involved in pharmaceutical science and technology and, consequently, inhibits the improvements that policy makers try to achieve.

Bringing Everyone Together: Infrastructure for Collaboration

It is in this context that policy makers and state agencies are trying to facilitate collaborative links between various actors, that is, to develop an institutional environment conducive to the success of the initiatives to boost local innovative drug development and production.

Etzkowitz and Leydesdorff (2000) suggest that different national innovation systems can be characterized in terms of varying institutional arrangements of academia-industry-government relations. They distinguish several Triple Helix forms; the most productive, in their opinion, is the Triple Helix that generates a knowledge infrastructure of overlapping institutional spheres, trilateral networks, and hybrid organizations that emerge at the interfaces. Here not only the state, academia, and industry are equal partners, but they also take on each other's functions. These authors also distinguish a "pseudo"-triple helix, where the state encompasses academia and industry and directs the relations between them. Etzkowitz and Leydesdorff (2000) elaborate that the latter model in its strong versions can be found in some of the countries of the former Soviet Union and is largely considered a "failed developmental model" because there is little room for bottom-up initiatives, and innovation is discouraged rather than encouraged (112).

Indeed, as is elaborated below, in Russia the state does not take the position of an equal partner of academia and business in development but rather positions itself on top of both and strongly directs their work and interactions and more generally the development of an innovative environment. But what are the current results of this arrangement, in particular, for collaboration?

As was already described, measures to encourage interaction between actors in the pharmaceutical innovation system, first of all academia and business, include state funding instruments that require investments from external sources. Also, these measures have involved a formation of clusters—groups of specialized companies, often small and medium-sized, working together in a particular location and benefiting from common infrastructure, shared expertise, and collaboration opportunities. In 2012, a countrywide competition between Russian regions for state funding for pilot innovative cluster development programs resulted in the selection of twenty-five clusters in twenty regions, among which six (and from 2014, eight) specialized in pharmaceuticals, biotechnology, and the medical industry. Many Russian regions set up centers for cluster development that are tasked with creating an environment for the productive interaction of different actors to boost innovation. Also, the number of state development institutes has risen, as shown in documents of the working group Territorial Activity of Development Institutes, Including Innovative Territorial Clusters, which was set up within the Intersectorial Commission for Implementation of the Strategy for Innovative Development of the Russian Federation: there are state funds, banks, and associations that are providing grants, investments, and expert support (as shown in the Protocol 3, July 22, 2013, of a meeting of this commission). Finally, nonstate venture funds, clinical trial organizations, and R&D companies also began to emerge and became part of the innovation environment. Below I investigate how actors involved in drug innovation in Russia perceive these developments and state-directed measures and also reflect on how the dominant position of the state reflects on the project of boosting innovative drug development and production in present-day Russia.

A director of one of the cluster development centers explained that the formation of clusters, which occurred quite quickly, was arranged in a top-down manner with (mostly) regional administration taking the lead in a countrywide competition for cluster funding. Those who won and obtained funding could use it for the formation and support of a particular type of cluster (medical, IT, or other). Given that the movement for cluster formation generally has not been at the grassroots level, forming and running a cluster proved to be challenging, as this director described:

> It is difficult for us to develop now because originally clusters have been a top-down initiative. And when clusters were created here, they were created based on the decree of the Ministry of Economic Development. Now it is a big obstacle, because based on the Ministry decree the cluster unites medicine and IT. Can you imagine? They are placed together not because of some joint projects, but because from XX region unfortunately two applications were submitted and the Ministry could not support both, so everyone was lumped together in one cluster. And when some money arrives or some support is given to someone, some jealousy arises between participants . . . so the center of cluster development is like a referee who does not have a special interest either in medicine or in IT. So we are an independent actor here and this is how we occupy this position in this cluster as a management company. (15IF 2014)

The same director further added that the cluster development center is tasked not only with mediating relationships and decision making among cluster participants but also with motivating actors to join:

> When people are coming and express the desire to become residents of a special economic zone, it is clear for them that there are tax deductions, customs deductions, cheaper rent, etc. So one can easily explain to them. And when one is coming and says, "What will I get if I become a cluster participant? What will you help me with?" we then say, "You know, it is important to unite, collaborate. . . ." I am telling you, I see this in Russia, here all this time people were taught to do their own business, independent of everyone, independent of the state, people learned how to evade the law, etc., not to trust each other, because this is market and everyone survives. And meanwhile the world has been establishing cooperative ties. (15IF 2014)

This person explained that the cluster development center is addressing the problem of motivating actors to join through making agreements with regional infrastructure organizations such as engineering centers, the commercialization office, and technology transfer centers and channeling state funding received to cluster participants to receive priority access to the services of these organizations.

A director of a larger biomedical cluster in another Russian region explained how the cluster has functioned as an intermediary between academia and pharmaceutical business. This director also stressed the lack of experience among academic actors with functioning in the market environment, which necessitates an intermediary that facilitates the collaboration processes between academia and the pharmaceutical business:

> Our role is an interesting one and it is a difficult one to practice. This model exists when project management is concentrated not in an academic structure but in some business structure. It [the business structure] can be an intermediary, working as, for example, a technology transfer center, which has to be capable of speaking the language of Big Pharma or the pharmaceutical business that can be attracted. So that they find a potentially interested party and then further develop this interest. So that we ask: "What do you want?" Sometimes companies themselves say, "We are interested in projects in these and these areas." Then we can negotiate based on this topic: "Ok, we have this. We sign a confidentiality agreement. We offer you options and try to organize a mutual collaboration." But it is better if this is done not by an [academic] institute. Because . . . possibly it is not the case in Moscow, but here very few organizations have sufficient business competence. And then the process first of all becomes in a manageable way. This process has a road map. Often this function is taken up by private venture funds, nanocenters, some departments of development institutes, or some objects of innovation infrastructure. Here, for instance, our private seed venture fund is doing this. It is 100 percent private, which puts potentially interested parties together and takes on itself the project management. (17IF 2014)

Importantly, this biomedical cluster director proposed that to be fruitful, academic-business collaborations in pharmaceuticals need to be long-term, starting early in the development process, because scientific academic competencies are not enough to produce a potentially commercially successful drug candidate: ". . . there is a need to work preliminarily with pharma, and not when we already have done everything and then realized that we did it wrong and not in a way that is needed" (17IF). This is why expectations apparently harbored by academics regarding short-term collaboration with business for the sole purpose of selling already developed candidate molecules are not realistic.

Actors involved in development institutes, clusters, and other initiatives to boost innovation in drugs suggested that an increase in interactions between business and academia is actually being facilitated by the government-designed measures and, in some instances, forced. Especially strong pressure to interact is being applied to the actor group that is most directly controlled by the state, that is, the academic actors working in state-financed institutions:

> Therefore, there are no any ways of intensification other than forcing them, creating conditions so that they communicate to each other from time to time. . . . [Academic] institutes at least in the course of the recent years based on the experiences of our colleagues in XX academic campus, made much progress, because they stopped closing down. Much positive influence was brought in by the RAS [Russian Academy of Science][2] reform, they themselves began to initiate contacts, to become more open in negotiations, become more interested. They understood that they cannot develop on their own. They need industry to that. They are ready for negotiations. Business is also different. There is business that wants collaboration and looks for it. They can find the possibilities. Of course after all it may take years and years of negotiations. But nonetheless the process has started. It intensified with the RAS reform, when everyone began to be not very comfortable. (17IF 2014)

The informants observe progress in the intensification of interactions between academic, business, and other actors in the pharmaceutical innovation arena brought by the top-down countrywide "clusterization," reform of the Russian Academy of Science, and new funding instruments such as Pharma-2020. As a result of these measures, actors gradually do come to seek collaboration, either because their acceptance of new rules has become a condition for survival (as it is for academic scientists) or because of the benefits offered, access to which depends on actors' willingness to establish new links.

Political Culture

Overall, many informants indicate that the attention and support measures from the state, including funding such as Pharma-2020 and the establishment of new development institutes and infrastructural organizations, are timely. While they do not observe immediate results of this in the form of novel local drugs on the market or in the late stage of development, they still predict that the quality of new projects in drug development will increase as the actors involved obtain more experience and build their networks and a wider local drug innovation environment forms. Yet the described position of the state, above both academia and business and controlling the development of the innovation environment, constitutes, together with continuous change and nontransparency, a core of local political culture that works in two ways that appear to contradict each other. On the one hand, the state decision makers may quickly devise, implement, and to a large extent force measures to realize pharmapolitical ambitions, including measures to stimulate collaboration in the institutional environment pertinent to pharmaceutical innovations. On the other hand, these same characteristics of political culture appear to inhibit self-organization in the local pharmaceutical arena and the initiative of the actors involved, both of which are important for developing a collaborative institutional environment.

While Etzkowitz and Leydesdorff (2000) suggest that a situation where the state encompasses academia and industry and directs the relations between them is a dead end for innovative development, the guiding role of the state may not necessarily be a problem in itself. Guennif and Ramani (2012), who investigated the development of the pharmaceutical industry in India and Brazil, highlight the role of the state in these two countries as a catalyst of change, which at least in the case of India resulted in the development of indigenous capabilities in pharmaceuticals. However, as the same authors argue, the directing role of the state must be complemented by multiway interaction, dialogue, and feedback loops from other involved actors. They argue that whether or not actors productively use the windows of opportunity created by policy makers to stimulate innovation very much depends on the actors' perceptions of the emerging opportunities and threats.

The views and practices of those involved in the Russian pharmaceutical innovation system reported in this chapter suggest that they experience difficulties in productively using the windows of opportunity created by policy makers. Guennif and Ramani (2012) argue that the state actors must involve others to arrive at policy arrangements that match the situation and expectations of various players to induce positive responses as much as possible, open up to communication and exchange for more coordinated development, and actively scan for and encourage self-organized activity and networking among actors. However, the Russian state, concerned with quickly addressing the urgent problem of lack of locally developed and produced drugs on the country market, minimally complements its directing role with such inclusive approaches. This facilitates the atmosphere of disorientation and distrust among actors in the local pharmaceutical arena that is detrimental for collaboration and, thus, innovating.

In the previous chapters, I elaborated how vision production, value generation, and problem definition matter for shaping the directions of pharmapolitical processes. In Russia, the development and implementation of the Pharma-2020 policies have contributed to envisioning the independent and self-sufficient Russian nation. The mechanisms of constructing this vision included defining the problem to be addressed by Pharma-2020 in economic terms as that of the (internal country) market and of the inability of Russian industry to dominate it, which have led to untying the value of pharmaceutical science and technology from public health improvements. In the local political culture, characterized, as I suggest in this chapter, by nontransparency, continual change, and top-downness, this problem definition and vision of the national future were translated into quick, state-defined measures to rapidly produce needed results, including developing a productive, collaborative innovation environment. However, the haste and unidirectional mode of the implementation of measures to support innovative drug development appear to negatively affect the relations that animate interactions in the pharmaceutical innovation system. These relations, consequently, unfold in a climate of closedness, restricted information flows, and distrust between the key actor groups, inhibiting the collaboration necessary for the productive functioning of innovation systems. Therefore, collaboration as a process central to pharmapolitics can be characterized as a two-way dynamic whereby opportunities for collaboration are structured by the dominant political culture, while the implementation of the national pharmapolitical agenda is being affected by the ways in which the actors on the ground choose to engage and collaborate with each other.

Russian Drug Innovation Infrastructure in 2018

<u>Pharmaceutical innovation clusters</u>: Twelve, of which two are in Saint-Petersburg, three in Moscow and the Moscow region, and others are in the Kaluga, Belgorod, Penza, Tomsk, Kemerovo, Altai, and Irkutsk regions.

<u>Technology transfer centers</u>: Seventy, most of which are established by academic organizations and fewer by private companies as well as regional and municipal governing bodies. Some of the technology transfer centers specialize in pharmaceutical technologies, such as Yaroslavl Center named after Dorogov, which began work in 2016 with funding from the Pharma-2020 program.

<u>Business incubators and accelerators</u>: A total of 363 (260 business incubators and 103 accelerators). Few specialize in (bio)pharmaceuticals or medicine; rather, these organizations and programs in Russia tend to be more generalist. Types of incubators and accelerators are described below.

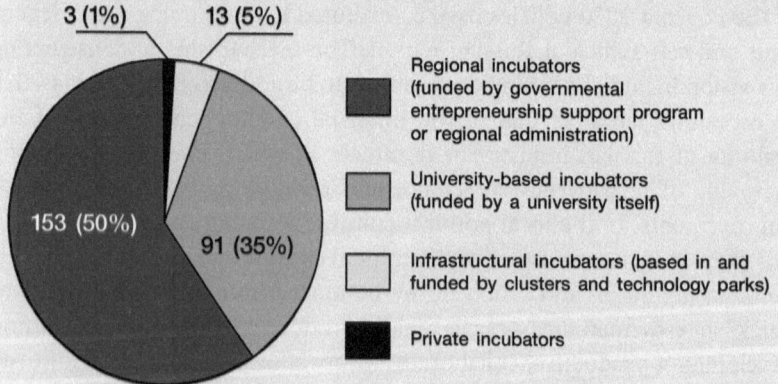

Figure 5.2. Types of incubators.

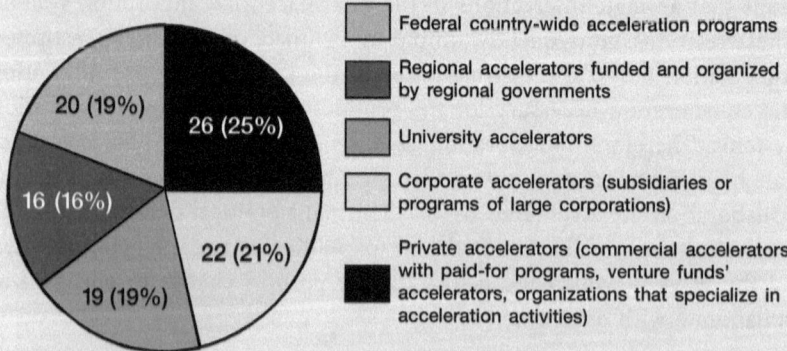

Figure 5.3. Types of accelerators.

Development institutions: Influential development institutions in Russia that are most directly related to drug innovation are Russian Venture Company, Agency for Strategic Initiatives to Promote New Projects, Skolkovo Foundation, Rusnano, Innovation Promotion Foundation, and Industry Development Fund. These development institutions build infrastructure for making necessary resources accessible for companies engaged in innovating, including innovating in (bio)pharmaceuticals, and support specific projects through funding provision.

Investors: Most often investments for novel drug projects come from partly publicly owned venture funds or from state funds in partnership with corporations or private funds. For instance, half of the eight venture funds most active in the domain of drug development in Russia were established with funding from the governmental Russian Venture Company (RVC). These venture funds are RVC Biopharmaceutical Investments and Maxwell Biotech, which invest in Russian (bio)pharmaceutical companies, Bioprocess Capital Ventures, with investment portfolio consisting mostly of high-risk biopharmaceutical projects by Russian companies, and RVB Capital, which invests in biomedical projects globally. The remaining four are Chemrar Ventures, which invests in early-stage innovative drug development; Rusnanomedinvest, which invests in promising foreign-developed medicines and technologies for their subsequent production in Russia; Inbio Ventures, which belongs to Pharmstandart (the largest Russian pharmaceutical company) and invests in innovative therapies globally and in Russia; and Gurus BioPharm, which coinvests with private investors in Russian (bio)pharmaceuticals.

Data presented here were obtained from the following sources: Rossiiskaia klasternaia observatoriia 2018; Ministry of Higher Education and Science of the Russian Federation 2018; Assotsiatsia akseleratorov i biznes-inkubatorov Rossii 2018.

Chapter 6

Pharmapolitics in Russia and Beyond

The preceding chapters traced how pharmaceutical innovation in Soviet and post-Soviet Russia has become entangled with rebuilding the nation and reimagining its identity and future, merging into pharmapolitics. The investigation of this merger led us from Soviet pharmaceutical industry functioning through post-Soviet reforms of this industry and the arrival of international commercial clinical trials to Russia, to recent attempts to boost drug development in the country and some consequences of these attempts. The steps taken in the investigation bridge bioethical guidance, the organization of the pharmaceutical sector, innovation policies, clinical trial conduct, and collaborative practices, which together attest to the coproduction of politics and pharmaceutical science and technology.

    In this last chapter, I bring together the processes of producing visions, generating value, defining problems, and collaborating that were explored in the previous chapters to identify exactly how this coproduction occurs and how specific pharmapolitical practices and trajectories take shape. Then I analyze the implications of the current pharmapolitical regime in Russia for governing drug innovation there, taking account of the multiple roles pharmaceuticals play in society. Finally, I reflect on the resemblance between the Russian case and the global pharmaceutical arena dominated by multinational companies and suggest that both are characterized by oppressive imagination practices that prevent alternatives to the dominant visions of the pharmaceutical futures from emerging and inhibit linking pharmaceutical science and technology and people's health.

> While final reports on results of implementation of Pharma-2020 remain in the future, representatives of the Russian Ministry of Industry and Trade provide the following estimates that by 2017:
>
> - more than 100 billion rubles were spent within the framework of the Pharma-2020 Program;
>
> - more than four hundred drug development projects were financed;
>
> - more than ninety drugs by Russian companies were registered to enter the country market; and
>
> - more than twenty new pharmaceutical production sites began operating.
>
> - Data presented here were obtained from the following sources: Tsib 2016; Mansurov 2016; Osipov 2019.

Constituting Pharmapolitics

The analytical framework of coproduction provided a starting point for this investigation of pharmapolitics by cautioning against using political interests as an exhaustive explanation for the state of pharmaceutical science and technology, or the other way around. Then, throughout this book, it became possible to further specify how particular directions that coproductive processes take are shaped. To understand how the contemporary pharmapolitical regime in Russia (or elsewhere) emerged and how exactly it works now, we need to analyze four constituent processes: vision production, problem definition, collaboration, and value generation. These processes span political ambitions and agendas, on the one hand, and technological opportunities and constraints, on the other. Attending to vision production makes it possible to trace how, in the interaction between drug research and development (R&D) systems and political programs, imaginaries of the societal futures emerge and how these imaginaries affect pharmaceutical governance. Analyzing problem definition makes visible how drug innovations are shaped by ways in which societal problems to be addressed through pharmaceutical technoscience are formulated. Attention to collaboration makes apparent the influences of political culture on how pharmaceutical sector actors engage with each other and thus on the kinds of output they produce. Considering value generation highlights how distribution of power affects what kinds of value are produced by pharmaceutical science and technology and for whom.

Let us take a closer look at how the four processes defining for pharmapolitics have played out in Russia. First, *vision production* is explored in chapter 2, using the case of early post-Soviet reforms of the Russian pharmaceutical industry. Chapter 2 traced the emergence, rise, and fall of the neoliberal vision of the Russia's future. This vision was rooted in a set of neoliberal ideas championing the market, which is to be safeguarded from state intervention, and placed entrepreneurship at the center of economic and societal development. Correspondingly, this vision portrayed Russia's future as one in which well-being and prosperity are brought to life through the initiative and creativity of entrepreneurial individuals living and working in a free market environment. Chapter 2 traced how, in the early 1990s from the very first days of the new Russia after the end of the Soviet Union, the neoliberal vision of the Russian future became quickly integrated with national policy instruments and governance infrastructures. Strong support on the highest national political level provided the neoliberal vision with an impetus to take hold nationwide, resulting in, among other things, the speedy privatization and decentralization of the local pharmaceutical industry. Yet the pharmaceutical industry was not simply molded in accordance with the neoliberal aspirations of the policy makers. Rather, national regulatory agendas interacted in a coproductive process with the state of the local pharmaceutical science and technology, which proceeded to deteriorate rapidly. While initially the neoliberal policies significantly changed the Russian pharmaceutical industry, soon the technoscientific deterioration of the sector supported the widespread rejection of the neoliberal vision of the Russian future among those involved with pharmaceuticals in the country. This rejection prepared a receptive ground for a major turn in the regulation of the pharmaceutical industry in Russia away from neoliberal aspirations, a turn grounded in the newly assembled vision of the independent and self-sufficient nation.

Second, *problem definition* contributes to shaping the processes of coproduction of pharmaceutical technoscience and politics and is analyzed in chapter 4, using as a central example Pharma-2020, the set of policies recently adopted in Russia to direct the development of the pharmaceutical industry in the country. Through Pharma-2020, the Russian government aims to boost the development and production of drugs, including innovative ones, by the local pharmaceutical industry. In chapter 4, it becomes clear that it is not only that trajectories of drug innovation define possibilities for solving societal problems; simultaneously, the ways in which societal problems to be solved through pharmaceutical science and technology are defined affect the trajectories of drug innovation. Pharma-2020 proclaims the lack of locally developed and produced drugs as a threat to national security, and the failure of local companies to harvest profits from the growing Russian pharmaceutical market as a long-term risk factor. This pharmapolitical problem definition draws on preexisting, historically rooted aspirations with respect to self-sufficiency, on recent national experiences of living through drastic reforms, and on novel technoscientific opportunities in the field of pharmaceuticals. The problem to be solved through the employment of pharmaceutical science and technology has been defined in economic terms and has focused largely on the local market. Consequently, the implementation of Pharma-2020 has so far concentrated on enhancing research, development, and production capacities of the local industry, while leaving out the issue of translating the newly built industrial capacities into the improvement of public health, and has also inhibited the internationalization of Russian pharmaceutical business practices. The development and implementation of Pharma-2020 has, then, worked to articulate, rehearse, and strengthen a particular vision of the nation and its future: that of an independent and self-sufficient Russian nation. Thus, the problem definition contributes to directing pharmapolitical processes along particular paths and also concurrently supports the production of specific visions of the nation and its future.

Third, *collaboration* also impacts the directions coproductive processes take and is analyzed in chapter 5, which maps the collaboration between various actors involved in the drug innovation domain, such as academic scientists, pharmaceutical businesses, and state decision makers. It is commonly accepted that collaboration is crucial for generating innovations, especially in medicine and pharmaceuticals. Chapter 5 highlights how the local political culture influences the ways in which collaborations in the Russian pharmaceutical arena proceed, while actual collaboration practices, in turn, mediate the state of pharmaceutical science and technology. The political aspirations of Pharma-2020 suggest that the current situation in which foreign pharmaceutical companies dominate the internal country market is considered problematic because it is the Russian pharmaceutical industry that should be reaping the benefits from this market. To rectify this situation, Pharma-2020 was translated into quick, state-defined measures to rapidly produce the needed results. The measures have included the introduction of new pharmaceutical research funding schemes, the establishment of new infrastructural organizations, such as biomedical clusters, and the development of new rules for obtaining state support. These measures have been characterized by nontransparency, continual change, top-downness, and a lack of opportunities for dialogue between the actors working on drug development and regulators. It became clear that these characteristics contribute to the general atmosphere of disorientation and uncertainty that inhibits the opportunities for interaction and collaboration between actors involved in pharmaceutical science and technology. Such an atmosphere hinders the changes policy makers are trying to achieve, because the described lack of collaboration opportunities in the Russian pharmaceutical arena is inimical to drug innovation. Thus, the ways in which actors collaborate or refrain from collaboration in drug innovation affects the state of the pharmaceutical science and technology and, thus, the implementation of the national pharmapolitical agenda.

Finally, *value generation* feeds into shaping the pharmapolitical coproductive processes as analyzed in chapter 3, using the case of international commercial clinical trial conduct in Russia. Value generation is central to pharmaceutical science and technology, because the development and production of drugs entangles multiple kinds of value, including potential therapeutic benefits for patients, soaring profits for industry, and opportunities to advance academic research and promote state interests. Correspondingly, questions loom large about what kind of value is being generated and for whom in drug development and production. Chapter 3 showed that while the rhetoric of improving public health is central in the pharmapolitical arena, the value in pharmapolitical processes is not a given, but rather it is multiply configured in the clinical, scientific, and economic domains. In the case of international clinical trials, this means that medical experimentation may generate such diverse value types as new medicines, monetary profits, the enhancement of local academic research capacity, and opportunities to fill some gaps in local health care; actors involved actively engage in translations between the different value types. The kinds of value generated in clinical trials and through pharmaceutical science and technology more generally depend on which visions of the future animate drug development efforts, how the problems to be solved with the use of pharmaceutical science and technology are defined, and how the relevant actors in the drug innovation domain engage with each other—that is, on the directions of pharmapolitical processes. At the same time, in a coproductive process, potential and actual value generated through pharmaceutical science and technology contributes to formulating political agendas and interests and, in doing so, also directs pharmapolitical processes. Importantly, according to analysis of value generation in the pharmaceutical arena, public health benefits do not follow automatically from developments in national or international pharmaceutical science and technology, but require targeted efforts to link these developments and people's health concerns.

Vision production, problem definition, collaboration, and value generation together help to elucidate how exactly pharmaceutical technoscience and politics underwrite each other's existence and to what effects. This list is not intended to be exhaustive; rather, it reflects what has emerged from my exploration of the mutual shaping of politics and pharmaceutical technoscience in post-Soviet Russia. Such an approach offers a more comprehensive explanatory account than analyzing industrial development apart from wider political aspirations or analyzing the political work of nation building in isolation from technoscientific change. The first would risk portraying pharmaceutical innovation as entirely determined by progress in science and technology and missing the influences of power and culture on specificities of drug innovation processes in particular settings. The second would fail to question the role of pharmaceutical science and technology in building the nation and imagining its future and to scrutinize the processes whereby this engagement between technoscientific change and nation building takes place. The analytical framework developed here can be adapted and employed in research on innovations in other settings as well to understand their development trajectories and to analyze the corresponding implications.

Markets and Health Needs in Russian Pharmapolitics

The multinational pharmaceutical industry helps create demand for its products through direct-to-consumer advertising and through clinical trials that aim to research a treatment in such a way that it can be indicated for the largest possible market. The critique of such practices mounted by multiple studies indicates that now, when health has become a market to be grown, it would be naive to view pharmaceuticals simply as a way to respond to people's health needs (Sismondo and Green 2015). It is, and for good reasons, commonplace in social science scholarship to argue that pharmaceuticals are embroiled in a redefinition of health and illness.

This redefinition entails presenting the risk of the disease as a disease itself, posing questions in clinical trials about more and more minutiae and distant health risks, and then convincing everyone that all risks are conditions to be treated with drugs (Dumit 2012). As a result, we witness continual growth in diagnoses, drugs, and costs.

At the same time, it is important to bear in mind that this growth maps onto patterns of power and inequality globally. Astonishing numbers, for instance, those cited by Joseph Dumit in his book *Drugs for Life*—that the average American is prescribed and purchases between nine and thirteen prescription drugs per year, totaling more than 4 billion prescriptions in 2011 and growing—certainly raise well-grounded concerns about overuse of pharmaceuticals driven by a market-based notion of health. The public health value of this dynamic is questionable at best. Still, examples such as antiretroviral drugs for HIV that turned a deadly disease into a manageable chronic condition; insulin, the first hormone-replacement therapy, which allowed type I diabetics to live their lives instead of rapidly wasting away; and pain relief medications that help some people suffering from cancer, trauma, and other conditions spend their days without agonizing pain, show that pharmaceuticals do play a vital role in the alleviation of human suffering. And it is of utmost concern that access to such essential drugs as antiretrovirals is still problematic for many (WHO 2016), and that the burden of diseases that affect mostly the world's poor has been largely neglected by pharmaceutical R&D (Utzinger and Keiser 2013). These latter cases reinforce that in the contemporary global pharmaceutical regime, expansive growth in lifelong consumption of multiple pharmaceuticals coincides with persistent dire need for lifesaving medicines.

This book recognizes the multiplicity of the roles pharmaceuticals perform in society. This perspective highlights the entanglement of pharmaceuticals in a whole range of value-producing processes, some of which can be tied to saving lives and improving well-being. Below, in summarizing the implications of pharmapolitical processes as they unfold currently in Russia for governing drug innovation there, I rely on this understanding.

The Russian pharmapolitical regime relies heavily on the notion of market. This centrality of the market seemingly aligns with the above-mentioned mode of operation of the Western-centric multinational pharmaceutical industry. Yet there is an important difference. In Russia, it is the state sector that sets the aim of capturing the market by defining and developing measures to address the problem of the inability of the local industry to dominate the sizable local market and harvest profits from it.

The implications of this move are twofold: on the one hand, they concern the development of the Russian pharmaceutical industry itself, and on the other, they concern public health and its precarious relationship with pharmaceuticals.

In chapter 4, I investigated how the problem definition and vision production processes have operated in the case of the Pharma-2020 initiative to solidify the closing-down strategy of the local pharmaceutical industry. Many Russian industry actors hesitate to work internationally, not seeing internationalization as beneficial to them, while some also fear that relying on foreign counterparts at any stage of drug development, production, or commercialization creates risks for national security. Surely, some Russian companies involved in drug development and production do work with foreign partners: they receive licenses for local production of foreign-developed drugs, arrange transfers of foreign-developed molecules to Russia, and attempt to develop strategies to enter international markets. However, generally the vision of an independent and self-sufficient Russia as articulated and strengthened by Pharma-2020 limits the possibilities and motivations to internationalize among Russian actors. The ensuing dominance of the closing-down strategy may have negative consequences for the actual innovative development of the local pharmaceutical industry that the state has aimed to achieve through devising and implementing Pharma-2020. This is because development of pharmaceutical industry capacities such as employment of modern technologies, access to financial resources, and knowledge of international regulatory regimes has been shown to follow the internationalization of pharmaceutical companies (Chittoor et al. 2008; Hoskisson et al. 2000). That is, the excessive focus on self-sufficiency inadvertently impedes the strengthening of the ability of the Russian pharmaceutical industry to develop and produce novel drugs and, thus, to address what the Pharma-2020 policy defined as a problem of the dominance of the foreign companies on the Russian market.

Apart from the focus on independence and self-sufficiency, other important characteristics of the currently dominant approach to drug innovation governance in Russia are haste and top-downness in making and implementing decisions. In chapter 5, I highlighted that the speedy and continuous regulatory change, including the shifts in opportunities for receiving state support for drug development and production, may exceed the capacity of the organizations active in the pharmaceutical arena to adapt (as demonstrated to be the case in other settings by Guennif and Ramani 2012). Actors involved in drug innovation fail to recognize windows of opportunity created by policy makers to support the Russian pharmaceutical industry and consequently do not use these to build their capacities and advance their work. Furthermore, when developing and implementing drug innovation governance measures in a rushed way, state decision makers do not have an opportunity to solicit input and feedback from others involved to better match these measures with the situation on the ground and with the expectations of relevant actors. This top-down approach further deters those who work in the field of drug innovations from actively responding to and productively using the new opportunities created by the state. Although introducing more dialogue and multiple feedback loops into the drug innovation governance process might slow down the implementation of measures to support pharmaceutical research, development, and production, such a more collaborative approach would likely lead to more sustainable development of the Russian pharmaceutical industry in the long run.

As for health and pharmaceuticals, public and public health needs are being silenced in the currently dominant approach to drug innovation governance in Russia. This means that measures introduced by the government to support pharmaceutical R&D do not involve specific efforts that link pharmaceutical industry development with citizens' health. Rather, these measures focus on the research, development, and production capacities of the Russian pharmaceutical industry with the goal of increasing the share of the internal country market it occupies. The reigning assumption is that the development of the capabilities of the pharmaceutical industry, supported by the state, will automatically lead to meeting population drug needs in a better way and thus will positively affect public health. However, in chapter 3, I highlight that public health benefits do not follow automatically from developments in national or international pharmaceutical science and technology. Rather, they require targeted efforts by regulators and others involved to link these developments with people's health. Scholars interested in the issues of linking technoscientific advances with societal needs have observed that developments in sectors other than pharmaceuticals, for example in biotechnology, also are not by themselves sufficient for achieving major positive impacts on people's lives (Reid and Ramani 2012). Therefore, the pervasive rhetoric of national security embedded in the current state efforts to boost drug development and production in Russia in practice is unlikely to result in national security in terms of meeting the essential drug needs of the population. Without clear mechanisms linking technoscientific advances and the development of industry capabilities with actually improving public health, efforts to boost local drug development and production in Russia will result in no major improvements in people's access to medicines or in their health.

Oppressing Imagination: Russian and Global Pharmapolitics

Innovation in contemporary science and technology is intensely future oriented. It is driven by and gives rise to a variety of visions and expectations regarding new opportunities, capabilities, and risks to societies (Van Lente 2012; Brown, Rappert, and Webster 2000). The Human Genome project, for example, has inspired discussions about the future of health care, in which positive visions of the opportunities to prevent diseases were negotiated with negative visions that portrayed the threat to privacy and freedom by genomic knowledge (Jasanoff 2005, 13–41). Moreover, the visions of the future not only depict what is attainable through science and technology, but also have a normative character, because they encode understandings of how societies ought or ought not to live (Jasanoff 2015). Previous research on the topic has documented how visions of the future emerge and mediate relationships between various actor groups through, for example, attracting the interest of allies such as investors, users, and regulators and building agendas (Abrishami, Boer, and Horstman 2014). Often, in the process of such mediation, competing innovation futures are promoted and conflict tend to be high (Borup et al. 2006). Existing research on imagination and science, technology, and innovation highlights the processes of negotiation and contestation involved in the formation of the future.

Characteristic of the pharmapolitics in Russia is the absence of negotiation and contestation. The shaping of vision production, problem definition, collaboration, and value generation has barely been challenged by actors involved in the drug innovation field, despite the multiple difficulties they experience, and no alternative directions for pharmapolitical processes have been formulated. This absence is not accidental. In the field of pharmaceuticals, it is rooted in the decades when the Soviet state played a controlling and directing role in the field of science, technology, and innovation. Its prominence is also facilitated by the already mentioned contemporary continuous change, including change in the regulations governing the pharmaceutical sector and in institutions involved in the governance, and by the top-down decision making by the Russian state actors on priority setting in drug development and on the design and functioning of support mechanisms for research and production of drugs.

The combination of top-down steering and continuous, often unpredictable change impedes the formulation of alternatives to the current pharmapolitical trajectory, because it hinders dialogue between the state decision makers and others working in the pharmaceutical sector, and also between those involved in drug research, development, and production themselves, such as academic and business actors. In the shifting environment, the nonstate actors tend to be concerned primarily with adapting to changes initiated by the government and ensuring their own survival. Consequently, they become too isolated and disconnected from each other to conceive and articulate alternative directions for pharmapolitical processes, while their practices appear to be too fragmented and hampered by underlying tensions between actor groups to exert any significant influence on the dominant state-defined directions. Notably, publics, including current and future patients, are disengaged from shaping pharmapolitical processes in any direct or indirect ways. They are implicated actors referenced as the ultimate beneficiaries of the state support of national drug development, but lacking real opportunities to learn the details of state efforts or to participate in any way in developing and defining them. Through limiting opportunities for the elaboration of coordinated alternative approaches to the governance of drug innovations and for the mobilization of bottom-up initiatives in the field, the state actors preserve full control over pharmapolitical processes and their directions.

Pharmapolitics in Russia, then, has turned to suppressing the emergence of a variety of visions of the future. In the case of the recent government efforts to boost local drug innovation in Russia, pharmapolitical processes hindered the formulation of any prominent visions of national futures alternative to the one offered by the development and implementation of the Pharma-2020 policies. In the absence of competing visions, the only available, state-formulated version of a national future, grounded in the materiality of pharmaceutical science and technology, has been much more likely to become accepted by those concerned. This leads to the conclusion that expectations and visions of the future do not always emerge in conjunction with innovation and advances in science and technology. In situations with strong power inequalities and lack of coordination and collaboration within and among actor groups, society at large may fail to react to technoscientific developments and refrain from formulating and advancing any alternative visions of their promises, risks, and ways of engaging these developments in society. Pharmapolitics in Russia hinders public imagination.

But what about pharmapolitics globally? Global pharmapolitics are much more similar to pharmapolitics in Russia than may be evident at first, and I suggest that the core of this similarity lies in oppressive imagination practices. In his book *Pharmocracy* (2017), Kaushik Sunder Rajan diagnoses a narrowing scope of imaginable alternatives to monopolistic corporatization of pharmaceutical production instituted by the "multinational, Euro-American, research and development (R&D)-driven pharmaceutical industry."[1] Sunder Rajan points out that now, in the discussions about bridging pharmaceutical innovation and people's health, an alternative of, for example, a public sector pharmaceutical industry is not even on the table. Imagining a political horizon in which health and health care are not accountable only to the logic of capital appears inconceivable. The globally dominant pharmapolitical regime, with its hegemonic imaginary of a monopolistic, corporatized pharmaceutical industry together with a commercialized metric of innovation, then, is no less detrimental to public imagination than pharmapolitics in Russia, with its sole imaginary of an independent and self-sufficient nation. Of course, Big Pharma companies are regularly on the receiving end of criticisms regarding advertising aggressively, propagating health risks, and exploiting disadvantaged populations in clinical trials. Yet the structure of the domain they constitute has become the norm, one that is so powerful and pervasive that it hinders carving out alternatives that truly break with its logic.

One of the alternatives or at least alternative directions for global pharmapolitics discussed in the scholarly literature is an enhanced state control. This book illustrates, though, that in itself, transfer of control to the state or even a public sector pharmaceutical industry may not be an alternative at all in the sense of better alignment of pharmaceutical science and technology with public health and of more public accountability. It is not different sources of control, be it state or market entities, that need to be discussed, but ways of opening up control over defining the problems to be addressed through innovation, over generating guiding visions of the futures attainable through advances in science and technology, over the arrangement of collaboration, and over the specification of the value to be generated through innovating. Too much and too concentrated control restricts experimentation and learning from the experiences by the actors involved and, thus, limits flexibility in using innovation to address the changing public health challenges. Moreover, excessive control complicates the critical appraisal of health innovations, their use, and the ways to govern them, increasing the risk of making decisions that would not fit with the realities innovations are intended for and the needs of innovation developers and users. Finally, excessive control hinders imagination and generates apathy and inaction.

This book puts forward the argument that productive pharmapolitics are those that nourish and open up ways for public imagination to flourish. Such pharmapolitics would entail creating conditions for engagement between different visions of the future being produced, versions of the problems to be addressed, collaboration practices, and forms of value. Maintaining the current oppressive imagination practices evident in both the Russian and globally dominant pharmapolitical regimes risks propagating stillborn innovations that make little positive difference for societal well-being.

In the introduction to this book, I mentioned the resemblance between common critiques of the profit-pursuing capitalist multinational pharmaceutical industry and of nondemocratic states' interference in science and innovation. The resemblance lies in the shared ideal of technoscience untainted by market influences or authoritarian intrusions. These critiques give rise to governance approaches that, in an attempt to purge pharmaceutical R&D from politics, focus on either substituting markets for state, where the problem is seen in authoritarian state interference, or substituting state for markets, where the problem is seen in excessive influence of capital. Yet the choice between market and state is inherently limited, as both approaches may end up diverging pharmaceutical technoscience and public health needs. It is rather in the direction of acknowledging the interconnections between pharmaceutical science and technology and politics and finding new ways of collectively responding to them in a more transparent and equitable way that positive change can be brought about.

Notes

Introduction

1. See, for example, a package of procedures developed by FDA to speed up "the availability of drugs":

Fast track is a process designed to facilitate the development and expedite the review of drugs to treat serious conditions and fill an unmet medical need;

Breakthrough therapy is a process designed to expedite the development and review of drugs that may demonstrate substantial improvement over available therapy;

Accelerated improvement. These regulations allowed drugs for serious conditions that filled an unmet medical need to be approved based on a surrogate endpoint;

A Priority Review designation means the FDA's goal is to take action on an application within six months.

Information on these procedures is taken from the FDA website: http://www.fda.gov/ForPatients/Approvals/Fast/ucm20041766.htm.

EMA also introduced "special regulatory pathways to facilitate market access," such as conditional marketing authorization, approval under exceptional circumstances, and accelerated assessment, with an adaptive licensing initiative being currently piloted.

2. Retrieved from the FDA website: http://www.fda.gov/ScienceResearch/SpecialTopics/CriticalPathInitiative/ucm076689.htm.

3. http://www.ich.org/about/history.html

4. The ICH website states, "To date, six Regional Harmonisation Initiatives (RHIs) namely, APEC, ASEAN, EAC, GCC, PANDRH and SADC, in addition to

eight Drug Regulatory Authorities/Department of Health (DRAs/DoH) namely Australia, Brazil, China, Chinese Taipei, India, Republic of Korea, Russia and Singapore are invited in the ICH bi-annual meetings. RHI/DRA/DoH representatives participate in the Global Cooperation session of the ICH Steering Committee (SC) to discuss capacity-building and share experience/challenges on the implementation of ICH Guidelines. Representatives also listen to ICH technical topics discussed by the SC during meetings and are invited to nominate technical experts in Expert Working Groups/Implementation Working Groups to contribute to the development of ICH Guidelines."

Chapter 1

1. Council of People's Commissars of the USSR. O Proizvodstve i Vypuske Novykh Farmatsevticheskikh Preparatov [About Production and Prescription of New Pharmaceutical Drugs]. November 16, 1937.

2. Instruction to the circular order by the People's Commissariat for Health, May 25, 1926, #74 "Regulation of registration of finished pharmaceutical products and new medicines."

3. As was mentioned previously, about 80 percent of pharmaceutical products commercialized from 1800 to 1990 came from the United States, Germany, Switzerland, the United Kingdom, and France (Achilladelis and Antonakis, 2001), signaling a strong concentration of drug development activities in these countries, with more recent output from other European countries and Japan.

4. By "deep experimental research" is meant preclinical research.

Chapter 3

1. Numbers of trials increase because of the "me-too" business: many not especially innovative drugs, with minimal pharmacological alteration from an existing drug, are being tried and launched; they also increase because of regulatory demands in relation to long-term safety for drugs for chronic diseases. Competition to get drugs approved and marketed intensifies the search for subjects. Also, there is growth in the number of new chemical entities (Petryna 2015, 211).

2. Decree of the Ministry of Health of the RSFSR No. 235, of August 25, 1992, "About the Organization of Departments for Clinical Trials of Medicines with Healthy Volunteers," 1. While this decree is still in force, in 2010 the Federal Law No. 61 "On Circulation of Medicines" prohibited phase 1 clinical trials with healthy volunteers to be conducted by foreign entities. Russian pharmaceutical companies are still allowed to conduct phase 1 clinical trials with healthy volunteers.

3. The CRO was called Evidence Clinical and Pharmaceutical Research and was acquired by Worldwide Clinical Trials.

4. Industry Standard OST 42-511-99.

5. Russian National Standard GOST R 52379-2005 "Good Clinical Practice"

6. State-funded free health care is provided in Russian cities mainly through polyclinics. These are primary care outpatient facilities where general practitioners and other medical specialists, including cardiologists, are housed. Other elements of the state health-care system include specialized outpatient centers and hospitals of various types.

7. The "press lunch" was organized by the association Innovative Pharma (inpharma.info). A list of press releases can be found at inpharma.info/resursy/spravochnaya-informatsiya/.

8. The article published in the electronic professional journal www.pharmvestnik.ru was based on an interview with Vladimir Gurdus, CEO of RMI Partners, Management Company of RusnanoMedInvest LLC and NovaMedica LLC.

Chapter 4

1. These two views on development are in no way incompatible. The pharmaceutical industry, for instance, uses policy makers' fascination with innovation to push for more deregulation.

2. For example, Viktor Dmitriev, director of the Association of the Russian Pharmaceutical Manufacturers (ARPM), explained his vision of how production of these strategically important drugs could have been ensured. Officials from the Ministry of Industry and Trade should have arranged a meeting with producers and scientists and discussed who would assume responsibility for which of the strategic drugs. "Then we will see whether companies, science, have desire to do so or not. And if yes, then what is needed. . . . Somebody would need a production line, others will need money to increase turnover volume so that from this turnover they finance the science part themselves. I think we need to begin from a meeting, where we would clearly work from the list: Bupivacaine—responsibility for its development is taken by such research center or such company. Agree between each other, who does what, in which stage, make a business plan, which can be controlled via benchmarks, according to dates: what and when is done, when we will see the finalized drug. The most important is a plan. Each company that takes part in it needs to understand how it is going to develop the process, for which a business plan is needed. For each drug we need to appoint a responsible entity, deadlines . . . and work accordingly. To distribute resources to develop drugs without specific details is equivalent, I think, to sending money

into a black hole" (Shevchenko 2010, "Strategically important medicines according to the list." Pharmatsevticheskoe obozrenie, n.9.

Chapter 5

1. Drugs Registration Department is another name used for the Center for Expertise (Pharm Committee is another such name). This multiplicity of names is also a result of the regulatory field's continuous change that occurs so quickly that multiple names for key authorities remain in use in communication.

2. RAS is the Russian Academy of Sciences. Interestingly, its reform, while praised by the informant (the director of a biomedical cluster), is being fiercely criticized by academic actors; for example, a scientist interviewed described the reform as "knocking down" the Academy and science altogether (2SE).

Chapter 6

1. The quote is from Kaushik Sunder Rajan's page on the University of Chicago website: https://anthropology.uchicago.edu/people/faculty_member/kaushik_sunder_rajan/.

Bibliography

Abraham, J., and C. Davis. 2007. "Deficits, Expectations and Paradigms in British and American Drug Safety Assessments." *Science, Technology & Human Values* 32: 399–431.

Abraham, J., and G. Lewis. 2000. *Regulating Medicines in Europe: Competition, Expertise and Public Health*. London: Routledge.

Abraham, John. 2010. "Pharmaceuticalization of Society in Context: Theoretical, Empirical and Health Dimensions." *Sociology* 44 (4): 603–22. https://doi.org/10.1177/0038038510369368.

———. 2011. "Evolving Sociological Analyses of 'Pharmaceuticalization': A Response to Williams, Martin and Gabe." *Sociology of Health and Illness* 33 (5): 726–28.

Abrishami, Payam, Albert Boer, and Klasien Horstman. 2014. "Understanding the Adoption Dynamics of Medical Innovations: Affordances of the Da Vinci Robot in the Netherlands." *Social Science and Medicine* 117: 125–33. https://doi.org/10.1016/j.socscimed.2014.07.046.

Achilladelis, Basil, and Nicholas Antonakis. 2001. "The Dynamics of Technological Innovation : The Case of the Pharmaceutical Industry." *Research Policy* 30: 535–88.

Anderson, B. 2006. *Imagined Communities. Reflections on the Origin and Spread of Nationalism*. London: Verso.

Anderson, James a. 2010. "Clinical Research in Context: Reexamining the Distinction between Research and Practice." *The Journal of Medicine and Philosophy* 35 (1): 46–63. https://doi.org/10.1093/jmp/jhp054.

Anokina, Anna, and Dmitry Meshkov. 2007. "Going Further East in CEE." *International Clinical Trials* (Summer): 24–29.

Appelbaum, Paul S. 2010. "Clarifying the Ethics of Clinical Research : A Path toward Avoiding the Therapeutic Misconception." *American Journal of Bioethics* 2 (2): 22–23.

Appelbaum, Paul S., Charles W. Lidz, and Thomas Grisso. 2004. "Therapeutic Misconception in Clinical Research: Frequency and Risk Factors." *IRB* 26 (2): 1–8.

Association of Accelerators and Business Incubators of Russia. 2018. "Karta Akseleratorov and Biznes-Inkubatorov RF [Map of Accelerators and Business-Incubators in Russia]." http://www.oneup.ru/analytics/innomap.

Association of Clinical Trials Organizations. 2010. "Obzor Rynka Klinicheskikh Issledovanii v Rossii v 2009 Gody [Review of the Clinical Trials Market in Russia in 2009]." *Remedium*, no. S13: 128–33.

———. 2016. "ACTO Newsletter № 14: Summary of 2016 Results." Moscow. http://acto-russia.org/files/ACTO_Newsletter_14.pdf.

Babayan, E. A., and O. B. Ytkin. 1982. *Osnovnie Polozheniia Aprobatsii Lekarstvennikh Sredstv s SSSR i Zarubezhnikh stranakh [General Principles of Assessment of Medicines in USSR and Other Countries]*. Moscow: Meditsina.

Balashov, Aleksei. 2012. *Formirovanie Mekhanisma Ustoichivogo Razvitiia Farmatsevticheskoi Otrasli: Teoriia i Metodologiia [Forming a Mechanism of Sustainable Development of Pharmaceutical Industry: Theory and Methodology]*. St. Petersburg: Saint-Petersburg State University of Economy and Finance.

Balázs, Katalin, Wendy Faulkner, and Uwe Schimank. 1995. "Transformation of the Research Systems of Post-Communist Central and Eastern Europe: An Introduction." *Social Studies of Science*, no. 25: 613–32.

Belmont Report. 1979. "The Belmont Report: Ethical Principles and Guidelines for the Protection of Human Subjects of Research."

Borup, Mads, Nik Brown, Kornella Konrad, and Harro van Lente. 2006. "The Sociology of Expectations in Science and Technology." *Technology Analysis and Strategic Management* 18 (3/4): 285–98.

Brown, Julie V., and Nina L. Rusinova. 1997. "Russian Medical Care in the 1990s: A User's Perspective." *Social Science & Medicine* 45 (8): 1265–76.

Brown, N., and M. Michael. 2003. "A Sociology of Expectations: Retrospecting Prospects and Prospecting Retrospects." *Technology Assessment and Strategic Management* 15: 3–18.

Brown, N., B. Rappert, and A. Webster, eds. 2000. *Contested Futures: A Sociology of Prospective Techno-Science*. Aldershot, UK: Ashgate.

Brown, Patrick, Sabine de Graaf, Marij Hillen, Ellen Smets, and Hanneke van Laarhoven. 2015. "The Interweaving of Pharmaceutical and Medical Expectations as Dynamics of Micro-Pharmaceuticalisation: Advanced-Stage Cancer Patients' Hope in Medicines alongside Trust in Professionals." *Social Science and Medicine* 131: 313–21. https://doi.org/10.1016/j.socscimed.2014.10.053.

Busfield, Joan. 2015. "Assessing the Overuse of Medicines." *Social Science and Medicine* 131: 199–206. https://doi.org/10.1016/j.socscimed.2014.10.061.

Carpenter, Daniel P. 2010. *Reputation and Power: Organizational Image and Pharmaceutical Regulation at the FDA*. Princeton Studies in American Politics. Princeton: Princeton University Press.

Chittoor, Raveendra, Sougata Ray, Preet S. Aulakh, and M. B. Sarkar. 2008. "Strategic Responses to Institutional Changes: 'Indigenous Growth' Model of the

Indian Pharmaceutical Industry." *Journal of International Management* 14 (3): 252–69. https://doi.org/10.1016/j.intman.2008.05.001.
Clarke, Adele E., and Susan Leigh Star. 2008. "The Social Worlds Framework: A Theory/Methods Package." In *The Handbook of Science and Technology Studies*, edited by Edward J. Hackett, Olga Amsterdamska, Michael Lynch, and Judy Wajcman, 3rd ed., 113–39. Cambridge, MA: MIT Press.
Collier, Stephen J. 2011. *Post-Soviet Social: Neoliberalism, Social Modernity, Biopolitics*. Princeton: Princeton University Press.
Conroy, Mary Schaeffer. 2006. *The Soviet Pharmaceutical Business during Its First Two Decades (1917–1937)*. New York: Peter Lang.
Consoli, Davide, and Andrea Mina. 2009. "An Evolutionary Perspective on Health Innovation Systems." *Journal of Evolutionary Economics* 19 (2): 297–319. https://doi.org/10.1007/s00191-008-0127-3.
Consoli, Davide, and Ronnie Ramlogan. 2008. "Out of Sight: Problem Sequences and Epistemic Boundaries of Medical Know-How on Glaucoma." *Journal of Evolutionary Economics* 18 (1): 31–56. https://doi.org/10.1007/s00191-007-0074-4.
Cooper, Melinda. 2008. "Experimental Labour—Offshoring Clinical Trials to China." *East Asian Science, Technology and Society: An International Journal* 2: 73–92. https://doi.org/10.1007/s12280-008-9040-y.
Davis, C., and J. Abraham. 2013. *Unhealthy Pharmaceutical Regulation: Innovation, Politics and Promissory Science*. Basingstoke: Palgrave Macmillan.
Deloitte. 2017. "Russian Pharmaceutical Market Trends in 2017. Track & Trace System: Additional Costs or Opportunities?" Moscow. https://www2.deloitte.com/content/dam/Deloitte/ru/Documents/life-sciences-health-care/russian-pharmaceutical-market-trends-2017-eng.pdf.
Dorofeev, Valerii. 1995. *Farmatsevticheskaia Promishlennost Rossii v Usloviiakh Perekhodnogo Perioda [Russian Pharmaceutical Industry under Conditions of Transition]*. Moscow: Meditsina.
DSM. 2017. "Russian Pharmaceutical Market 2016." Moscow. https://www.dsm.ru/docs/analytics/Annual_Report_2016.pdf.
———. 2018. "Russian Pharmaceutical Market 2017." Moscow. https://dsm.ru/docs/analytics/Annual_Report_2017_EN_R.pdf.
DSM group. 2006. "Russian Pharmaceutical Market in 2006." Moscow.
Dumit, J. 2012. *Drugs for Life: How Pharmaceutical Companies Define Our Health*. Durham: Duke University Press.
Emanuel, Ezekiel J., David Wendler, Jack Killen, and Christine Grady. 2004. "What Makes Clinical Research in Developing Countries Ethical? The Benchmarks of Ethical Research." *The Journal of Infectious Diseases* 189 (5): 930–37. https://doi.org/10.1086/381709.
Epstein, S. 1996. *Impure Science: AIDS, Activism and the Politics of Knowledge*. Berkeley: University of California Press.

Etzkowitz, Henry, and Loet Leydesdorff. 2000. "The Dynamics of Innovation: From National Systems and 'Mode 2' to a Triple Helix of University–Industry–Government Relations." *Research Policy* 29 (2): 109–23. https://doi.org/10.1016/S0048-7333(99)00055-4.

Felt, Ulrike. 2015. "Keeping Technologies Out: Sociotechnical Imaginaries and the Formation of Austria's Technopolitical Identity." In *Dreamscapes of Modernity: Sociotechnical Imaginaries and the Fabrication of Power*, edited by Sheila Jasanoff and Sang-Hyung Kim, 103–25. Chicago: Chicago University Press.

Fisher, J. A. 2015. "'Ready-to-Recruit' or 'Ready-to-Consent' Populations? Informed Consent and the Limits of Subject Autonomy." In *The Pharmaceutical Studies Reader*, edited by I. S. Sismondo and J. A. Green, 195–207. Malden, MA: Wiley-Blackwell.

Fisher, Jill A. 2009. *Medical Research for Hire: The Political Economy of Pharmaceutical Clinical Trials*. New Brunswick, NJ: Rutgers University Press.

Freeman, C. 1995. "The National System of Innovation in Historical Perspective." *Cambridge Journal of Economics* 19 (1): 5–24.

Fujimura, Joan H. 1992. "Crafting Science: Standardized Packages, Boundary Objects, and 'Translation.'" In *Science as Practice and Culture*, edited by Andrew Pickering, 168–211. Chicago: University of Chicago Press.

Gagliardone, Iginio. 2014. "'A Country in Order': Technopolitics, Nation Building, and the Development of ICT in Ethiopia." *Information Technologies & International Development* 10 (1): 3–19.

Gaponenko, Nadezhda. 1995. "Transformation of the Research System in a Transitional Society: The Case of Russia." *Social Studies of Science* 25: 685–703.

Gassmann, Oliver, Gerrit Reepmeyer, and Maximilian Von Zedtwitz. 2008. *Leading Pharmaceutical Innovation. Leading Pharmaceutical Innovation*. https://doi.org/10.1007/978-3-540-77636-9.

Gay, Brigitte, and Bernard Dousset. 2005. "Innovation and Network Structural Dynamics: Study of the Alliance Network of a Major Sector of the Biotechnology Industry." *Research Policy* 34 (10): 1457–75. https://doi.org/10.1016/j.respol.2005.07.001.

Gelijns, A., and N. Rosenberg. 1994. "The Dynamics of Technological Change in Medicine." *Health Affairs* 13 (3): 28–46. https://doi.org/10.1377/hlthaff.13.3.28.

Geltzer, Anna. 2012. "In a Distorted Mirror: The Cold War and U.S.-Soviet Biomedical Cooperation and (Mis)Understanding, 1956–1977." *Journal of Cold War Studies* 14 (3): 39–63. https://doi.org/10.1162/JCWS_a_00247.

Gibbons, Michael, Camille Limoges, Helga Nowotny, Simon Schwartzman, Peter Scott, and Martin Trow. 1994. *The New Production of Knowledge: The Dynamics of Science and Research in Contemporary Societies*. London: SAGE Publications.

Glickman, S. W., J. G. McHutchison, E. D. Peterson, C. B. Cairns, R. A. Harrington, R. M. Califf, and K. A. Schulman. 2009. "Ethical and Scientific Implications

of the Globalization of Clinical Research." *New England Journal of Medicine* 360 (5): 816–23.
Gordeev, A I. 2009. "The Pharmaceutical Industry in Russia: Reality and Prospects." *Acta Naturae*, no. 3: 6–9.
Granovetter, M. 1985. "Economic-Action and Social-Structure—the Problem of Embeddedness." *American Journal of Sociology*. https://doi.org/Doi 10.1086/228311.
Greene, J. A., and S. H. Podolsky. 2009. "Keeping Modern in Medicine: Pharmaceutical Promotion and Physician Education in Postwar America." *Bulletin of the History of Medicine* 83 (2): 331–77.
Guennif, Samira, and Shyama V. Ramani. 2012. "Explaining Divergence in Catching-up in Pharma between India and Brazil Using the NSI Framework." *Research Policy* 41 (2): 430–41. https://doi.org/10.1016/j.respol.2011.09.005.
Hecht, Gabrielle. 2001. "Technology, Politics, and National Identity in France." In *Technologies of Power*, edited by Michael Thad Allen and Gabrielle Hecht, 253–94. Cambridge, MA: MIT Press.
———. 2009. *The Radiance of France. Nuclear Power and National Identity after World War II*. Cambridge, MA: The MIT Press. https://doi.org/10.1017/CBO9781107415324.004.
Hedgecoe, Adam, and Paul Martin. 2003. "The Drugs Don't Work: Expectations and the Shaping of Pharmacogenetics." *Social Studies of Science* 33 (3): 327–64. https://doi.org/10.1177/03063127030333002.
Henderson, R., L. Orsenigo, and G. P. Pisano. 1999. "The Pharmaceutical Industry and the Revolution in Molecular Biology." In *Sources of Industrial Leadership: Studies of Seven Industries*, edited by D. C. Mowery and R. Nelson, 267–312. Cambridge: Cambridge University Press.
Hoebert, J., R. Laing, and P. Stephens. 2011. "The World Medicines Situation 2011: Pharmaceutical Consumption." Geneva.
Hogarth, Stuart. 2015. "Neoliberal Technocracy: Explaining How and Why the US Food and Drug Administration Has Championed Pharmacogenomics." *Social Science and Medicine* 131: 255–62. https://doi.org/10.1016/j.socscimed.2015.01.023.
Hoskisson, R., L. Eden, C.-M. Lau, and M. Wright. 2000. "Strategy in Emerging Economies." *Academy of Management Journal* 43: 249–67.
Höyssä, Maria, Henrik Bruun, and Janne Hukkinen. 2004. "The Co-Evolution of Social and Physical Infrastructure for Biotechnology Innovation in Turku, Finland." *Research Policy* 33: 769–85. https://doi.org/10.1016/j.respol.2003.12.003.
Iudanov, A., E. Volskaia, and S. Lagunov. 1998. *Biznes-Putevoditel' Po Farmatsevticheskomy Rinku Rossii [Business-Guide for Russian Pharmaceutical Market]*. Moscow: Classic-Consulting.
Ivanov, Konstantin. 2002. "Science after Stalin: Forging a New Image of Soviet Science." *Science in Context* 15 (2): 317–38.

Jack, D. B., and N. P. Mason. 1987. "The Pharmaceutical Industry in the USSR." *Journal of Clinical Pharmacy and Therapeutics* 12: 401–7. https://doi.org/10.2166/wh.2013.221.

Jasanoff, Sheila, ed. 2004. *States of Knowledge: The Co-Production of Science and Social Order*. London: Routledge.

———. 2005. *Designs on Nature: Science and Democracy in Europe and the United States*. Princeton: Princeton University Press.

Jasanoff, Sheila, and Sang Hyun Kim. 2009. "Containing the Atom: Sociotechnical Imaginaries and Nuclear Power in the United States and South Korea." *Minerva* 47 (2): 119–46. https://doi.org/10.1007/s11024-009-9124-4.

Jasanoff, Sheila, and Sang-Hyun Kim, eds. 2015. *Dreamscapes of Modernity: Sociotechnical Imaginaries and the Fabrication of Power*. Chicago: The University of Chicago Press.

Kalinin, Iu, A. Machula, M. Grigor'ev, M. Sapovskii, and V. Padalkin. 2000. "Poteria Promishlennogo Potentsiala Proizvodstva Farmatsevticheskih Substantsii—Factor Ugrozi Strategicheskoi Bezopasnosti Rossii. Problema i Predlagaemie Puti Resheniia [The Loss of Industrial Potential for Production of Pharmaceuticals as a Challenging Factor for the Strategical Security of Russia: Problem and Proposed Solutions]." *Khimiko-Pharmatsevticheskii Zhurnal* 34 (9): 49–54.

Karlberg, Johan. 2008. "Sponsored Clinical Trial Globalization Trends." *Clinical Trial Magnifier* 1 (2): 13–18.

———. 2011. "The Establishment of Emerging Trial Regions." *Clinical Trial Magnifier* 4 (1): 7–23.

Kash, Don E., and Robert W. Rycoft. 2000. "Patterns of Innovating Complex Technologies: A Framework for Adaptive Network Strategies." *Research Policy* 29 (8062): 819–31. https://doi.org/10.1016/S0048-7333(00)00107-4.

Kelly, Ann H., David Ameh, Silas Majambere, Steve Lindsay, and Margaret Pinder. 2010. "'Like Sugar and Honey': The Embedded Ethics of a Larval Control Project in the Gambia." *Social Science & Medicine (1982)* 70 (12): 1912–19. https://doi.org/10.1016/j.socscimed.2010.02.012.

Kimmelman, Jonatan. 2007. "The Therapeutic Misconception at 25: Treatment, Research and Confusion." *Hastings Center Report* 37 (7): 36–42.

Kneller, Robert. 2003. "Autarkic Drug Discovery in Japanese Pharmaceutical Companies : Insights into National Differences in Industrial Innovation." *Science and Technology* 32: 1805–27. https://doi.org/10.1016/S0048-7333(03)00062-3.

Krementsov, Nikolai. 1997. *Stalinist Science*. Princeton, NJ: Princeton University Press.

Lairumbi, Geoffrey Mbaabu, Sassy Molyneux, Robert W. Snow, Kevin Marsh, Norbert Peshu, and Mike English. 2008. "Promoting the Social Value of Research in Kenya: Examining the Practical Aspects of Collaborative Partnerships Using an Ethical Framework." *Social Science & Medicine (1982)* 67 (5): 734–47. https://doi.org/10.1016/j.socscimed.2008.02.016.

Lakoff, Andrew. 2004. "The Anxieties of Globalization: Antidepressant Sales and Economic Crisis in Argentina." *Social Studies Of Science* 2 (April): 247–69. https://doi.org/10.1177/0306312704042624.

Law, J. 2006. *Big Pharma: How the World's Biggest Drug Companies Control Illness.* London: Constable & Robinson Ltd.

Lente, H. Van. 2012. "Navigating Foresight in a Sea of Expectations: Lessons from the Sociology of Expectations." *Analysis & Strategic Management* 24 (8): 789–802.

Lichterman, Boleslav. 2002. "Conflict or Harmony? Clinical Research and the Medical Press in Russia." *Science and Engineering Ethics* 8: 383–86.

Lin, A., B. Sokolov, and D. Slepnev. 2013. "Farmatsevticheskiy Rynok: Proizvodstvo Lekarstvennyh Sredstv v Rossii [Pharmaceutical Market: Production of Medicines in Russia]." *Problemi Sovremennoi Ekonomiki* 1 (45): 191–95.

Livanskii, Stanislav. 2017. "Farmatsevticheskaya Promyshlennost: Predvaritel'nye Itogi 2016 Goda [Pharmaceutical Industry: Preliminary Results of 2016]." Moscow. https://gmpnews.ru/wp-content/uploads/2017/03/Tendentsii-rynka-2016-po-GILS-i-NP.pdf.

Lundvall, B. 1992. *National Systems of Innovation: Towards a Theory of Innovation and Interactive Learning.* London: Pinter.

———. 2002. "National Systems of Production, Innovation and Competence-Building." *Research Policy* 31 (2): 213–31.

Magidson, Onisim. 1967. "Stanovlenie Sovetskoi Khimiko-Farmatsevticheskoi Promishlennosti [Establishment of the Soviet Chemical-Pharmaceutical Industry]." *Khimiko-Pharmatsevticheskii Zhurnal* 1 (10): 10–14.

———. 1970. "Istoriia Razvitiiya Khimiko-Farmatsevticheskoi Promyshlennosti in SSSR [History of Development of Chemical-Pharmaceutical Industry in USSR]." *Khimiko-Pharmatsevticheskii Zhurnal* 4 (5).

Mansurov, Denis. 2016. Idem s operezheniem grafika [We are ahead of schedule] Kommersant. https://www.kommersant.ru/doc/3155972.

Marcelle, G. 2015. "Science, Technology and Innovation Policy That Is Responsive to Innovation Performers." In *International Research Handbook on Science, Technology and Innovation Policy in Developing Countries: Rationales and Relevance*, edited by S. Kuhlmann and G. O. Matamoros. Cheltenham, UK: Edward Elgar Publishing Ltd.

Markina, Nadezhda. 2013. "Esli Ne Rabotaet Elektronnaia Zapis', Zhaluites v Minzdrav [If Electronic Appointment Booking Does Not Work, Complain to the Ministry of Health]." *Gaseta.Ru*, December 7. https://www.gazeta.ru/health/2013/07/12_a_5425073.shtml.

Marsh, Vicki, Dorcas Kamuya, Yvonne Rowa, Caroline Gikonyo, and Sassy Molyneux. 2008. "Beginning Community Engagement at a Busy Biomedical Research Programme: Experiences from the KEMRI CGMRC-Wellcome Trust Research Programme, Kilifi, Kenya." *Social Science & Medicine* 67 (5): 721–33. https://doi.org/10.1016/j.socscimed.2008.02.007.

Martin, Ben R. 2012. "The Evolution of Science Policy and Innovation Studies." *Research Policy* 41 (7): 1219–39. https://doi.org/10.1016/j.respol.2012.03.012.

Martin, Paul, John Abraham, Courtney Davis, and Alison Kraft. 2006. "Understanding the 'Productivity Crisis' in the Pharmaceutical Industry: Over-Regulation or Lack of Innovation?" In *New Technologies in Health Care: Challenge, Change and Innovation*, edited by Andrew Webster, 177–93. Palgrave Macmillan.

Mashkovskii, Mikhail. 2000. "K 80-Letiiu Tsentra Po Khimii Lekarstvennykh Sredstv—Vserossiiskogo Nauchno-Issledovatalskogo Khimiko-Farmatsevticheskogo Instituta (TsKhLS-VNIKhFI) [80th Anniversary of the Center for Chemistry of Medicines—All-Russian Pharmaceutical Chemical Scientific Research Institute (TsKhLS-VNIKhFI)]." *Khimiko-Pharmatsevticheskii Zhurnal*, no. 12: 48–50.

Melo-Martín, I. de, and a Ho. 2008. "Beyond Informed Consent: The Therapeutic Misconception and Trust." *Journal of Medical Ethics* 34 (3): 202–5. https://doi.org/10.1136/jme.2006.019406.

Metcalf, Peter. 2001. "Global 'Disjuncture' and the 'Sites' of Anthropology." *Cultural Anthropology* 16 (2): 165–82.

Metcalfe, Stan, and Ronnie Ramlogan. 2008. "Innovation Systems and the Competitive Process in Developing Economies." *Quarterly Review of Economics & Finance* 48 (2): 433–46. https://doi.org/10.1016/j.qref.2006.12.021.

Miller, Franklin G. 2004. "Research Ethics and Misguided Moral Intuition." *Journal of Law, Medicine and Ethics* 32: 111–16.

Miller, Franklin G., and Howard Brody. 2003. "A Critique of Clinical Equipoise: Therapeutic Misconception in the Ethics of Clinical Trials." *The Hastings Center Report* 33 (3): 19–28.

Ministerstvo meditsinskoi promishlennosti. 1971. "Pamiati O.Iu.Magidsona [In Commemoration of O.Iu.Magidson]" 5 (11): 62–63.

Ministry of Higher Education and Science of the Russian Federation. 2018. "Portal 'Natsional'nii Tsentr Po Monitoringu Innovatsionnoi Infrastrukturi Nauchno-Tekhnicheskoi Deiatel'nosti i Regional'nih Innovatsionnih Sistem' [Website 'National Center for Monitoring of Innovation Infrastructure for Technoscientific Activities and Regional Innovation Systems']." http://www.miiris.ru.

Minpromtorg. 2009. *Strategy for the Development of the Pharmaceutical Industry in the Russian Federation to 2020*. Moscow.

———. 2012. *State Programme of the Russian Federation "Development of the Pharmaceutical and Medical Industry" for 2013–2020*.

Morreim, E. Haavi. 2005. "The Clinical Investigator as Fiduciary: Discarding a Misguided Idea." *The Journal of Law, Medicine & Ethics: A Journal of the American Society of Law, Medicine & Ethics* 33 (3): 586–98.

Moynihan, R., I. Heath, and D. Henry. 2002. "Selling Sickness: The Pharmaceutical Industry and Disease Mongering." *British Medical Journal* 324 (7342): 886–91.

Natradze, Aleksandr. 1957. "Khimiko-Farmatsevticheskaia Promyshlennost' Za 40 Let [Chemical-Pharmaceutical Industry during 40 Years]." *Meditsinskaia Promyshlennost' SSSR* 10: 5–13.

———. 1967. *Ocherk Razvitiia Khimiko-Farmatsevticheskoi Promyshlennosti SSSR [An Outline of Development of the Soviet Chemical-Pharmaceutical Industry].* Moscow: Meditsina.

Nelson, R. R. 1993. *National Innovation Systems: A Comparative Analysis.* Oxford University Press.

Newman, K. L. 2000. "Organizational Transformation during Institutional Upheaval." *Academy of Management Review* 25 (3): 602–19.

Niosi, J., P. Saviotti, B. Bellon, and M. Crow. 1993. "National Systems of Innovation: In Search of a Workable Concept." *Technology in Society* 15 (2): 207–27.

Novas, Carlos. 2006. "The Political Economy of Hope: Patients' Organizations, Science and Biovalue." *BioSocieties* 1: 289–305. https://doi.org/10.1017/S1745855206003024.

OECD (Organization for Economic Cooperation and Development). 1994. "Accessing and Expanding the Science and Technology Base." Paris.

Osipov, Aleksandr. 2019. "Gora Rodila Misl': Chto Opyat' Pomeshalo Voploshcheniiu Svetloi Idei o Lekarstvennom Importozameshchenii [What Again Interfered with Realizing the Bright Idea of Drug Import Substitution]." *Vademecum*, April 1. https://vademec.ru/article/gora_rodila_mysl-_chto_opyat_pomeshalo_voploshcheniyu_svetloy_idei_o_lekarstvennom_importozameshchen/.

Parker, J. N., N. Vermeulen, and B. Penders, eds. 2010. *Collaboration in the New Life Sciences.* Aldershot: Ashgate.

Participants in the 2001 Conference on Ethical Aspect of Research in Developing Countries. 2004. "Moral Standards For Research in Developing Countries. From 'Reasonable Availability' to 'Fair Benefits.'" *The Hastings Center Report* 34 (3): 17–27.

Petryna, Adriana. 2009. *When Experiments Travel: Clinical Trials and the Global Search for Human Subjects.* Princeton: Princeton University Press.

Rabeharisoa, V., and M. Callon. 2004. "Patients and Scientists in French Muscular Dystrophy Research." In *States of Knowledge: The Co-Production of Science and Social Order*, edited by S. Jasanoff, 142–60. London: Routledge.

Ramlogan, Ronnie, Andrea Mina, Gindo Tampubolon, and J. Stanley Metcalfe. 2007. "Networks of Knowledge: The Distributed Nature of Medical Innovation." *Scientometrics* 70 (2): 459–89. https://doi.org/10.1007/s11192-007-0212-7.

Reid, Susan E., and Shyama V. Ramani. 2012. "The Harnessing of Biotechnology in India: Which Roads to Travel?" *Technological Forecasting and Social Change* 79 (4): 648–64. https://doi.org/10.1016/j.techfore.2011.12.008.

Romanova, Svetlana. 2017. "Delovaia Activnost' Predpriiatii Farmpromyshlennosti: Reiting Po Vyruchke Ot Realizatsii Za 2016 God [Business Activities of Pharmaceutical Companies: Rating Based on Sales Revenue in 2016]." *Remedium*.

Russian cluster observatory. 2018. "Karta Klasterov Rossii [Map of the Russian Clusters]." http://map.cluster.hse.ru.

Rycroft, R. W., and D. E. Kash. 1999. "Managing Complex Networks—Key to 21st Century Innovation Success." *Research-Technol-Ogy Management* 42 (3).

Sariola, Salla, Deapica Ravindran, Anand Kumar, and Roger Jeffery. 2015. "Big-Pharmaceuticalisation: Clinical Trials and Contract Research Organisations in India." *Social Science and Medicine* 131: 239–46. https://doi.org/10.1016/j.socscimed.2014.11.052.

Schecter, Kate. 1992. "Soviet Socialized Medicine and the Right to Health Care in a Changing Soviet Union." *Human Rights Quarterly* 14 (2): 206–15.

Schroeder, Doris, and Eugenijus Gefenas. 2012. "Realizing Benefit Sharing—the Case of Post-Study Obligations." *Bioethics* 26 (6): 305–14. https://doi.org/10.1111/j.1467-8519.2010.01857.x.

Serebrianyi, Roman. 2016. "Chlen-Correspondent RAN, Vidnyi Obschestvennyi i Gosudarstvennyi Deiatel,' Doktor Meditsynskikh Nauk, Professor D. D. Venediktov [Corresponding Member of the Russian Academy of Sciences, a Prominent Public Figure and Politician, Doctor of Medicine, Professor D. D. Venediktov]." *Biulleten' Natsional'nogo Nauchno-Issledovatelskogo Instituta Obschestvennogo Zdorov'ia Imeni N. A. Semashko*, no. 2: 326–329.

Sherstneva, Elena. 2018. "Gosudarstvennaia Politika v Farmatsevticheskoi Sfere v SSSR v 1930-e Godi [State Policy in the Sphere of Pharmaceutics in the USSR in the 1930s]." *Remedium*, no. 6: 50–53. http://dx.doi.org/10.21518/1561-5936-2018-6-50-53.

Sismondo, Sergio, and Jeremy Green, eds. 2015. *The Pharmaceutical Studies Reader*. Malden, MA: Wiley-Blackwell.

Sixteenth All-Russian Congress of Soviets. 1935. "15-23 January 1935, Moscow, Verbatim Report." Bulletin #11-17.

Star, Susan Leigh. 1989. "The Structure of Ill-Structured Solutions: Boundary Objects and Distributed Heterogeneous Problem Solving." In *Distributed Artificial Intelligence 2*, edited by L. Gasser and M. Huhns, 37–54. San Mateo, CA: Morgan Kauffmann.

Star, Susan Leigh, and James Griesemer. 1989. "Institutional Ecology, 'Translation' and Boundary Objects: Amateurs and Professionals in Berkeley's Museum of Vertebrate Zoology, 1907–30." *Social Studies of Science* 19: 387–420.

Stefanov, Igor. 2007. "Clinical Trials Come to Russia." *International Clinical Trials* (Fall): 43–50.

———. 2008. "Russian Revolution." *European Pharmaceutical Contractor* (Spring): 14–18.

Stefanov, Igor, and Pavel Tverdokhleb. 2008. "Russia Grows Its CRO Market." Applied Clinical Trials. http://www.appliedclinicaltrialsonline.com/applied-clinicaltrials/article/articleDetail.jsp?id=506846&pageID=1&sk=&date=.
Sunder Rajan, K. 2006. *Biocapital: The Constitution of Postgenomic Life*. Durham: Duke University Press.
Sunder Rajan, Kaushik. 2010. "The Experimental Machinery of Global Clinical Trials: Case Studies from India." In *Asian Biotech: Ethics and Communities of Fate*, edited by Aihwa Ong and Nancy N. Chen, 55–80. Durham: Duke University Press.
Timmermans, Stefan, and Marc Berg. 2003. *The Gold Standard: The Challenge of Evidence-Based Medicine and Standardization in Health Care*. Philadelphia: Temple University Press.
Timmermans, Stefan, and Tara McKay. 2009. "Clinical Trials as Treatment Option: Bioethics and Health Care Disparities in Substance Dependency." *Social Science & Medicine (1982)* 69 (12): 1784–90. https://doi.org/10.1016/j.socscimed.2009.09.019.
Tobbell, Dominique. 2009. "'Who's Winning the Human Race?' Cold War as Pharmaceutical Political Strategy." *Journal of the History of Medicine and Allied Sciences* 64 (4): 429–73.
Tsib, Sergei. 2016. Farma-2020: gosprogramma, kotoraia rabotaet [Pharma-2020: State Program That Works] Website of the Ministry of Industry and Trade of the Russian Federation. http://minpromtorg.gov.ru/press-centre/news/#!farma2020_gosprogramma_kotoraya_rabotaet.
Utzinger, Jürg, and Jennifer Keiser. 2013. "Research and Development for Neglected Diseases: More Is Still Needed, and Faster." *The Lancet Global Health* 1 (6): 317–18. https://doi.org/10.1016/S2214-109X(13)70148-7.
Vacroux, Alexandra Mary. 2005. "Formal and Informal Institutional Change: Evolution of Pharmaceutical Regulation in Russia, 1991-2004." Harvard University.
Varshavsky, Sergei. 2002. "Discover Russia for Conducting Clinical Research." *Applied Clinical Trials*, no. March: 74-80.
Venediktov, Dmitrii. 1977. *Mezhdunarodnie Problemi Zdravookhraneniia [International Problems of Health Care]*. Moscow: Meditsina.
Vries, Martine C. de, Mirjam Houtlosser, Jan M. Wit, Dirk P. Engberts, Dorine Bresters, Gertjan J. L. Kaspers, and Evert van Leeuwen. 2011. "Ethical Issues at the Interface of Clinical Care and Research Practice in Pediatric Oncology: A Narrative Review of Parents' and Physicians' Experiences." *BMC Medical Ethics* 12 (1): 18. https://doi.org/10.1186/1472-6939-12-18.
Wadmann, Sarah. 2014. "Physician-Industry Collaboration: Conflicts of Interest and the Imputation of Motive." *Social Studies of Science* 44 (4): 531–54. https://doi.org/10.1177/0306312714525678.

Wadmann, Sarah, and Klaus Hoeyer. 2014. "Beyond the 'Therapeutic Misconception': Research, Care and Moral Friction." *BioSocieties* 9 (1): 3–23. https://doi.org/10.1057/biosoc.2013.37.

WHO. 2016. "Progress Report 2016. Prevent HIV, Test and Treat All." *Progress Report 2016. Prevent HIV, Test and Treat All.* Geneva, Switzerland.

Williams, Simon J., Paul Martin, and Jonathan Gabe. 2011. "The Pharmaceuticalisation of Society? A Framework for Analysis." *Sociology of Health and Illness* 33 (5): 710–25. https://doi.org/10.1111/j.1467-9566.2011.01320.x.

World Health Organization. 2004. "The World Medicines Situation." *World Health Organization.* https://doi.org/10.1089/acm.2009.0657.

Zaitseva, Elena. 2001. "Aleksei Evgen'evich Chichibabin (1871–1945)." *Khimiia* 16: 1–4.

Zingerman, Boris. 2013. "Elektronnaia Meditsinskaia Karta i Printsipi Ee Organizatsii [Electronical Medical Record and Principles of Its Organization]." *IT v Zdravookhranenii*, March 28. https://www.osp.ru/medit/blogs/bz/bz_109.html.

Zvonareva, O., N. Engel, S. Martsevich, G. de Wert, and K. Horstman. 2015. "International Clinical Trials, Cardiovascular Disease and Treatment Options in the Russian Federation: Research and Treatment in Practice." *Social Science and Medicine* 128: 255–62.

Index

Abbott, 7, 50, 131
academia, 17, 95, 104, 133, 139–48, 152, 156, 159, 160, 162, 163
accelerators, 166, 167
access to drugs, 2, 11, 21, 64, 84, 92, 93, 102, 113, 115, 121, 175, 178
access to markets, 12, 82, 92, 100, 112, 124, 125, 134, 145, 163, 176, 183
access to research participants, 82, 95
adrenalin, 31
adverse reactions, 50, 91, 96, 97
advertising (drugs), 36, 37, 51, 174, 180
agora, 138
AIDS, 4
Akrikhin, 34, 66, 79
amendments, Kefauver-Harris, 8, 37, 44, 45, 50, 51, 63, 64
anesthesia, 68, 69
antibiotics, 8, 11, 35, 43, 69
antidepressants, 8
antihistamines, 11, 68
antimalarial, 34
antiprotozoals, 35
antipyretics, 35
antiretroviral, 175
anxiolytics, 8
ascorbic acid, 34
aspirin, 34, 123

Babayan, Eduard, 47–49, 102, 103
Bayer, 7, 130
Belmont Report, 46
benefits (clinical trial), 21, 84, 85, 95, 96, 101, 103, 105, 106, 173, 174, 177
bias, 3, 20, 48, 51, 52
big-pharmaceuticalization, 82
biotechnology, 9, 15, 121, 133–35, 160, 177
botanicals, 27, 32
Bristol-Myers Squibb, 74
bureaucrats, 19, 61
Burroughs–Wellcome, 7
business, Russian pharmaceutical, 22, 26, 27, 70, 71, 74, 78, 79, 108, 122, 123, 135, 140–46, 148–53, 156, 158–64, 172, 179

candidate drug, 36, 49, 140, 142, 143, 146, 147, 149, 162, 163
capabilities, industrial, 7, 23, 125, 134, 139, 164, 177, 178
capacity-building, 105, 184
capital, 3, 19, 83, 84, 122, 180, 181
capitalist pharmaceutical industry, 3, 4, 6, 9, 32, 83, 181
cardiovascular disease, 8, 52, 67, 68, 85
chemistry, 5, 7, 8, 27, 28, 32, 53, 147, 151

199

Chernomyrdin, Victor, 62
Chichibabin, Aleksei, 30
chronic diseases, 51–53, 99, 100, 175, 184
citizens' health needs, 60, 115, 118–21, 128, 177
clinicians, 100, 138, 139, 152
closing-down strategy, 124, 128, 176
cluster, biomedical, 156, 160–62, 186
cocaine, 32
collaboration
  between industry and academia, 7, 22, 23, 72, 84, 99, 140, 143–45, 148, 153, 159, 160, 162–65
  in drug development, 7, 134, 136, 137, 140, 181
  physician-industry, 94, 95
  process in pharmapolitics, 19, 22, 23, 81, 133, 135, 165, 170, 172–74, 178–81
commercialization, 6, 8, 150, 161, 176
communism, 32, 43, 51, 55
communist ideals, 26, 42, 43, 50, 53
companies
  Big Pharma, 7–9, 12, 17, 78, 87, 88, 112, 113, 117, 131, 146, 169, 180
  biotechnology, 9
  Russian pharmaceutical, 22, 26, 66, 67, 71–74, 79, 108, 113, 120, 126, 130, 131, 135, 145, 167, 170, 172, 176
competition, market, 8, 51, 67, 71, 74, 112, 113, 160, 184
competitiveness, industry, 2, 112, 119, 136
conflict between research and treatment, 46
Conroy, Mary Schaeffer, 27, 29–34, 40
consumer choice, 63, 116
consumption, drugs, 2, 11, 24, 116, 175

control, state, 15, 19, 28, 40, 65, 67, 75, 127, 128, 156, 179–81
cooperation, 41, 42, 80, 110, 137, 141, 145, 184
coproduction, 13–16, 18, 53, 169–71
corruption, 94, 155
crisis
  health crisis, 21, 83, 85, 103
  productivity, 11
  Russian pharmaceutical industry, 71, 74, 75, 77, 78, 85, 86, 107, 111
culture, political, 15, 16, 19, 135, 153, 159, 164, 165, 170, 172, 174
culture of collecting and evaluating evidence, 25, 44, 50, 53
CVD, 85, 86, 91, 94, 95, 97, 99–101

decentralization, 20, 60–62, 65, 171
decision-making, 60, 63, 154, 157
demand for drugs, 34, 63, 67, 68, 150, 151, 174
democracy, 60, 61
deregulation, 11, 63–65, 78, 109, 185
development institutes, 17, 157, 160, 163, 164
diagnostics, 92
disability, 100
disadvantaged populations, 103, 180
discovery, drug, 8, 9, 139
disintegration, USSR, 58, 59, 107
distrust, 52, 156, 165
double-blinding, 48, 49
downstream, research and development, 9
drug
  development, 1, 2, 5–9, 11–13, 17, 19–22, 26, 28, 32, 33, 36–39, 44–48, 50, 52, 53, 64, 72, 73, 75, 77, 81, 82, 84, 106, 108, 109, 120–22, 124–27, 133–35, 140–44,

Index

146, 148, 151, 155–60, 164, 165, 167, 169, 170, 173, 176, 178, 179, 184
discovery, 8, 9, 139
effectiveness, 17, 19, 37, 44, 45, 48, 52, 148
efficacy, 8, 11, 45–49, 52, 63, 81, 88
evaluation, 44, 46, 51
history, 5–7, 23, 56, 71, 122
lag, 64
registration, 154, 155, 158
safety, 48, 88
duplication, 9, 20, 30, 35, 37, 55

economic development, 61, 161
economic liberalization, 55–57, 69, 77, 78, 125
entrepreneurship, 20, 28, 60, 75, 166, 171
epistemic virtues of markets, 64
essential drugs, 114–18, 126, 129, 175
essential medicines, 11, 34, 117
ethics committees, 88, 89
Etzkowitz, Henry, 138, 159, 164
evidence, 2, 8, 25, 37, 44–48, 50, 52, 53, 63, 87, 88, 95
experimentation, medical, 49, 51, 83, 84, 103, 105, 173
expertise, 21, 38, 45, 78, 83, 93, 95, 104, 105, 134, 138, 151, 152, 156, 160
experts, 45, 48–50, 115, 138, 154, 184
exploitation, 20, 30, 50

FDA, 8, 11, 12, 37, 44–48, 50–52, 63–65, 67, 88, 93, 183
feasibility, 90, 91
financing, drug research and development, 73, 86, 92, 110, 113

galenicals, 28

Geltzer, Anna, 39, 40
generalizable knowledge, 46
generic drugs, 72, 74, 112–14, 144, 149, 151
glasnost, 58, 60
GlaxoSmithKline, 87, 130
globalization, 12, 82–84, 102
Gorbachev, Mikhail, 57, 58, 60
guidelines, ICH, 12, 184

harmonization, regulatory, 12, 89, 112, 128
health-care system, 41–43, 53, 97, 99, 102, 104, 185
health inequalities, 21, 83
health needs, 4, 11, 28, 43, 83, 106, 115, 121, 128, 129, 174, 177, 181
Helix, Triple, 138, 140, 153, 159
Hoechst

ICH, International Conference on Harmonisation, 12, 89, 183, 184
ICH guidelines, 12, 184
implicated actors, 129, 179
India, 67, 78, 82, 84, 87, 113, 125, 164, 184
inefficiencies in drug development, 26
inequalities, 21, 35, 53, 83, 103, 179
infectious diseases, 52, 53, 149
infrastructure, 17, 54, 71, 72, 75, 87–89, 91, 105, 116, 135, 159–62, 166, 167
innovation environment, 133, 135, 152, 160, 164, 165
firms, 6, 9, 22, 43, 52, 110, 125, 133, 134, 137–39, 151, 155
government, 15, 17, 19–21, 43, 56, 58, 60, 62, 63, 66, 76, 88, 109, 110, 113, 115, 117, 121, 138, 147, 171, 177, 179

innovation environment *(continued)*
  hospitals, 7, 68, 89, 134, 138, 139, 151, 185
  scientists, 7, 19, 22, 38–41, 44, 55, 123, 128, 138, 141, 150, 151, 156, 158, 163, 172, 185
  universities, 7, 110, 134, 138, 139
innovation governance, 176, 177
innovation studies, 108, 109, 111, 121, 124, 125, 129, 134–37, 139
innovation systems, 109–11, 134, 135, 137, 138, 140, 159
innovativeness, 6, 149, 150, 152
institution, 85, 86, 89, 94, 134
interaction, 23, 77, 104, 110, 126, 133, 134, 137, 140, 153, 159, 160, 164, 170, 173
interdependence, 123, 124
International Conference on Harmonisation, ICH, 12, 89, 183, 184
internationalization, 22, 122, 125, 126, 172, 176
investigators, 17, 21, 46, 90–94, 96–105
investors, 74, 139, 144, 150, 167, 178

Japan, 5, 12, 48, 81, 88, 89, 184
Jasanoff, Sheila, 15, 59, 135
justice, 25, 26, 29, 30, 32, 35, 53–55, 59, 87, 102

Kalinin, Yoryi, 75–77
Kefauver-Harris Amendments, 8, 37, 44, 45, 50, 51, 63, 64
Kefauver hearings, 36, 51

laboratories, 9, 25, 26, 36, 50, 71, 72
legislation, 8, 44, 51, 61, 66, 88, 154, 157
Leydesdorff, Loet, 40, 138, 159, 164

liberalization, 55–57, 62, 63, 65, 67, 69, 77, 78, 109, 125
local industry, 22, 74, 79, 82, 113, 114, 116, 117, 121, 125, 126, 145
localization, 116
local market, 22, 114, 116, 126, 129, 141, 172, 175

managers, 38, 66, 123, 141, 152
manufacturers, 37, 89, 117, 144, 145, 157, 185
market
  global market, 125, 127
  Russian, 79, 92, 93, 113, 115, 125, 130, 131, 146, 153, 176
market economy, 58, 60, 65, 90
marketization, 58, 61
meaning-making, 110, 111
medicine, 25, 33, 34, 42, 44, 49, 54, 134, 138, 139, 161, 166, 172
Mont Pelerin Society, 64, 65

nationalization, 26, 30, 66
national security, 2, 22, 77, 111, 116–18, 120–25, 128, 176, 177
nation building, 14, 16, 174
negotiation, 14, 178
neoliberal ideals, 21, 56, 65
neoliberalism, 20, 21, 55–57, 62–65, 74–76, 78, 79, 87, 109, 127, 171
network, 10, 22, 74, 106, 128, 134–38, 159, 164
norms, 13, 61, 110, 137
Novartis, 87, 130
Nowotny, Helga, 138

objectivity, 48
oncology, 67, 68
oppressive imagination practices, 23, 169, 180, 181
outsourcing, 12, 141

ownership, 65–67

partnerships, 84, 138
patent, 32, 51, 149, 150
payments, 93
penicillin, 123, 124
perestroika, 58, 60, 65, 69
pharmaceutical arena, 3, 19, 23, 26, 37, 83, 128, 133–35, 137, 140, 155, 164, 165, 169, 172–74, 176
pharmaceutical companies, 7–9, 12, 17, 22, 29, 50, 71, 73, 74, 78, 88, 90, 91, 95, 99, 117, 120, 167, 172, 176
pharmaceutical industry
 Indian, 78, 82, 87, 121, 125
 multinational, 4, 9, 87, 131, 169, 174, 175, 180, 181
 Russian, 1, 2, 21, 22, 29, 57, 65, 67, 75, 78, 79, 107, 111, 113, 114, 120, 124, 128, 130, 133, 171, 176, 177
 Soviet, 25–27, 30, 32, 35, 36, 39, 41, 52, 53, 55, 68, 127, 128, 169
pharmaceutical innovation, 3–6, 12, 15, 35, 63, 103, 124, 146, 148, 151, 152, 160, 165, 166, 169, 174, 180
pharmaceuticalization, 9, 10, 12, 82
pharmaceutical market, 1, 2, 22, 79, 87, 124, 130, 131, 149, 150, 172
pharmacology, 5, 7, 8, 52, 73, 139, 144, 147
pharmapolitical regime, 19, 25, 26, 35, 43, 44, 50, 53, 54, 169, 170, 175, 180
pharmapolitics, 3, 15–21, 23, 35, 41, 43, 53, 55, 56, 77, 83, 103, 105, 106, 108, 111, 125, 126, 129, 135, 165, 169, 170, 174, 178–81
phase, clinical trials, 45, 46, 49, 58, 63, 88, 184

physicians, 7, 22, 37, 45, 50–52, 85, 90, 93–97, 100, 102, 151, 152
placebo, 46, 49, 52
plasmocid, 34
political culture, 15, 16, 19, 135, 153, 159, 164, 165, 170, 172, 174
political imagination, 16, 19, 23, 55, 59, 62, 75, 169, 178, 180, 181
privatization, 20, 56, 60, 62, 65, 66, 71, 72, 76, 78, 109, 171
problem definition, 19, 22, 81, 108, 111, 122, 124–26, 129, 134, 165, 170–72, 174, 176
procurement, 1, 68, 131
production capacities, 22, 116, 125, 172, 177
profit, 6, 20, 28, 29, 32, 36, 45, 47, 51–53, 61, 70, 71, 83, 84, 104
public health, 4, 7, 12, 21–23, 64, 77, 88, 102, 103, 105, 106, 119–21, 165, 172–74, 176, 177, 180, 181
public health benefits, 21, 105, 106, 174
public imagination, 180, 181

quality, 1, 2, 19, 36, 38, 45, 46, 50, 52, 67, 71, 91, 105, 112–14, 118, 119, 129, 134, 138, 142, 164
quality control, 38, 67, 112, 138

radiopharmaceuticals, 39
randomization, 46, 48, 49
rationality, 35, 53, 55
recruitment, patient, 82, 87, 91, 96, 97, 101
reform, 26, 51, 163, 186
registration, drugs, 9, 12, 70, 87, 112, 143, 154, 155, 158, 184, 186
relevance, 95, 128, 129, 151
research and development, 55, 83, 111–13, 135, 170, 180

research ethics, 46, 49, 102
research institutes, 19, 25, 35, 71, 72, 79, 110, 134, 135, 138, 139
research participants, 20, 21, 46–48, 82–84, 90, 96–103
resistance, 20, 56, 58, 59
risk, 4, 15, 22, 86, 102, 116, 125, 133, 172, 174, 175, 181
RosZdravNadzor, 154, 158
Russian companies, 72, 108, 126, 130, 131, 167, 170, 176
Russian industry, 27, 29, 107, 113, 114, 165, 176

safety, drug, 8, 11, 15, 17, 19, 44, 45, 47–49, 51, 52, 63, 81, 88, 184
SANOFI, 130
scientific research institutes, 71, 72, 135
security, 2, 22, 74, 76, 77, 111, 114, 116–26, 128, 129, 172, 176, 177
self-interest, 28, 47, 99
self-sufficiency, 22, 116–18, 122–25, 128, 172, 176
Skolkovo Foundation, 135, 167
socialized health care, 6, 8, 32, 33, 42, 43
societal development, 30, 171
sociotechnical imaginary, 15, 16, 29, 30, 33, 59, 170
Soviet bioethics, 44, 48
Soviet drug development, 38, 44, 52, 127
Soviet health-care, 41, 42
Soviet state, 7, 15, 19, 25, 31, 40, 54, 58, 67, 69, 178
standards, 44–46, 51, 88, 89, 112, 120, 152, 157
state control, 15, 19, 28, 40, 65, 67, 75, 127, 128, 156, 179–81

state control, 52, 128
state interests, 21, 76, 81, 173
substances, pharmaceutical, 9, 66, 67, 69, 76, 77, 114, 117, 119, 122–24, 127, 144, 147, 151
superiority, 42, 44, 50, 53, 55
surveillance, 94

technopolitics, 14–16, 108
thalidomide, 8
therapeutic access, 84, 102
therapeutic benefits, 21, 173
toxicity, 46, 51, 148
trade, 27, 51, 60, 67, 76, 109, 127
Triple Helix, 138, 140, 153, 159
tuberculosis, 4, 67, 68

uncertainty, 23, 60, 61, 74, 78, 86, 154, 156, 159, 173
upstream, research and development, 9
users, 138, 139, 152, 178, 181

vaccines, 7, 35, 43, 114
Vacroux, Alexandra, 61
validity, 46, 49, 51
value generation, 19, 21, 81, 83, 103, 105, 121, 134, 173, 174, 178
Venediktov, Dmitrii, 41–43
vision production, 19, 55, 56, 62, 81, 134, 165, 170, 171, 174, 178
vitamins, 8, 35, 69
volunteers, healthy, 46, 48, 49, 88, 184

Washington consensus, 109
Western markets, 12, 146

Yeltsin, Boris, 58–60, 62

www.ingramcontent.com/pod-product-compliance
Lightning Source LLC
Chambersburg PA
CBHW020332240426
43665CB00043B/446